THE KEY TO UNDERSTANDING
U.S. HISTORY AND GOVERNMENT
(Fifth Edition)

JAMES KILLORAN

STUART ZIMMER

MARK JARRETT
Ph.D., Stanford University

JARRETT PUBLISHING COMPANY
The Gold Standard in Test Preparation

EAST COAST OFFICE
P.O. Box 1460
Ronkonkoma, NY 11779
631-981-4248

SOUTHERN OFFICE
50 Nettles Boulevard
Jensen Beach, FL 34957
800-859-7679

WEST COAST OFFICE
10 Folin Lane
Lafayette, CA 94549
925-906-9742

1-800-859-7679 ❖ Fax: 631-588-4722
www.jarrettpub.com

Jarrett Publishing Company
Post Office Box 1460
Ronkonkoma, New York 11779

ISBN 1-882422-49-X
ISBN 978-1-882422-49-4

Printed in the United States of America
Fifth Edition
10 9 8 7 6 5 4 3 2 1   12 11 10 09

ABOUT THE AUTHORS

James Killoran is a retired assistant principal. He has written *Government and You* and *Economics and You.* Mr. Killoran has extensive experience in test writing for the N.Y. State Board of Regents in social studies and has served on the Committee for Testing of the N.C.S.S. His article on social studies testing has been published in *Social Education,* the country's leading social studies journal. In addition, Mr. Killoran has won a number of awards for outstanding teaching and curriculum development, including "Outstanding Social Studies Teacher" and "Outstanding Social Studies Supervisor" in New York City. In 1993, he was awarded an Advanced Certificate for Teachers of Social Studies by the N.C.S.S. In 1997, he became Chairman of the N.C.S.S. Committee on Awarding Advanced Certificates for Teachers of Social Studies.

Stuart Zimmer is a retired social studies teacher. He has written *Government and You* and *Economics and You.* He served as a test writer for the N.Y. State Board of Regents in social studies, and has written for the National Merit Scholarship Examination. In addition Mr. Zimmer has published numerous articles on teaching and testing in social studies journals. He has presented many educational workshops at local, state and national teachers' conferences. In 1989, Mr. Zimmer's achievements were recognized by the New York State Legislature with a Special Legislative Resolution in his honor.

Mark Jarrett is a former social studies teacher and attorney in San Francisco. Dr. Jarrett has served as a test writer for the New York State Board of Regents, and has taught at Hofstra University. He was educated at Columbia University, the London School of Economics, the Law School of the University of California at Berkeley, and Stanford University, where he received his doctorate in history. Dr. Jarrett has received several academic awards including the Order of the Coif at Berkeley and the David and Christina Phelps Harris Fellowship at Stanford.

ALSO BY KILLORAN, ZIMMER, AND JARRETT

Mastering U.S. History and Government
Mastering New York's Grade 5 Social Studies Standards
Mastering World Regions and Civilizations
Mastering Ohio's Grade 8 Social Studies Achievement Test
Mastering the Grade 5 CRCT in Social Studies
Ohio, The Buckeye State
Ohio: Its Neighbors, Near and Far
Mastering the MCAS Grade 5 Social Studies Test
Texas: Its Land and Its People
Learning About New York State
North Carolina: The Tar Heel State
Michigan: Its Land and Its People
The Key to Understanding Global History
Mastering Global History
Mastering the Grade 10 TAKS Social Studies Assessment
Mastering the M.E.A.P. Test in Social Studies: Grade 5
Mastering the M.E.A.P. Test in Social Studies: Grade 8
Mastering Michigan's High School Test in Social Studies

ACKNOWLEDGMENTS

The authors would like to thank the following educators who reviewed the manuscript. Their comments, suggestions, and recommendations proved invaluable.

Alice D. Grant
Chair, Social Studies Department
Adjunct Prof., Pace University
Pelham High School
Pelham, New York

Ken Hilton, Ph.D
Executive Director of Organizational
and Professional Development
Rush-Henrietta CSD
Henrietta, New York

Maps and graphics by C.F. Enterprises, Huntington, New York.
Layout, graphics and typesetting: Burmar Technical Corporation, Sea Cliff, NY.

This book is dedicated:

to my wife Donna and my children Christian, Carrie, and Jesse
and my grandchildren Aiden, Christian, and Olivia   *— James Killoran*

to my wife Joan and my children Todd and Ronald and to my
grandchildren Jared and Katie   *— Stuart Zimmer*

to my wife Goska and my children Alexander and Julia

— Mark Jarrett

TABLE OF CONTENTS

PART 1: TEST-TAKING STRATEGIES

CHAPTER 1: How to Remember Important Information 1
CHAPTER 2: Interpreting Different Types of Data 5
**CHAPTER 3: How to Answer Multiple-Choice Questions
and Interpret Documents** 19
CHAPTER 4: How to Answer Essay Questions 27

PART 2: A REVIEW OF UNITED STATES HISTORY

CHAPTER 5: Tools for Mastering American History 47

CHAPTER 6: Constitutional Foundations 53
    What You Should Focus on 54
    Looking at Government 55
    From Colonies to Independent States 57
    The Origins of the U.S. Constitution 62
    Basic Principles of the U.S. Constitution 64
    The Federal Government: Its Structure and Functions 67
    Constitutional Protection of Individual Liberties 71

CHAPTER 7: The Constitution Tested 79
    What You Should Focus on 80
    Looking at the Impact of Geography 81
    The Young Republic 83
    The Civil War, 1861–1865 88
    The Reconstruction Era, 1865–1877 93
    The Aftermath of Reconstruction 96

CHAPTER 8: The Rise of Industry 111
    What You Should Focus on 112
    Looking at Economic Change 113
    The Rise of American Industry 116
    The Rise of Organized Labor 121
    Changing American Lifestyles 125
    The Last American Frontier 130

CHAPTER 9: The Progressive Era: Protest, Reform, and Empire 141
    What You Should Focus on 142
    Looking at the Arts 143
    The Agrarian Movement 147
    The Progressive Movement, 1900–1920 151
    The Women's Rights Movement, 1865–1920 158
    American Foreign Policy, 1898–1920 160

CHAPTER 10: Prosperity and Depression 183
    What You Should Focus on 184
    Looking at Economic Policy 185
    Boom Times: The 1920s 189
    The Great Depression, 1929–1940 195
    Franklin D. Roosevelt and the New Deal 198

CHAPTER 11: The Age of Global Crisis 209
    What You Should Focus on 210
    Looking at Foreign Policy 211
    Peace in Peril, 1920-1941 215
    The United States at War, 1941–1945 219
    The Start of the Cold War, 1945–1960 224

CHAPTER 12: The World in Uncertain Times 241
    What You Should Focus on 242
    Looking at our Legal System 243
    The Civil Rights Movement 247
    The Post-War Presidents: Eisenhower, Kennedy, and Johnson 250
    The Sixties: A Decade of Change 254
    The Vietnam War, 1954–1973 261

CHAPTER 13: Contemporary America 271
    What You Should Focus on 272
    Looking at Diversity 273
    The Presidency in Crisis 277
    The New Conservatism: Reagan and Bush 280
    The United States in Recent Times 286
    Toward a Post-Industrial World: Living in a Global Age 294

PART 3: FINAL REVIEW AND PRACTICE TEST

CHAPTER 14: A Final Review 303
    Glossary of Major Concepts 303
    Checklist of Important Terms 305
    Notable Americans 306
    Principles of the U.S. Constitution 307
    Milestones of U.S. Political and Social History 308
    Milestones of American Economic History 310
    Milestones of American Foreign Policy 312

CHAPTER 15: A Practice Examination Regents 315
    Multiple-Choice Questions 316
    Thematic Essay Question 325
    Document-Based Essay Question 326

Index 336

CHAPTER 1

HOW TO REMEMBER IMPORTANT INFORMATION

Examination questions will often test knowledge of key terms, concepts, and people. To learn and remember this information well, you have to engage your mind actively in the learning process. This chapter discusses how you can take a more active approach to studying. It will introduce you to a method that will make it easier for you to recall important information and to perform better on all your tests.

REMEMBERING IMPORTANT TERMS

The terms you are expected to know are of many different types:

★ **documents** — *Mayflower Compact*　　★ **policies** — *Monroe Doctrine*

★ **time periods** — *Progressive Era*　　★ **organizations** — *United Nations*

★ **events** — *Attack on Pearl Harbor*　　★ **wars** — *World War II*

What all these terms have in common is that they refer to a *specific* thing that actually happened or existed. Questions about a term will generally ask you about:

what it is (or was)　　*its purpose*　　*its causes and effects*　　*its significance*

It will be easier to remember a term if you jot down the main information about it and draw a simple illustration. Every time you read about an important term, concept, or famous person, you should therefore complete a 3" by 5" index card similar to the following example:

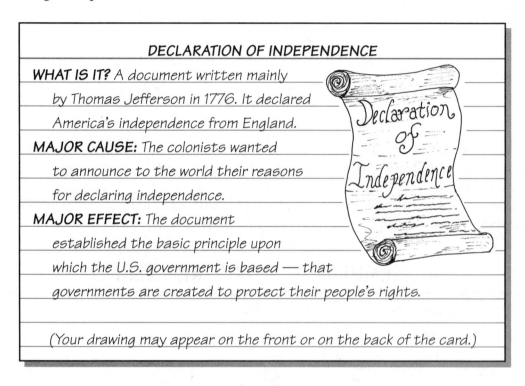

DECLARATION OF INDEPENDENCE

WHAT IS IT? *A document written mainly by Thomas Jefferson in 1776. It declared America's independence from England.*

MAJOR CAUSE: *The colonists wanted to announce to the world their reasons for declaring independence.*

MAJOR EFFECT: *The document established the basic principle upon which the U.S. government is based — that governments are created to protect their people's rights.*

(Your drawing may appear on the front or on the back of the card.)

**If you have access to a computer,
you might want to create a database of these terms.*

REMEMBERING KEY CONCEPTS

Concepts are the building blocks of knowledge. They are words or phrases that provide categories of information. Concepts allow us to organize vast amounts of information. Unlike terms — which identify specific things — concepts identify and explain relationships among groups of things. A concept identifies a structure that things in a particular group have in common. Questions about concepts typically ask for a definition or an example of the concept. Thus, when you study a concept, you should learn the following:

its definition   *an example*

It will be easier to remember a concept if you first jot down the definition, provide an example, and then draw an illustration on a 3" by 5" index card. Following is a sample card dealing with the concept *democracy*.

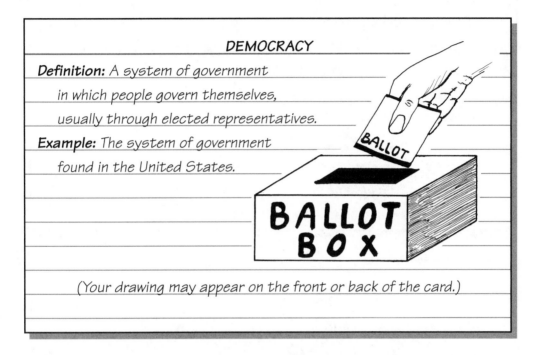

DEMOCRACY

Definition: *A system of government in which people govern themselves, usually through elected representatives.*

Example: *The system of government found in the United States.*

BALLOT

BALLOT BOX

(Your drawing may appear on the front or back of the card.)

REMEMBERING FAMOUS PEOPLE

In American history you will also learn about many famous people. Questions about these individuals will usually ask you who they were and why they were important. Therefore, when you study a famous person, you should focus on:

the place and time period in which the person lived **1**

his or her background or position **2**

the person's accomplishments and impact **3**

It will be easier to remember famous people if you jot down the main information about each of them and draw a simple illustration on a 3" by 5" index card, similar to the example on the next page for President Franklin D. Roosevelt:

FRANKLIN D. ROOSEVELT

TIME PERIOD: In the 1930s and early 1940s.

WHAT HE DID: As President, Roosevelt introduced New Deal legislation that helped bring the United States out of the Great Depression. Roosevelt also helped to steer the United States through World War II.

IMPACT:

(1) He advanced the idea that the federal government should ensure the smooth operation of the U.S. economy.

(2) Many of the laws he introduced, such as the Social Security Act, are still in effect today.

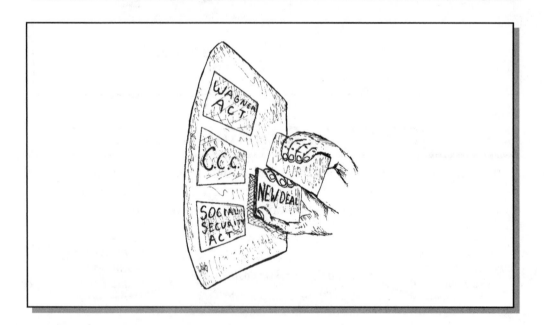

In each chapter of this book, important terms, concepts, and people will be highlighted in **bold** print. Make your own index card for each important term, concept, and person to clarify and reinforce your understanding. At the end of the school year, you will have a collection of cards that will be extremely helpful in preparing for class tests and for the U.S. History and Government Regents Examination.

CHAPTER 2

INTERPRETING DIFFERENT TYPES OF DATA

Data refers to facts or information. Many questions on the Regents Examination, including both multiple-choice and document-based questions, are based on interpreting data provided in the question itself. In this chapter, you will review the ten main types of data used by testmakers in designing these questions:

- ★ Maps
- ★ Bar Graphs
- ★ Line Graphs
- ★ Pie Charts
- ★ Tables

- ★ Timelines
- ★ Political Cartoons
- ★ Outlines
- ★ Speaker Questions
- ★ Reading Passages

MAPS

WHAT IS A MAP?

A **map** is a diagram or representation of an area. Different kinds of information can be shown on a map.

- ★ **Political maps** show the major boundaries between countries or states.

- ★ **Physical maps** show the physical characteristics of a region, such as its rivers, mountains, vegetation and elevation (*height above sea level*).

- ★ **Product maps** show the major natural resources and the chief agricultural and industrial products of an area.

- ★ **Theme maps** can provide information on almost any theme, such as rainfall, population density, languages spoken, or main points of interest.

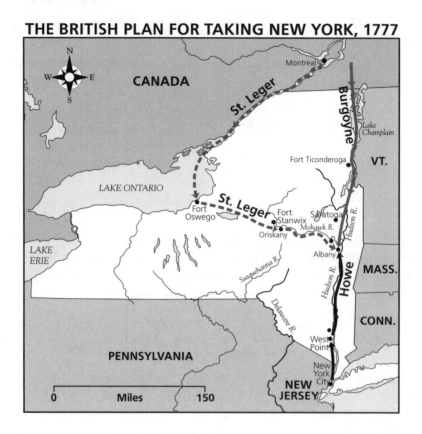

THE BRITISH PLAN FOR TAKING NEW YORK, 1777

KEYS TO UNDERSTANDING A MAP

Title. The title of the map usually identifies the area shown and any information that is presented. For example, the title of the map above is *The British Plan for Taking New York, 1777*. The map shows the plan that the British army had for capturing New York during the American Revolutionary War.

Legend. The legend (*or key*) unlocks the information on a map. The legend shows the symbols used and identifies what each one represents. Sometimes, as here, features of the map are directly labeled and there is no separate legend. In this map:

★ The **dotted line** shows the path that the army under Colonel St. Leger was meant to follow. (*Instead, St. Leger's forces were stopped at Oriskany.*)

★ The **black line** shows the path that the army under General Howe was meant to follow. (*Instead of following the plan, Howe marched south. Later, Howe marched up the Hudson when it was too late.*)

★ The **gray line** shows the path to be followed by the army under General Burgoyne's command. (*Burgoyne was defeated at the Battle of Saratoga.*)

Direction. To find directions on a map, you should look at its **direction indicator** (*compass rose*). The compass rose is used to indicate the four basic directions: north, south, east, and west. If no indicator is shown, assume north is at the top of the map.

Scale. A map would be impossible to use if it were the same size as the area it represents. Mapmakers use a scale to show how much the actual distances have been reduced. A map scale is often shown as a line marked in miles or kilometers. On this map, for example, 1$\frac{1}{2}$ inches are equal to 150 miles. The scale can be used to find the actual distance between two points on the map.

✔ CHECKING YOUR UNDERSTANDING ✔

1. In which city did the three British armies plan to meet?
2. In which general direction was Burgoyne's army moving?

BAR GRAPHS

WHAT IS A BAR GRAPH?

A **bar graph** is a chart made up of parallel bars with different lengths. A bar graph is used to compare two or more items. It can also show how items have changed over time.

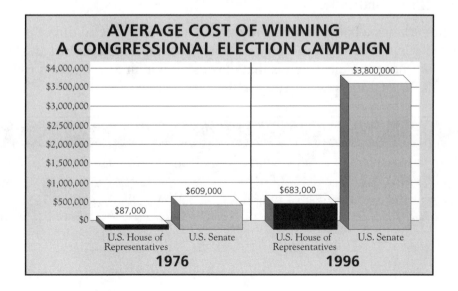

AVERAGE COST OF WINNING
A CONGRESSIONAL ELECTION CAMPAIGN

KEYS TO UNDERSTANDING A BAR GRAPH

Title. The title identifies the general topic of the graph. For example, the title of the bar graph on page 7 is *Average Cost of Winning a Congressional Election Campaign.* It shows how the cost of winning a seat in the U.S. Congress has changed in the twenty years between 1976 and 1996.

Legend. The legend shows what each bar represents. Sometimes, as here, the bars are labeled directly.

★ The **black bars** represent the average cost of winning election campaigns to the U.S. House of Representatives. This is calculated by taking the amount each winning candidate spent in the campaign and averaging them.

★ The **gray bars** represent the average cost of winning election campaigns to the U.S. Senate.

Vertical and Horizontal Axis. Each bar graph has a vertical and horizontal axis.

★ The **vertical axis** runs from the bottom to top. It allows the reader to measure the length of the bars. Here, the vertical axis lists the average cost in dollars. Thus, the first gray bar for 1976 represents an average cost of slightly more than $500,000.

★ The **horizontal axis** runs from left to right. It tells us what each bar or group of bars represents. Here, the horizontal axis indicates the two years being compared: 1976 and 1996.

Trends. Sometimes a bar graph will reveal a **trend** — a general direction in which events are moving. We can often identify a trend from the height of the bars. For example, one trend shown by the graph is that the cost of winning an election campaign in the House of Representatives has risen in the past 20 years.

✔ CHECKING YOUR UNDERSTANDING ✔

1. What was the average cost of winning an election to the House of Representatives in 1976?
2. What was the average cost of winning an election to the Senate in 1996?

LINE GRAPHS

WHAT IS A LINE GRAPH?

A **line graph** is a chart made of points connected in a line. A line graph is often used to show how something has changed over time. Many line graphs have more than one line, allowing the reader to make comparisons.

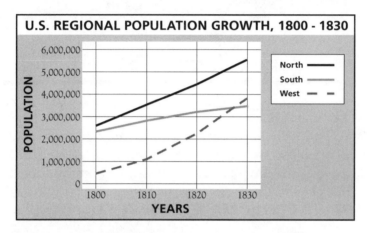

KEYS TO UNDERSTANDING A LINE GRAPH

Title. The title identifies the topic of the graph. For example, the title of the line graph above is *U.S. Regional Population Growth, 1800–1830*. The graph shows the changes in population in three regions of the United States — the North, South, and West — in the thirty year period between 1800 and 1830.

Vertical and Horizontal Axis. Each line graph has a vertical and horizontal axis.

- **Vertical Axis.** The vertical axis runs from *bottom* to *top*. It usually measures the size of items. Notice that as you move up the vertical axis, the numbers increase.

- **Horizontal Axis.** The horizontal axis runs from *left* to *right*. Often it measures the passage of time. In this graph, the horizontal axis shows years. The first year is 1800, and the dates continue in ten-year intervals until 1830.

Legend. If a line graph has many lines, a legend explains what each line represents. Sometimes the information is printed directly on the graph.

- the **black line** represents the population of the North
- the **gray line** represents the population of the South
- the **broken line** represents the population of the West

Trends. Often a line graph will reveal a trend or pattern. One trend shown in this graph is a sharp increase in the population of the Western United States.

✔ CHECKING YOUR UNDERSTANDING ✔

1. What was the approximate population of the North in 1815?
2. Which region of the nation was not growing as rapidly as the other regions between 1800 and 1830?

PIE CHARTS

WHAT IS A PIE CHART?

A **pie chart,** also called a **circle graph,** is a circle divided into sections of different sizes. A pie chart is often used to show the relationship between a whole and its parts. Sometimes several pie charts are placed side-by-side for comparisons.

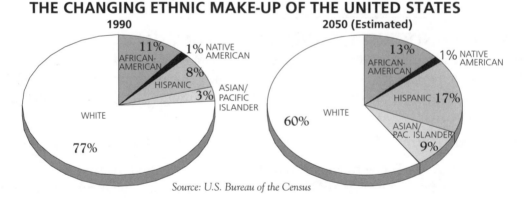

THE CHANGING ETHNIC MAKE-UP OF THE UNITED STATES

Source: U.S. Bureau of the Census

KEYS TO UNDERSTANDING A PIE CHART

Title. The title identifies the overall topic of the chart. For example, the title of the pie charts above is *The Changing Ethnic Make-up of the United States*. The charts show the major ethnic groups in the United States, the relative size of their populations in 1990, and their estimated size in 2050.

Slices of the Pie. Each slice of the pie shows us the size or relationship of the parts to the whole pie. Think of the pie as 100% of something. If you add all the slices together, they total 100%.

Size of each Slice. The size of each slice tells you the relative size of each ethnic group. For example, you can see that in 1990, *Whites* made up the largest ethnic group in the United States.

Legend. A pie chart may include a legend. In many pie charts, such as these, a legend is not necessary because information is displayed on the slices themselves.

✔ CHECKING YOUR UNDERSTANDING ✔

What trends in the ethnic make-up of the United States can you see developing between the years 1990 and 2050?

TABLES

WHAT IS A TABLE?

A **table** is an arrangement of words or numbers in columns and rows. Tables are used to organize many facts so they can be easily located and compared.

ESTIMATED AFRICAN-AMERICAN POPULATION IN THE THIRTEEN BRITISH COLONIES, 1690—1740			
Year	**New England Colonies**	**Middle Colonies**	**Southern Colonies**
1690	905	2,472	13,307
1700	1,680	5,361	22,476
1710	2,585	6,218	36,063
1720	3,956	10,825	54,058
1730	6,118	11,683	73,220
1740	8,541	16,452	125,031

Source: *Historical Statistics of the United States*

KEYS TO UNDERSTANDING A TABLE

Title. The title identifies the general topic of the table. The title of this table is *Estimated African-American Population in the Thirteen British Colonies, 1690–1740*. The table provides information showing the population of African Americans living in the thirteen British colonies between 1690 and 1740.

Categories. A table is made up of various categories of information. Each column represents a category named in the headings found across the top. Here, there are four different categories: *Year, New England Colonies, Middle Colonies,* and *Southern Colonies.* Each row represents a different year.

Making Inferences from the Data. By examining a table, it is often possible to identify trends or draw conclusions. For example, between 1730 and 1740, the African-American population in the Southern colonies increased dramatically. This might indicate an increased use of enslaved workers brought over by the Trans-Atlantic slave trade.

✔ CHECKING YOUR UNDERSTANDING ✔

Which section of the colonies had the largest number of African Americans in 1730?

TIMELINES

WHAT IS A TIMELINE?

A **timeline** presents a series of events arranged in chronological order along a line. **Chronological order** is the sequence in which the events actually occurred. Thus, the event that occurred earliest is the first event on the timeline. The distances between events on a timeline are usually in proportion to the passage of actual time between the events they represent. A timeline can span anything from a short period of time to thousands of years. The purpose of a timeline is to show how events are related to each other.

KEY EVENTS IN AMERICAN HISTORY, 1887 TO 1920						
1887	1901	1906	1909	1912	1917	1920
Interstate Commerce Act passed	Theodore Roosevelt becomes President	Pure Food and Drug act passed	N.A.A.C.P. formed	Woodrow Wilson elected President	United States enters World War I	Women gain the right to vote

KEYS TO UNDERSTANDING A TIMELINE

Title. The title identifies the general topic of the timeline. For example, the title of this timeline is *Key Events in American History, 1887 to 1920*. The timeline lists important milestones in American history during the Progressive Era.

Events. All of the events on the timeline are related in some way to the title.

Dates. Events are placed on the timeline in chronological order according to their date. This timeline starts with the passage of the Interstate Commerce Act in 1887 and continues until 1920, when women gained the right to vote.

Special Terms. To understand questions about timelines or time periods, you should be familiar with some special terms:

- A **decade** refers to a 10-year period.

- A **century** represents a 100-year period.

> **A Note About Centuries.** Identifying centuries may seem confusing at first. For example, the 20th century actually refers to the 1900s — the 100 years from 1901 to 2000. This numbering system came about because we start counting from the year it is believed that Christ was born. Thus, the first one hundred years after the birth of Christ were the years 1–100. This time period is called the first century. The second century went from 101–200. The next millennium will therefore officially begin on January 1, 2001, even though most people celebrated it on January 1, 2000.

✔ CHECKING YOUR UNDERSTANDING ✔

Which event happened first: Theodore Roosevelt became President or the N.A.A.C.P. was formed?

POLITICAL CARTOONS

WHAT IS A POLITICAL CARTOON?

A **political cartoon** is a drawing that expresses an opinion about a topic or issue. Political cartoons may be humorous, but usually have a serious point. The use of political cartoons dates back to colonial times, when many people could not read or write, but could still enjoy the message of a good cartoon.

KEYS TO UNDERSTANDING A POLITICAL CARTOON

Title or Caption. Most political cartoons have a title or caption. The title or caption helps explain the message the cartoonist is trying to get across. In this cartoon, the caption asks, *Are you sure we're on the right road?*

Medium. Cartoonists want to persuade readers to follow their point of view. To achieve this, a cartoonist will use the size of objects, facial expressions, exaggerations, or words spoken by characters to satirize (*poke fun at*) some positions and to support others.

Symbols. Cartoonists often use symbols. A **symbol** can be any object that stands for, or *represents,* something else.

Are you sure we're on the right road?

Library of Congress

People. A cartoonist may want to draw attention to a particular issue by portraying a famous person closely associated with it. The cartoonist will often draw the person in the form of a caricature. A **caricature** is a drawing in which a subject's features are deliberately exaggerated for a comic effect.

✔ CHECKING YOUR UNDERSTANDING ✔

What is the main idea of the cartoon?

OTHER FORMS OF VISUAL DATA

Other types of visuals that may appear on the U.S. History and Government Regents Examination are pictures, illustrations, and diagrams. Unlike cartoons, these do not usually express an opinion, but depict a scene, person, situation, or process.

PHOTOGRAPHS AND ILLUSTRATIONS

Photographs or illustrations are especially useful for understanding the past. They show how people looked, dressed, and lived. A photograph can give us a feeling for an earlier time period or a different place. Since photographs only came into being in the mid-1800s, we rely on drawings and paintings for a glimpse of what life was like before that time. Examine the photograph on the right of children after a typical day of work in a coal mine in 1870. What does this photograph tell us about the lifestyles of children working in coal mining areas at that time?

National Archives

Children after a day in a coal mine in 1870

✔ CHECKING YOUR UNDERSTANDING ✔

What kinds of work do you think these boys performed in the mine?

DIAGRAMS

A **diagram** is a symbolic picture that shows how something is organized or how a particular process works. Examine the diagram to the right. It shows how members of our federal government are chosen.

The diagram indicates that both the legislature and the chief executive are elected by voters. The diagram also reveals the method used for selection of federal judges.

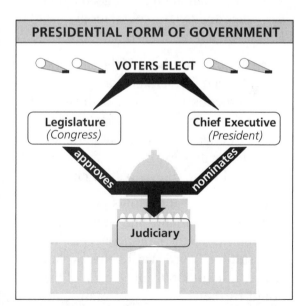

PRESIDENTIAL FORM OF GOVERNMENT

VOTERS ELECT

Legislature
(Congress)

Chief Executive
(President)

approves

nominates

Judiciary

✔ CHECKING YOUR UNDERSTANDING ✔

How is the judiciary selected for our federal government?

OUTLINES

WHAT IS AN OUTLINE?

An **outline** is a brief plan in which a topic or major idea is divided up into smaller units. The main purpose of an outline is to show the logical relationships between a topic (*major idea*) and its parts. This serves as a "blueprint" to help organize the thoughts of the writer.

KEYS TO UNDERSTANDING AN OUTLINE

Title. The title identifies the general topic of the entire outline.

Format. Most outlines follow a format that allows you to easily understand how the main topic is divided into sub-sections.

★ **Roman Numerals.** The first major divisions are given by Roman numerals (I, II, III, etc.).

★ **Capital Letters.** If the topic covered by a Roman numeral needs to be further divided, its subtopics are listed by capital letters (A, B, C, etc.).

★ **Arabic Numbers.** If the sub-topics are divided further, they are given Arabic numerals (1, 2, 3). To illustrate this process, assume you want to write about America's involvement in major wars during the early 20th century. It might be outlined as shown to the right.

TITLE:
Major Wars Involving the U.S. in the Early 20th Century

I.   World War I
    A. Causes
    B. Course of the War
    C. Results

II. World War II
    A. Causes
        1. Nazi Aggression
        2. Attack on Pearl Harbor
    B. Course of the War
    C. Results

Remember that outlines go from the general to the specific. They break down a larger idea into smaller and smaller units. In this example, each smaller unit (*sub-topic*) helps to develop the larger concept. For example, information about the causes, course, and results of World War I helps explain what the war was all about. The outline might then go into further detail on each of these sub-topics. For example, under "causes" you should further identify the main causes of World War I, such as nationalism, the alliance system, and European militarism. Knowing how to outline not only can help you to answer questions on examinations, but will also provide a useful tool for taking notes or for organizing your thoughts when writing an essay.

✔ **CHECKING YOUR UNDERSTANDING** ✔

If you were to add details about the "Results" of World War II, which would you use: Roman numerals, letters, or Arabic numerals?

SPEAKER QUESTIONS

WHAT IS A SPEAKER QUESTION?

A *speaker question* presents a series of statements by different speakers. There will usually be four speakers, identified by the letters A, B, C, and D. The main function of this type of question is to present a discussion of differing viewpoints.

Speaker A: We must provide arms to the legitimate governments of Greece and Turkey. Only with this help can they defend their nations against Soviet-sponsored subversion.

Speaker B: Now that the war against Germany is over, our first priority must be to help rebuild the economies of European countries so that democratic governments can survive and flourish.

Speaker C: Our main goal should be to create a system of collective security in which peaceful nations can deal with any military threat.

Speaker D: We must build up both our nuclear and conventional arsenals if we are to have any hope of achieving world peace.

KEYS TO UNDERSTANDING A SPEAKER QUESTION

To better understand speaker questions, you should recognize that each speaker's statement usually expresses an opinion about an important term or concept. Often these views were held by an important individual or group in history. Start by asking yourself the following questions about each speaker:

★ What term or concept is being described or discussed by the speaker?

> *Speaker A is describing the Truman Doctrine, a plan announced by President Truman to provide aid to any free people resisting a Communist takeover.*

★ What is the speaker saying about the term or concept?

★ Note how some speakers have contrasting opinions. Why do they disagree?

★ Do the opinions of the speakers remind you of the views of any individuals or groups you are already familiar with?

✔ CHECKING YOUR UNDERSTANDING ✔

Circle the decade in which the speakers' remarks would have been made:

1900–1910   1930–1940   1945–1955   1980–1990

READING PASSAGES

WHAT IS A READING PASSAGE?

Questions based on a reading require you to understand a quotation or paragraph about some topic. This type of question focuses on testing your understanding of someone's views.

"To the Honorable Senate and House of Representatives in Congress Assembled: We the under-signed, citizens of the United States, but deprived of some of the privileges and immunities of citizens, among which is the right to vote, beg leave to submit the following Resolution ...."

— *Susan B. Anthony and Elizabeth Cady Stanton (1873)*

KEYS TO UNDERSTANDING A READING SELECTION

In a reading, the writer presents a series of statements to express his or her ideas about a topic. Ask yourself the following questions about each reading selection:

What do you know about the writer?

What is the historical significance of the passage?

What is the main idea of the passage?

✔ CHECKING YOUR UNDERSTANDING ✔

Based on the excerpt, what did Anthony and Stanton propose to Congress in their Resolution of 1873?

CHAPTER 3

HOW TO ANSWER MULTIPLE-CHOICE QUESTIONS AND INTERPRET DOCUMENTS

The purpose of this chapter is to familiarize you with answering multiple-choice questions and interpreting historical documents. Let's begin by examining the basic types of multiple-choice questions.

ANSWERING MULTIPLE-CHOICE QUESTIONS

Multiple-choice questions will make up a large part of the U.S. History and Government Regents Examination. They can be grouped into two major types:

★ **Statement Questions** begin with a question or an incomplete statement. This is followed by either a list of possible answers to the question or by a list of different ways in which the statement can be completed.

★ **Data-based Questions** present some type of data or information as part of the question. You are then asked to select the correct answer from a list of four choices. In the previous chapter, you already reviewed how to understand various forms of data.

Multiple-choice questions test your mastery of both the content of American history and fundamental social studies thinking processes. Testmakers do this with a variety of question types, some of which are identified on the following pages.

KNOWLEDGE OF IMPORTANT INFORMATION

Statement questions test your knowledge of important terms, concepts, and people. The following examples illustrate some of the ways in which these questions may be phrased:

★ The concept of [*democracy*] is best illustrated by ...

★ Which statement about the [*Progressive Era*] is most accurate?

★ List two beliefs of the [*Populists*].

> *To help you recognize major terms, concepts, and people, these will be high-lighted in* **bold type** *in each content chapter.*

COMPREHENSION

Comprehension questions apply to data-based questions. These questions test whether you understand the information or data presented as part of the question. A comprehension question may take any of the following forms:

★ Which [*political party*] does the [*donkey*] in the cartoon represent?

★ According to the table, in [*which war were casualties*] the greatest?

★ According to the graph, which [*nation had the largest population*]?

> *The crucial factor in answering comprehension questions is your understanding of the information given in the data. Data-based questions appear frequently throughout this book to help you practice answering this type of question.*

CONCLUSION OR GENERALIZATION

Some questions ask you to make a generalization or draw a conclusion based on your knowledge of American history. The following are typical examples of conclusion or generalization questions:

★ Which is a valid conclusion that can be drawn about the [*causes of war*]?

★ The idea that our nation's [*geography can greatly influence its economy*] is best illustrated by ...

★ In an outline, one of these is the main topic, and the other three are sub-topics. Which is the main topic?

To help you answer generalization questions, important generalizations are identified throughout the book. They often summarize the "big idea" or main theme found in each section. Generalizations are treated in greater detail in Chapter 4, which deals with answering essay questions.

COMPARE AND CONTRAST

The act of comparing and contrasting allows us to separate and highlight particular events, ideas, and concepts, placing them into sharper focus. Compare-and-contrast questions might appear as follows:

★ Presidents [*Richard Nixon*] and [*Ronald Reagan*] were similar in that both ...

★ A major difference between the [*Democratic Party*] and [*Republican Party*] is that ...

★ A study of [*World War I*] and [*World War II*] shows that both events ...

*As you read through each content chapter, test yourself by comparing and contrasting **new** names and terms with those you already know. It is important to understand what things have in common as well as how they differ.*

CAUSE AND EFFECT

History consists of a series of conditions and events leading to other conditions and events. Causal explanations give history much of its meaning. Cause-and-effect questions test your understanding of the relationship between an action or event and its corresponding effect. In answering these questions, be careful to understand what answer is being asked for — the *cause* or the *effect*. These types of questions might appear as follows:

★ Which was a significant cause of [*the Great Depression*]? (asks for a *cause*)

★ Which was a direct result of the [*Civil War*]? (asks for an *effect*)

★ If the trend in the chart continues, what will be its effect on [*U.S. trade*]?

To help you answer cause-and-effect questions, important cause-and-effect relationships are identified in each content chapter. In addition, cause-and-effect relationships are found in graphic organizers throughout the book.

CHRONOLOGY

As you learned on page 12, **chronology** refers to the order in which events occurred. A list of events in chronological order starts from the earliest event and progresses to the latest one. This arrangement allows us to see patterns and sequences in the events taking place. Chronological questions might appear as follows:

- Which sequence best describes [*the events leading to World War II*]?

- Which group of events is in the correct chronological order?

> *To help you with these types of questions, timelines are presented at the beginning of each content chapter. In addition, to help bolster your understanding of chronology, some chapters will have a multiple-choice question dealing with chronology.*

FACT AND OPINION

Certain questions will ask you to distinguish between facts and opinions.

- ◆ A **fact** is a statement that can be proven to be true. An example of a factual statement would be: "World War II began in 1939." We frequently verify the accuracy of a fact by looking at other sources.

- ◆ An **opinion** is an expression of someone's belief and *cannot* be verified. An example of an opinion would be: "The greatest American general of World War II was Douglas MacArthur."

Questions asking you to distinguish facts from opinions might be phrased as follows:

- ★ Which statement about [*President Lincoln*] would be the most difficult to prove? (*asks you to identify an opinion among a group of facts*)

- ★ Which statement about [*U.S. foreign policy*] expresses a fact rather than an opinion? (*asks you to identify a fact among a group of opinions*)

> *To answer this type of question, it is important to remember the difference between a fact and an opinion. To help you practice this type of question, multiple-choice questions asking you to distinguish between facts and opinions are found throughout the book.*

USE OF REFERENCE BOOKS

Historians and social scientists consult a wide variety of sources in order to discover what has happened in the past. Some questions ask you to identify a specialized book of information. One standard reference book is an **atlas,** which contains a collection of maps. Other standard reference books are **encyclopedias** and **almanacs.** Questions asking you about reference books could be phrased as follows:

★ To find information about a region's [*topography*], which source would you most likely consult?

> *To answer this type of question you need to know the differences among standard reference books. To help you practice answering such questions, multiple-choice questions about standard references are found throughout the book.*

READING HISTORICAL DOCUMENTS

The U.S. History and Government Regents Examination will require you to read and interpret actual historical documents as part of the test. This section looks at what is involved in reading and interpreting original historical sources. These skills are important for document-based essay questions as well as for some multiple-choice questions.

THE SEARCH FOR MEANING

Most document-based questions on the Regents will present short passages of only a few sentences. These passages will often be excerpts taken from longer speeches or writings. Remember when reading historical documents, you must use your imagination to send yourself back in time to understand someone else's point of view. A writer in the past often had very different attitudes and concerns than we have today.

UNDERSTANDING DIFFERENT POINTS OF VIEW

In reading a historical document, you must be a critical reader. It will help if you know something about the writer's social position and background, so that you can see how these factors affected the writer's ideas.

On the next page are some of the main questions you should ask yourself when reading a historical document or passage:

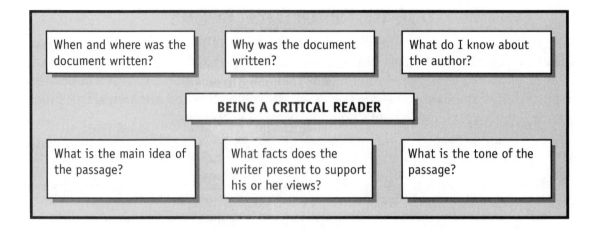

When and where was the document written?

Why was the document written?

What do I know about the author?

BEING A CRITICAL READER

What is the main idea of the passage?

What facts does the writer present to support his or her views?

What is the tone of the passage?

DETERMINING WORD MEANINGS FROM CONTEXT CLUES

Sometimes you may come across unfamiliar words or phrases in a historical document. **Context clues** will help you to figure out what they mean. Think of yourself as a detective. The surrounding words, phrases, and sentences provide clues that can help you uncover the meaning of the unfamiliar word.

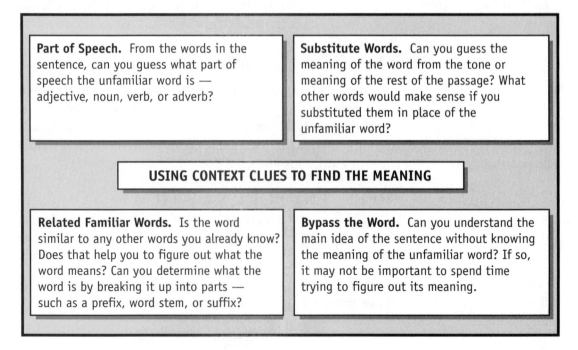

Part of Speech. From the words in the sentence, can you guess what part of speech the unfamiliar word is — adjective, noun, verb, or adverb?

Substitute Words. Can you guess the meaning of the word from the tone or meaning of the rest of the passage? What other words would make sense if you substituted them in place of the unfamiliar word?

USING CONTEXT CLUES TO FIND THE MEANING

Related Familiar Words. Is the word similar to any other words you already know? Does that help you to figure out what the word means? Can you determine what the word is by breaking it up into parts — such as a prefix, word stem, or suffix?

Bypass the Word. Can you understand the main idea of the sentence without knowing the meaning of the unfamiliar word? If so, it may not be important to spend time trying to figure out its meaning.

PRACTICE IN INTERPRETING DOCUMENTS

Let's practice the process of interpreting historical documents by examining the viewpoints of an imperialist and an anti-imperialist just after the Spanish-American War. This practice will help you to answer the questions that accompany documents in the document-based essay question as well as some multiple-choice questions.

DOCUMENT 1

"Think of the thousands of Americans who will pour into Hawaii and Puerto Rico when [our] republic's laws cover those islands with justice and safety. Think of the tens of thousands of Americans who will invade mine and field and forest in the Philippines when … the government of [our] republic shall establish order and equity!"

—*Albert Beveridge, U.S. Senator (1898)*

Suppose you did not understand the word *equity* in the last sentence. Below is a method for figuring out the meaning of this word.

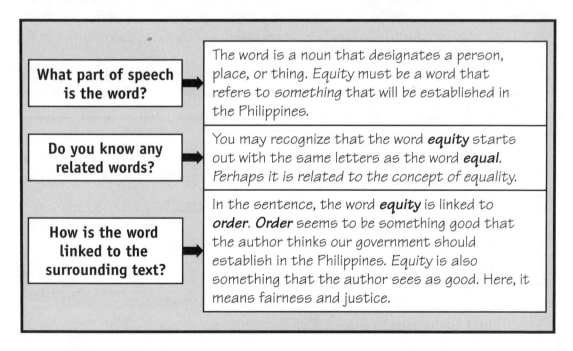

Now let's look at the document as a whole. Consider the background of the author and what the author is trying to say in this document.

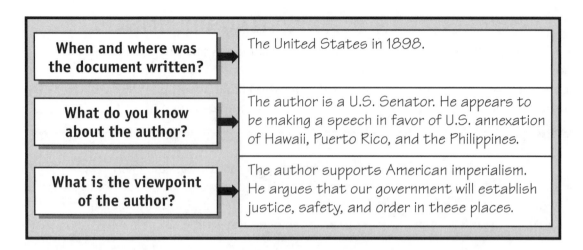

When and where was the document written?	The United States in 1898.
What do you know about the author?	The author is a U.S. Senator. He appears to be making a speech in favor of U.S. annexation of Hawaii, Puerto Rico, and the Philippines.
What is the viewpoint of the author?	The author supports American imperialism. He argues that our government will establish justice, safety, and order in these places.

Now let's compare Senator Beveridge's views with those of an anti-imperialist.

DOCUMENT 2

"We assume that what we like and practice, [will] come as a welcome blessing to Spanish-Americans and Filipinos. This is grossly and obviously untrue. They hate our ways. They are hostile to our ideas. Our religion, language, institutions, and manners offend them."

William G. Sumner, Yale University Professor (1898)

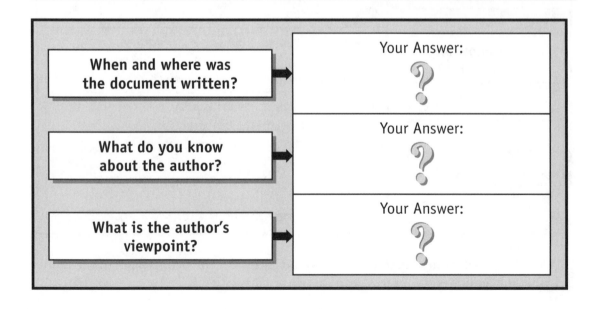

When and where was the document written?	Your Answer: ?
What do you know about the author?	Your Answer: ?
What is the author's viewpoint?	Your Answer: ?

CHAPTER 4

HOW TO ANSWER ESSAY QUESTIONS

The U.S. History and Government Regents will contain **two** essay questions. An essay question tests your ability to answer a question in depth by organizing and presenting relevant information in written form. This chapter focuses on the two types of essay questions that will appear on the test: *thematic essay questions* and *document-based essay questions*.

THEMATIC ESSAYS

One essay question will focus on a particular theme or generalization. This is known as a **thematic essay question.** Let's look at a typical question:

Directions: Write a well-organized essay that includes an introduction, several paragraphs addressing the task below, and a conclusion.

Theme: Diversity

> Throughout American history, important groups of people have faced prejudice.

Task:

Choose **two** groups from your study of United States history and government.

For *each* group:
• Explain how that group was treated unfairly.

You may use any example from your study of U.S. history and government. Some suggestions you might wish to consider include: Native American Indians, African Americans, Irish Americans, "New Immigrants," Latinos, Japanese Americans, persons with disabilities, and women.

You are *not* limited to these suggestions.

Notice that a thematic essay question opens with directions. The directions tell you the form in which your answer must be written. Next, you are provided with a theme or generalization. Here, the generalization is about groups of people facing prejudice. The question then gives you a task to complete. The question may suggest helpful examples which you might use in your essay to support the generalization. You are not limited, however, to those examples. Thus, what you are essentially asked to do is:

★   to show your understanding of a generalization by giving specific examples to support it as required by the *Task;* and

★   to write a well-organized essay that includes an introduction, several paragraphs as explained in the *Task,* and a conclusion.

WHAT IS A GENERALIZATION?

To answer a thematic essay question, you first must understand what a generalization is and how to support it. **Generalizations** are powerful organizing tools that allow us to summarize large amounts of information in a simple form. To understand what a generalization is, read the following list of facts:

★   New York City borders the Atlantic Ocean.

★   Albany is located on the Hudson River.

★   Buffalo is next to Lake Erie.

★   Geneva borders Seneca Lake.

These are four separate facts about cities in New York State. However, they have something in common: all of these cities are located next to a body of water. When a general statement identifies a common pattern, it is called a generalization. A **generalization** shows what several facts have in common. Let's see how this generalization might be presented in a diagram:

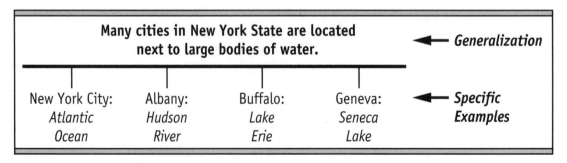

As we have seen, each thematic essay question opens with just such a generalization. Your job will be to provide examples and details to illustrate or support it. Your exact assignment will be defined by the **action words** in the **Task** part of the question.

THE "ACTION WORDS"

Essay questions require you to understand certain key words. The exact instructions for what you are supposed to do in writing your answer are contained in the "action words" in the *Task*. The most common "action words" are:

Describe or Discuss   Explain or Show How   Explain or Show Why   Evaluate

Let's examine each of these "action words" to see what they require you to do in answering an essay question.

DESCRIBE OR DISCUSS

Describe or *discuss* means to "illustrate something in words or to tell about it." *Describe* or *discuss* is used when you are asked for the *who, what, when,* and *where* of something. Of course, not every *describe* or *discuss* question requires all four of these elements, but your answer must go beyond just a single word or sentence. The following are examples of *describe* and *discuss* questions:

★ *Describe* an achievement of the Progressive Era.

★ *Discuss* the differences between the approaches of Herbert Hoover and Franklin D. Roosevelt for overcoming the Great Depression.

Here is what your answer might look like if you answered the first *describe* question:

Sample Answer: *In the early 20th century, the Progressive Movement led to the introduction of many important political reforms. Progressives introduced reforms to make government more efficient and responsive. One of the most important reforms they introduced was the direct primary, an election in which party members vote on which individuals to nominate as party candidates. In many states, direct primaries replaced a system in which party leaders picked candidates.*

Notice how the answer describes a particular achievement of the Progressive Era. The description creates a verbal picture of **who** (*Progressives*), **what** (*introduced direct primaries*), **when** (*early 20th century*), and **where** (*in many states*). *A helpful hint:* Go through your own mental checklist of *who, what, where* and *when* whenever you are asked to *describe* or *discuss* something.

EXPLAIN AND SHOW

Explain and *show* are often linked to the additional word *how* or *why*. Sometimes these action words are even used interchangeably. The key to approaching any question with these words is to determine whether the question requires you to tell *how* something happened or *why* it happened.

EXPLAIN HOW/SHOW HOW

In this type of question, the phrase *explain how* or *show how* is followed by a generalization. The general statement may ask you to illustrate *how* something works or *how* it relates to something else. It focuses on events or effects, not causes. Let's look at a few examples:

★ *Show how* the New Deal had a lasting impact on the nation.

★ *Explain how* improvements in technology can affect a country's social and economic development.

In each case you are expected to provide facts and examples that show that the generalization is true. Look at the *show how* question about the New Deal. Following is an example of how this question might be answered:

Sample Answer: *The New Deal inspired sweeping changes in the style of Presidential leadership and in the federal government's responsibilities. Americans gave up their traditional belief in "making it on their own" and turned to the government for help. Under President Roosevelt's "New Deal," the government intervened in several major ways in the nation's economy. Programs like the Civilian Conservation Corps put millions of people back to work. The Social Security Act provided new federal unemployment insurance, while the Federal Deposit Insurance Corporation guaranteed bank deposits. Finally, the New Deal increased public hopes and expectations. Voters now looked to the President to create programs and solve problems.*

Notice that the answer provides specific factual information and examples to *show how* the statement is true. These facts include: (1) that Americans had to give up their traditional belief in making it on their own; (2) that the federal government intervened more directly in the economy with programs like the C. C. C. and Social Security; and (3) that public expectations of the Presidency changed. *A helpful hint:* Think of a *show how* answer as several columns supporting the generalization you are explaining.

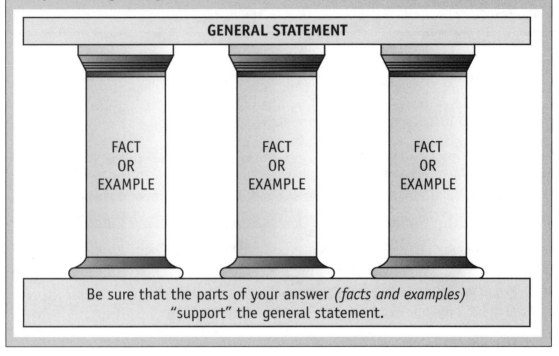

GENERAL STATEMENT

FACT OR EXAMPLE

FACT OR EXAMPLE

FACT OR EXAMPLE

Be sure that the parts of your answer *(facts and examples)* "support" the general statement.

EXPLAIN WHY/SHOW WHY

To explain *why* means to give reasons why an event took place or why a relationship identified in the question occurred. *Explain why* questions focus on causes. Your answer should identify the reasons why the event or relationship took place and briefly describe each reason. Two examples of such questions are:

★ *Explain why* the United States created the Marshall Plan.

★ *Show why* Southern states seceded from the Union in 1860–1861.

In each case, you must present reasons or causes to explain *why* the event occurred. Let's look at a sample answer to the question about the Marshall Plan.

Sample Answer: *By 1947, Communism was a growing threat. Americans feared that Communists might take over a number of countries in Europe. In addition, the United States was seeking to create future markets for its goods by building strong trading partners. In an attempt to help European countries rebuild their war-torn economies, Secretary of State George Marshall proposed a plan to pump millions of dollars of American aid into the economic recovery of European nations. The main reasons for the plan were to help European nations resist Communism and to help them to rebuild their economies.*

Notice how the answer provides reasons that *explain why* the United States created the Marshall Plan:

(reason) (1) fear that Communism would spread

+

(reason) (2) desire to build future trading partners for the United States

+

(reason) (3) desire to help European nations rebuild their economies

---

= **(conclusion)** The United States proposed the Marshall Plan
for a number of important reasons.

A helpful hint: When asked to *explain why,* go through a checklist of various reasons or causes. Be sure they add up to a satisfactory explanation.

EVALUATE

Evaluate means "to examine and judge carefully." *Evaluate* questions ask you to make a judgment. Consider the advantages and disadvantages of the policy or action you are evaluating. Then decide whether the advantages outweigh the disadvantages or the reverse. Let's look at a typical *evaluate* question: *Evaluate* the policy of interning Japanese Americans during World War II.

In order to answer this question, you must:

1. Explain why Japanese Americans were interned during World War II.
2. Identify the good and bad effects of this policy.
3. Make a judgment about whether the overall impact was positive or negative.

Let's look at a sample answer to this question:

Sample Answer: *Japanese Americans made up only a tiny minority of the population in the United States when World War II broke out. However, they suffered some of the worst discrimination during the war. Most of the Japanese American population was concentrated on the West coast. Anti-Japanese sentiment exploded after Japan attacked Pearl Harbor in December 1941. In 1942, President Roosevelt signed an Executive Order removing all Japanese Americans from the West coast to internment camps further inland.*

IF YOU THOUGHT FRANKLIN D. ROOSEVELT'S ACTION WAS

justified, you might continue as follows:	**unjustified, you might continue as follows:**
Although the conditions in the camps were harsh, there were good reasons for this policy. There was a genuine fear that some Japanese Americans might dynamite dams, choking off California's water supply, or commit other acts of sabotage. Many Americans reasonably believed that some Japanese Americans were sympathetic to Japan and might act as spies. With the Japanese navy threatening the coast of California, the entire West coast was officially a combat zone that could turn into a battlefield at any moment. Although unfortunate, the security needs of the nation justified the temporary suffering of this minority.	Although the President was concerned with national security, this step was not really justified. Roosevelt's Executive Order unfairly singled out one group of Americans based on their ancestry. It was unfair to pick on Japanese Americans, two-thirds of whom were born in the United States. There was no evidence that these were anything other than loyal American citizens. Yet, they were relocated so quickly that most had no time to sell their businesses, homes, or property. Italian Americans and German Americans did not face similar treatment, even though America was at war with Italy and Germany. Therefore, the government's persecution of Japanese Americans was clearly unjustified.

Notice how the first part of the answer provides background information and explains how the decision came about. The response then focuses on the positive and negative effects of the decision to send Japanese Americans to internment camps. Finally, the response makes an overall judgment about the wisdom of the policy. Note how one essay emphasizes the nation's security, while the other focuses on fairness. Once you take a position, be sure to provide information to support it.

PLANNING YOUR ESSAY

Now you should be ready to answer a thematic essay question. Start by examining the *Task* (on page 27). Spend a few moments thinking about how you will approach the question. Then start by making notes for your essay.

The example below is one way to approach taking notes for answering a thematic essay question.

Framework: Declaration of Independence and U.S. Constitution promised equality, but not always achieved.

Thesis: Groups of Americans have been treated unfairly.

Example/Action Words	Facts, Examples, and Details
African Americans Explain how treated unfairly	• African Americans were once slaves • Discrimination continued after end of slavery • Jim Crow Laws — Segregated in schools and public places; prevented from voting and serving on juries • *Plessy v. Ferguson* (1896) — Supreme Court upheld separate but equal treatment
Japanese Americans Explain how treated unfairly	• Gentleman's Agreement (1907) showed U.S. prejudice • Japan attack on Pearl Harbor — leads to W.W. II with Japan and increased discrimination • Forced relocation away from West coast into concentration camps • *Korematsu v. U.S.* (1944) — forced relocation upheld by U.S. Supreme Court

---

WRITING YOUR ESSAY

Now use the information from your notes to write your essay.

★ Be sure to include an introduction that goes beyond a mere restatement of the task by providing the historical context.

★ In the body of your essay, be sure to provide the number of examples required by the task (in this case it is two examples).

★ Be sure to include specific names, details, and facts. Organize this information into chronological order or some other logical order.

★ Finish your essay with a conclusion that relates the information in the body of your essay to your opening thesis.

> Notice how the opening sentence provides the historical context.

> The next two sentences provide the thesis statement. Here the student gives a particular view about the theme's generalization.

The Declaration of Independence and U.S. Constitution held out the promise of equal treatment for all Americans. Despite this lofty ideal, throughout our history certain groups of Americans have experienced prejudice and unfair treatment. Such discrimination has only lessened in the past few decades. This discrimination can be seen from an examination of the experiences of both African Americans and Japanese Americans.

Africans first came to the American colonies as slaves. Even after the Declaration of Independence was issued, slavery continued. Under slavery, African Americans faced cruel treatment: overwork, physical punishment, and the break up of their families. The Civil War ended slavery in America, but not prejudice and discrimination. After Reconstruction, Southern states passed "Jim Crow" laws. These laws separated African Americans from whites in schools, public transportation, and other public places. African Americans were also barred from serving on juries. The U.S. Supreme Court upheld this system of racial segregation in *Plessy v. Ferguson* (1896), permitting the policy of 'separate but equal' treatment.

> The second paragraph discusses the first example of the task: how African Americans were treated unfairly.

> This paragraph explores the second example required by the thesis statement.

Japanese Americans also faced prejudice in the United States. In the late 19th century, some Japanese began migrating to America for work, but they were stopped by racial prejudice on the West coast. The Japanese government agreed to stop Japanese immigration to the United States in the Gentleman's Agreement of 1907. Japanese Americans suffered even more during World War II. Japan launched a surprise attack on Pearl Harbor in 1941. Afterwards, many Americans feared acts of sabotage. Japanese Americans on the West coast were forced to give up their homes and businesses and sent to inland concentration camps where they were housed for the duration of the war. In 1944, the Supreme Court upheld this forced relocation in *Korematsu v. United States*.

We can see from the experiences of African Americans and Japanese Americans that the United States has not always lived up to its ideals. Several groups have faced prejudice and discrimination. However, in more recent times conditions have improved for both groups as America moves closer to the ideals stated in the Declaration of Independence and the U.S. Constitution.

> The conclusion relates information in the body of the essay to the thesis statement.

ADVANCED ESSAY-WRITING HINTS

These essay writing hints apply to both thematic and document-based essay questions. After you have developed a plan for your essay, you must carry it out by putting it into writing. Each major heading of your notes or outline will become one or more **paragraphs**, a group of related sentences that deal with the same topic or theme. A good paragraph displays three important characteristics:

1 Unity 2 Completeness 3 Order

UNITY

All of the sentences in a paragraph should deal with a single topic, even if they deal with different aspects of that topic. Sentences not related to the topic of a paragraph should not be included in the paragraph. The topic should cover the paragraph like an umbrella.

Writers use several techniques to give a paragraph unity. They use a topic sentence, which identifies, in a single sentence, what the main idea of a paragraph is. Through proper planning, all of the sentences in a paragraph should be clearly related to its topic sentence. Examine the following paragraph:

> *One of the most important causes of the Civil War was a basic disagreement over the future of slavery. Slavery was an important economic institution in the South. It was less important in the North, where the economy was based on free labor. Southerners did not think slavery was wrong. They pointed to slavery in the Bible and in other societies. Slave owners also felt their slaves were better treated than many factory workers in the North. Many Northerners detested slavery. Abolitionists opposed slavery on both humanitarian and religious grounds. They did not see how the nation could continue to be half-slave and half-free. Eventually, these conflicting attitudes over slavery led to the outbreak of war.*

Notice how several sentences in this paragraph specifically use the word "slavery" to tie the paragraph together. Each sentence also relates to the topic sentence.

COMPLETENESS

A second characteristic of good paragraphs is completeness. Each paragraph should thoroughly develop the idea expressed in its topic sentence. In general, you should provide enough details and supporting facts for your reader:

(1) to understand the main idea of your topic sentence, and
(2) to have enough details to conclude that your main idea could be correct.

Pretend you are the reader and re-read each paragraph to yourself. Does it meet the criteria for completeness mentioned above, or do you have to add more information to make your point sufficiently clear to your reader? A related consideration is paragraph length. If there is not enough relevant information presented in the paragraph to completely support the main idea, then the paragraph is probably too short. If the paragraph is very long, it may deal with two aspects of the same topic and should probably be broken up.

Following is an example of a paragraph with a topic sentence and supporting details:

> *The Civil Rights Movement of the 1960s was a major turning point in transforming America into a more just society. The Civil Rights Movement brought equal rights to millions of African Americans. It ended racial discrimination in public schools, public transportation, and public places. It also gave African Americans in fact, as well as law, voting rights and the right to serve on juries. The movement did not stop with helping African Americans. It later led to campaigns for equal rights for women, other ethnic minorities, and the disabled.*

Do you think this paragraph is complete? Do the details show that the Civil Rights Movement was a major turning point in transforming America?

ORDER

All the sentences in a paragraph should be presented in a logical order. In other words, the paragraph should move in a consistent direction. This is one of the hardest but most essential aspects of writing. The direction in which the paragraph moves will depend upon the purpose of the paragraph. Here are some of the most common ways for logically presenting information in a paragraph.

★ **Sequential (Chronology).** This paragraph presents a series of events (or *steps in a process*) in the order in which they have occurred (or *should occur*).

★ **From General to Specific.** This kind of paragraph opens with a general topic sentence and then provides examples or details to support or explain it. The examples can be presented in order from the most important to the least, or from the least important to the most. Sometimes the topic sentence will be restated in different words as a conclusion at the end of the paragraph.

★ **From Specific to General.** A paragraph may start with a series of examples or details that lead to a more general conclusion. The conclusion at the end of the paragraph can actually serve as the topic sentence.

★ **Parts to a Whole.** Here, the purpose of the paragraph is to identify or describe a number of "parts" to something. The parts should be described in any order that will make sense to the reader. If describing the details of a scene, you might describe items in the scene moving from right to left, or from the least to the most important. Often, we start with the least important item so that we can end the paragraph with the item having the most importance.

★ **Cause and Effect.** Another way to organize a paragraph is to begin with an effect, stated in the topic sentence, followed by its causes. The causes are identified in chronological order or in their order of importance. The topic sentence can be stated either as a question, such as "Why did Americans go to war in 1941?" or as a thesis statement: "There were many reasons why Americans went to war in 1941."

Good writers also rely on **transition words** to help make their order more obvious. Transition words serve as signposts, letting readers know exactly what to expect. This enables them to process new information more easily as they read.

Transitional Phrase	Function
Moreover, in addition, also, furthermore, then, similarly, again, next, secondly, finally	To explain a new point about the same idea or topic
For example, thus, to illustrate, in this case	To introduce an example
Therefore, in conclusion, thus, to sum up, as a result, in consequence	To introduce a conclusion or effect
Nevertheless, on the other hand, nonetheless, however, despite	To introduce a contrast or qualification

DOCUMENT-BASED ESSAY QUESTIONS

As you know, the Regents Examination will require you to answer a **document-based essay question,** also known as a "D.B.Q." This type of question tests your ability to interpret historical documents. Let's look at a typical "D.B.Q.":

Directions: Read the documents in Part A and answer the questions after each document. Then read the directions for Part B and write your essay.

Historical Context:

Beginning in the 1890s, Americans set out to correct the problems caused by rapid industrial growth. Reformers worked to eliminate a whole range of abuses.

Task:

Discuss **three** specific problems caused by rapid industrial growth, and explain how reformers sought to eliminate these problems.

After reading the documents, complete Part A.

PART A — Short Answer

NOTE: Most document-based questions will present five to eight documents. At least two will be documents other than reading passages — such as cartoons or pictures.

Directions: Analyze the documents and answer the questions that follow each document in the space provided.

DOCUMENT 1

"Old sausages that had been rejected and were moldy would be [sprayed] with borax and glycerine, and dumped into the hoppers for home sale as sausages. In the factory, sausage meat would be used that had fallen on the floor, in the dirt and sawdust, where workers had trampled and spit their billions of germs. The sausage meat was stored in great piles in rooms where water from leaky roofs would drip on it, and thousands of rats would race about on the piles of meat. It was too dark in these storage places to see well, but a man could run his hand over these piles of meat and sweep off handfuls of dried rat dung."

— Upton Sinclair, *The Jungle*

1. According to the document, what was the condition of meat being prepared for sale as sausages? _____

DOCUMENT 2

"[Congress hereby] prohibits the manufacture, sale, or transportation of adulterated or misbranded or poisonous or deleterious [harmful] *foods, drugs, medicines, and liquors."*

— Pure Food and Drug Act of 1906

2. How did this law try to correct one of the abuses of rapid industrial growth ?

_____

DOCUMENT 3

3. What problems are revealed by this photograph?

_____

_____

_____

_____

_____

Museum of the City of New York

Children at work in a textile factory

DOCUMENT 4

"My boss paid me three dollars [a week], *and for this he hurried me from early* [morning] *until late* [at night]. *He gave me only two coats at a time to do. When he handed me new work he would say quickly and sharply, "Hurry!" Late at night when the people would stand up and begin to fold their work away, and I too would rise, feeling stiff in every limb and thinking with dread of our cold empty little room and the uncooked rice, he would come over with still another coat."*
— Rose Cohen, 12-year old sweatshop worker describing her 12-hour workday

4. How would you describe Ms. Cohen's working conditions? _____

DOCUMENT 5

"Resolved: That we sympathize with the efforts of organized workingmen to shorten the hours of labor, and demand a rigid enforcement of the existing eight-hour law on work, and ask that a penalty clause be added to the said law."
— The Populist Platform of 1892

5. How did this proposal in the Populist Platform try to eliminate one of the abuses of rapid industrial growth ? _____

PART B-ESSAY

Directions: Write a well-organized essay that includes an introduction, several paragraphs, and a conclusion. Use evidence from at least **four** documents in the body of the essay. Support your response with relevant facts, examples, and details. Include additional outside information.

Task:

Using information from the documents and your knowledge of United States history and government, write an essay in which you:
- Discuss three specific problems caused by rapid industrial growth.
- Explain how reformers sought to eliminate these problems.

Notice that document-based questions have the following parts:

(**1**) directions on how to write the essay and how many documents to use;

(**2**) a historical generalization that sets the stage for the essay question;

(**3**) a task you must perform, stated in the form of a question;

(**4**) Part A, with up to eight documents that must be analyzed; and

(**5**) Part B, where you write the final essay.

To do well on a document-based essay question, you need to follow three steps: (1) look at the question; (2) analyze the documents; and (3) write the essay. An easy way to remember this approach is to think of the word "**L·A·W.**"

"L" — LOOK AT THE QUESTION

Let's use the "**L·A·W**" approach to answer the *Task* question above.

Task:

Using information from the documents and your knowledge of United States history and government, write an essay in which you:
- Discuss three specific problems caused by rapid industrial growth.
- Explain how reformers sought to eliminate these problems.

Notice how the task contains **two** sets of directions. Each set includes:

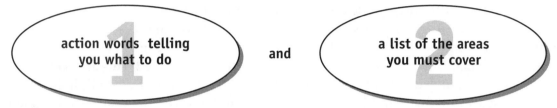

action words telling
you what to do

and

a list of the areas
you must cover

Action Words	*Discuss* and *Explain How*
Areas to Cover	You must discuss **three** specific problems caused by rapid industrial growth, and explain how reformers sought to eliminate these problems.

This information gives you an indication of how many paragraphs you should write. All essays must have an introduction and a conclusion. What varies from one essay to another is the number of paragraphs needed in the body of the essay to answer the *requirements of the question*. In this example, you need **at least** three paragraphs in the body of the essay — one to discuss each problem created by industrial growth and to explain how reformers sought to eliminate the problem. Therefore, your final written essay should contain at least five paragraphs:

Paragraph 1	should include your thesis statement and a transition sentence
Paragraph 2	should deal with one problem and how reformers sought to eliminate it
Paragraph 3	should deal with a second problem and how reformers sought to eliminate it
Paragraph 4	should deal with a third problem and how reformers sought to eliminate it
Paragraph 5	should end the essay with your conclusion

Some students also find it helpful to jot down what they know about the topic of the question before turning to the documents.

"A" — ANALYZE THE DOCUMENTS

You are now ready for the second part of the "**L•A•W**" approach — analyzing the documents.

Each document is followed by at least one "scaffolding" question related to the **Task**. Use the skills you have learned for interpreting different types of data and historical documents (see Chapters 2 and 3) to help you answer these "scaffolding" questions. With such a large amount of data, you need a way to organize your analysis. One recommended method is to use an **Analysis Box.** Fill in the boxes as you answer the questions that accompany the documents. The *Part A* questions will help guide you to what is important in the document. Note that the box also has space for related supplementary information.

	Document	Main Idea	Problem	Reform
SAMPLE ANALYSIS BOX	**The Jungle**	Describes conditions in a meat packing plant—the reuse of spoiled food, food falling on the floor, leaky roof water dripping on food, and rat droppings.	Unsanitary conditions in a sausage plant	
	Pure Food Act	Congress acted to prohibit many of the abuses pointed out by Upton Sinclair in *The Jungle*.		Protect against selling harmful products
	Photo	A young child at work in a factory, operating a large textile machine.	Child labor	
	Rose Cohen's Testimony	Rose, a child, labored 12 hours a day under miserable conditions.	Long workday; poor working conditions; child labor	
	Populist Platform	A part of the Populist Platform that demanded that the work day be reduced to eight hours.		Institute an eight-hour workday
	Related Supplementary Information:			

- Muckrakers drew attention to the abuses of Big Business.
- Samuel Gompers formed the American Federation of Labor, a union that fought against long hours, low wages, and poor working conditions.
- The Progressives called for legislation to abolish child labor.

Let's examine each of the items in the Analysis Box:

★ In the **Document** column, you should write a brief phrase to identify each document. Since the first document was from Upton Sinclair's book, *The Jungle,* you might identify it by writing "The Jungle" in the first box.

★ In the **Main Idea** column, briefly describe the main idea of each document.

★ The last columns will depend on what you must cover in your essay answer. In this example, since you must cover both a problem and attempts by reformers to correct it, you will need two additional columns.

★ The directions ask you to use **related supplementary information** based on your knowledge of American history. This is where you need to draw on your knowledge of related, outside information as shown in the examples in the Analysis Box.

You must be sure to answer every question that follows the documents. You will get a separate score for answers to these **Part A** questions.

"W"— WRITING THE ESSAY

In the last part of the "L•A•W" approach, you must plan and write your essay. You can use your Analysis Box as the basis for your plan. You should follow the same general rules as you do for writing thematic essays, except that now you must also include references to the documents in your answer.

OPENING PARAGRAPH

In a document-based essay question, you need one or more opening sentences that identify the historical context (*sets the time and place*). This sets a framework to your answer that goes beyond merely restating the **Task**. This opening should be followed by your thesis statement, based on the question. Your thesis statement should clearly state what you are trying to show in your essay. For example:

> During the late 19th and early 20th centuries, Americans faced new problems caused by rapid industrial growth. In the Progressive Era, reformers sought to eliminate some of these problems. Americans were not prepared for the congestion of cities, the sale of unhealthy foods by distant manufacturers, and the abuses of workers that occurred in each industrial society.

MAIN PARAGRAPHS

Each paragraph in the body of your essay should deal with one aspect of the thesis statement. In this example, each paragraph could deal with one problem and attempts to eliminate it. Use your analysis of the documents and related outside information to support your conclusions, just like a good lawyer would refer to evidence in court.

For a high score, you should richly support your thesis statement and main ideas with facts, examples, and details. Try to give specific names and dates. Tell about each fact or example with the *how*, *what*, *where*, *when*, *who*, and *why*.

CONCLUSION

How you close your essay will depend on the action words used in the question.

★ **Discuss or Explain.** If the question asks you to *discuss* or *explain* a topic, one approach is to begin your conclusion by restating your thesis statement. For example,

> Thus, we can see that during the late 19th and early 20th centuries, reformers attempted to overcome the new problems caused by rapid industrial growth.

You might add a short summary of what you have written already, to reinforce your case:

> Muckrakers and others promoted simple solutions to some problems, like unsafe food and child labor. Intervention by the government showed that in a democracy, legislation can be an effective tool for resolving certain social problems.

★ **Evaluate.** If the question asks you to *evaluate* a policy or program, you should weigh its positive and negative effects and then make a final judgment. For example, if you had to *evaluate* the reforms sponsored by the Progressives, you might conclude as follows:

> In conclusion, the reforms sponsored by the Progressives generally had a positive impact in making American society more democratic in curbing the worst abuses of industrialization. Passage of the Pure Food and Drug Act, state and local political reforms, and new laws against child labor were significant accomplishments whose advantages outweighed the dangers of governmental intervention.

TOOLS FOR MASTERING AMERICAN HISTORY

WHAT IS HISTORY?

History is the story of the past. People who write about history are known as **historians.** Historians are concerned with understanding events that happened in the past and with learning about the ideas, actions, and beliefs of people who lived before our time. The study of history helps a society remember what it is and where it is going. Just as your own life would be meaningless if you had no memory of who you were or what you had done, each society looks to its history for a sense of identity and direction.

SOURCES OF HISTORY

In one sense, a historian acts like a detective gathering clues. To find information about the past, historians rely on two kinds of sources:

★ **Primary Sources** are original records of an event. They include documents left by eyewitnesses, records created at the time of the event, speeches, reports, letters by people involved in the event, photographs, and artifacts.

★ **Secondary Sources** are the later writings and interpretations of historians and other writers. Often secondary sources, like history books and articles, provide summaries of the information found in primary sources.

HISTORICAL PERIODS

When writing history, historians divide the past into **historical periods.** Each period is a span of time unified by some common characteristics, circumstances, events, or people. There is no exact agreement on historical periods and their dates. Different periods begin and end in different places at different times. Traditionally, historical periods have been tied to a particular region or culture. For example, the Middle Ages is a historical period closely tied to Europe, while the Ming Dynasty refers to a period in the history of China.

Although the United States is a relatively young nation — just over 200 years old — people have been living in this region for thousands of years. Since the first "encounter" among Europeans, Native American Indians, and Africans about 500 years ago, American culture has been strongly influenced by a mixture of heritages. The main focus of the Regents Examination is on the last 140 years of American history. To help review for the test, this book is organized into the following chronological periods:

PERIODS OF AMERICAN HISTORY

★ Constitutional Foundations

★ Young Republic, Civil War, and Reconstruction, 1790–1870

★ Industrialization of the United States, 1870–1890

★ The Progressive Response to Industrialization, 1890–1920

★ Prosperity and Depression, 1920–1940

★ The United States in the Age of Global Crisis, 1940–1960

★ America in Uncertain Times, 1950–1970

★ Contemporary America, 1970 to the Present

GEOGRAPHY AND AMERICAN HISTORY

The Regents Examination will test your knowledge of the history of human activity in the area now known as the United States. This area consists of several distinct geographical regions. The diversity of America's geography has played an important role in its history. Because of this role, it is important to be familiar with this physical setting.

LOCATION, TOPOGRAPHY, AND CLIMATE

The United States is located in the middle of the continent of North America and extends from the Atlantic Ocean to the Pacific Ocean. In addition to the continental United States, the United States includes Alaska and Hawaii.

Cut off from many parts of the world by two large oceans, America's location separated Native American Indians from the cultures of Africa and Eurasia. Even in modern times, Americans have often felt protected from the problems and wars of the rest of the world by these vast oceans.

The continental United States has been described as a giant saucer, with a lower central plain in the middle, flanked by higher mountain ranges on each side. The two mountain ranges are the **Appalachian** and **Rocky Mountains.** In between these mountain chains are the central lowlands, while a wide coastal plain extends along the Atlantic coast. Both the lowlands and the coastal plain, as well as the Central Valley in California, have very fertile soil.

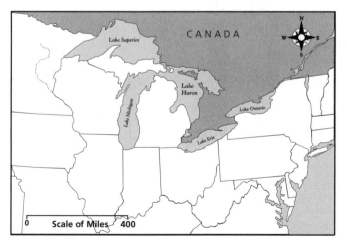

The United States also has some important waterways. The **Great Lakes** are some of the largest fresh water lakes in the world. In addition, the United States contains several major river systems. The largest is the **Mississippi River** system, with the Missouri, Ohio, and other tributaries draining almost half the continental United States. Other major river systems include the Rio Grande, Colorado River, and Hudson River. Important mineral resources include iron ore, coal, and oil.

The United States benefits from plentiful rainfall in the East and Midwest, with moderate temperatures. The Western United States is more dry, and areas of the Southwest, including parts of Texas, New Mexico, Arizona, Nevada, Utah, and California, are desert.

PHYSICAL REGIONS OF THE UNITED STATES

A **region** is an area that shares certain features and that has greater contact with other places within the region than outside it. Because of its diverse topography and climate, the continental United States can be thought of as one nation consisting of several geographic regions. Indeed, there are many ways to divide the United States into regions — one way of doing so is as follows:

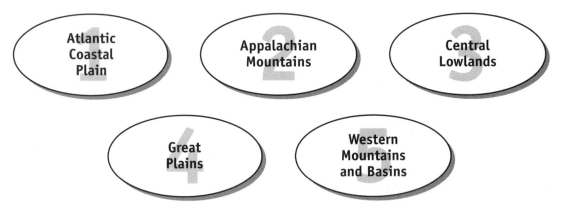

The locations of these five regions are indicated on the map below:

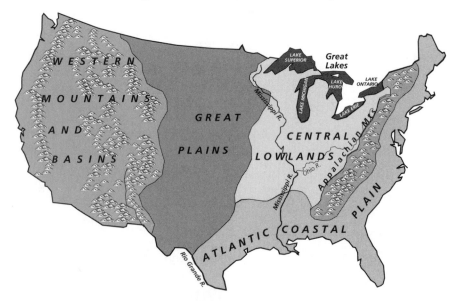

THE ATLANTIC COASTAL PLAIN

The **Atlantic Coastal Plain** is one of the world's largest coastal plains. It stretches southward from New England to Georgia. From Georgia it widens out to Texas while continuing southward. This was the region first settled by colonists from Europe in the seventeenth century. Much of this area was forest before settlers turned it into farmland. Today, it is the area with the highest concentration of people. The Atlantic Coastal Plain rises up to a hilly area, known as the **Piedmont,** as it approaches the Appalachian Mountains.

THE APPALACHIAN MOUNTAINS

The **Appalachian Mountains** cover much of the eastern part of the United States. They extend from Maine in the north to Alabama in the south, where they are cut off by the coastal plain. The Allegheny Mountains, the Blue Ridge Mountains, and the Great Smoky Mountains are all part of the Appalachians. The ancient Appalachian Mountains were formed by the folding and wrinkling

The Great Smoky Mountains in Western North Carolina

N.C. Travel and Tourism

of the earth's crust. Thousands of years ago, the Appalachians were higher than they are today. Over time, their peaks eroded and became rounded. They were difficult for the first settlers to pass through because they presented an almost unbroken chain with few gaps.

THE CENTRAL LOWLANDS

To the west of the Appalachians are the **Central Lowlands.** The northern part of this region was once scraped by **glaciers** (*huge moving sheets of ice*) and is a continuation of a sheet of ancient rocks extending southward from Canada. The Superior Uplands in Minnesota and Northern Michigan and the Adirondack Mountains in Northern New York are part of the system. Farther south, where the elevation is lower, glaciers and winds deposited soil and silt, making the land well suited for farming. Windblown topsoil, known as loess, makes parts of the Central Lowlands among the most fertile regions of the United States. The eastern part of the Central Lowlands are flat grasslands known as **prairies.** The Mississippi, Missouri, and Ohio Rivers drain this vast region.

THE GREAT PLAINS

West of the Mississippi, the grasslands become much drier and more hilly. This region is known as the **Great Plains**. These plains were covered with sod and thick grasses. The Central Lowlands and the Great Plains provide some of the world's most productive farmland — growing vast amounts of corn and wheat, and raising large amounts of cattle, hogs,

Early settlers used the dense sod of the plains as the building material for their roofs

and other livestock. If you were flying over this area, the rectangular fields would look much like a giant quilt spread out below and stretching as far as the eye can see.

THE WESTERN MOUNTAINS AND BASINS

To the west of the Great Plains, the land rises sharply, forming the **Rocky Mountains.** These mountains extend from western Canada as far south as New Mexico. Still further west are the peaks of the **Cascade** and **Sierra Nevada Ranges,** and the **Pacific Coastal Ranges.** Some of these mountains were formed by volcanoes. Most of them, like the Appalachian Mountains in the east, were formed by the shifting

A California lumber mill processes redwood trees

and folding of the earth's crust. These western areas receive little rainfall.

The **Great Basin,** separating the Rocky Mountains and the Sierra Nevada, is dry and desert-like. California's Central Valley, located between the Sierra Nevada and the Coastal Range, has excellent soils, almost continuous sunshine, and a long growing season. Although the Central Valley gets little rainfall in summer, irrigation has been made it into very productive farmland. The Pacific Northwest has frequent rain and is home to vast forests.

CHAPTER 6

CONSTITUTIONAL FOUNDATIONS

George Washington presides over the signing of the U.S. Constitution (1787)

National Archives

TIMELINE OF IMPORTANT EVENTS

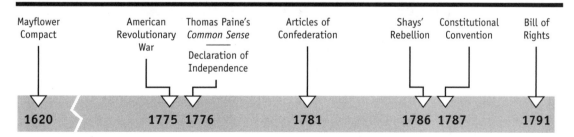

| Mayflower Compact | American Revolutionary War | Thomas Paine's *Common Sense* —— Declaration of Independence | Articles of Confederation | Shays' Rebellion | Constitutional Convention | Bill of Rights |

| 1620 | 1775 | 1776 | 1781 | 1786 | 1787 | 1791 |

WHAT YOU SHOULD FOCUS ON

In this chapter, you will learn how thirteen English colonies formed an independent nation. The main challenge of this era was to create a democratic government strong enough to meet the nation's needs without also threatening citizens' individual liberties. To meet this challenge, Americans drafted two documents — the Declaration of Independence and the U.S. Constitution. As you read this chapter, you will learn about:

National Archives

*The Declaration of Independence
is read for the first time*

★ **From Colonies to Independence.** American colonists objected to British attempts to impose new taxes without their consent, setting off a conflict that led to their independence from Great Britain. In the Declaration of Independence, Americans asserted that the purpose of government was to meet the needs of the governed.

★ **The Critical Period.** Under our first system of national government, the Articles of Confederation, most governmental powers were left to the states. This system of government proved too weak to deal with the problems facing the new nation.

★ **The U.S. Constitution.** The Constitutional Convention provided a strong government. Federalism, the separation of powers, and a system of checks and balances assured that no one branch of government would become too strong. To protect the rights of individual citizens, the first Congress added a Bill of Rights.

★ **The Principles of American Government.** The system of government we enjoy today is part of the legacy of the U.S. Constitution.

In studying this period, you should focus on the following questions:

★ What were the basic ideas of the Declaration of Independence?
★ How did the Constitution create a stronger central government without threatening individual liberties?
★ How does our federal system of government work?
★ How are individual rights protected by the Constitution and Bill of Rights?

LOOKING AT GOVERNMENT

n this chapter, you will learn about the American system of government. This introduction examines what government is and what the goals of government are.

WHAT IS GOVERNMENT?

By nature, human beings are communal. They live in communities to survive. All communities need to make rules, resolve disputes, and protect their members from aggressors. The body given the authority to carry out these binding decisions for a community is called **government.** Governments possess three powers to implement their authority:

Legislative Power
(to make laws)

Executive Power
(to carry out the laws)

Judicial Power
(to apply the laws to specific situations)

In fact, the word *govern* comes from the ancient Greek word for steering a ship. Just as a pilot guides a ship, a government guides the conduct of the members of a community in their dealings with each other and with outsiders.

CREATION OF A GOVERNMENT

The creation of governmental authority is a matter of great concern to each of us. Why do we give people whom we hardly know such immense power over our lives? And how much power can we give to government officials without threatening our own personal liberties? Asking such questions helps us to appreciate the complexity of the problems that faced the authors of the American system of government.

THE FORMS OF GOVERNMENT

Americans had several types of government from which to choose after independence. They could have created a **monarchy** (*rule by a king*), a **constitutional monarchy** (*where a king and parliament share power*), or a **representative democracy** (*rule by popularly elected representatives*). In 1776, the colonists chose a representative democracy. The delegates to the Constitutional Convention in 1787 remained committed to this choice. Ultimate power would remain in the hands of the people.

(continued)

THE GOALS OF THE U.S. GOVERNMENT

Members of the Constitutional Convention had to decide on the aims of the new federal government they were creating. The Declaration of Independence already stated that all governments should aim at protecting the rights and liberties of the individual members of the community. The Preamble of the U.S. Constitution spelled out the specific goals of our national government in more detail:

Declaration of Independence	The U.S. Constitution
Right to life	To Insure Domestic Tranquility To Provide for the Common Defense
Right to Liberty	To Secure the Blessings of Liberty To Establish Justice
Right to Pursue Happiness	To Promote the General Welfare To Form a More Perfect Union

You should note two important things about these statements of aims:

★　First, most of these aims are quite broad. For example, one of the goals of our national government is to "establish justice." What people believe to be "just" may change over time. In the late 1800s, Americans did not consider it "unjust" to place children of different races in separate schools. Attitudes gradually changed. Racial segregation became unconstitutional.

★　Secondly, it is possible for some of these goals to come into conflict. For example, in taking measures for the "common defense," the government may be forced to deny some citizens the "blessings of liberty."

THE STRUCTURE OF THE U.S. GOVERNMENT

Once they had decided on the aims of government, members of the Constitutional Convention had to design a government that could fulfill those aims. They wanted to strike a balance between the powers of the government and the rights of the individual. The central problem in forming a government was thus seen to be the following: *How much power should be given to government officials — so that they can carry out their duties effectively — without endangering the liberties of citizens?* The framers created a new government strong enough to meet national goals, but not so powerful that it would threaten individual liberties. How they achieved this miraculous result is the theme of this chapter.

FROM COLONIES TO INDEPENDENT STATES

This first section provides essential background for your understanding of American history. For thousands of years, what is now the United States was occupied by Native American Indians. Starting in the sixteenth century, European colonists began establishing settlements in North America. Most early colonists came in search of wealth, property, or religious freedom. One exception were the African slaves, brought to the colonies by force as captive laborers.

THE THIRTEEN ENGLISH COLONIES

By the 1730s, all of the Atlantic Coastal Plain between Florida and Canada had been divided into thirteen separate English colonies. Geographic, religious, and social differences created three distinct colonial regions.

NEW ENGLAND

New England's population grew quickly. Its soils were less fertile than those of the other colonies. New England colonists tended to work on small farms where they primarily grew crops for their own use. Others became merchants, sailors, shipbuilders, and fishermen. New England also emerged as a center for finished goods.

MIDDLE COLONIES

Fertile soil drew settlers to the Middle Colonies — New York, New Jersey, Pennsylvania, Delaware, and Maryland. Farmers in this region grew wheat, oats, corn, and other grains. The Middle Colonies especially benefited from trade between New England and the Southern Colonies. The region was noted for its religious diversity.

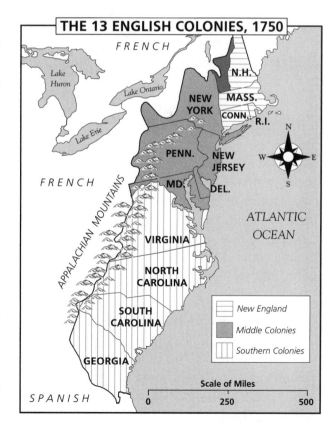

THE 13 ENGLISH COLONIES, 1750

FRENCH

Lake Huron

Lake Ontario

Lake Erie

N.H.

NEW YORK

MASS.

CONN. R.I.

PENN.

NEW JERSEY

FRENCH

MD. DEL.

APPALACHIAN MOUNTAINS

VIRGINIA

NORTH CAROLINA

ATLANTIC OCEAN

SOUTH CAROLINA

GEORGIA

SPANISH

New England

Middle Colonies

Southern Colonies

Scale of Miles

0   250   500

SOUTHERN COLONIES

Virginia was the oldest English colony in the New World. The Carolinas were settled by a chartered company formed by English nobles. Georgia was founded as a place for imprisoned debtors and convicts sent from England. Plantations in the Southern Colonies produced tobacco, rice, and indigo for shipment to England in exchange for manufactured goods. Although most Southerners did not own slaves, Southern plantations largely relied on slave labor.

DEMOCRATIC TRADITIONS EVOLVE IN THE COLONIES

Many of the democratic institutions found in the colonies were rooted in the English political tradition. In the **Magna Carta** of 1215, for example, the English king had promised not to take away property or imprison his nobles except according to the laws of the land.

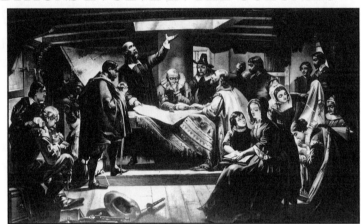

Pilgrims sign the Mayflower Compact

Library of Congress

Special democratic traditions also developed among the colonists themselves. In 1620, Pilgrims crossing the Atlantic signed the **Mayflower Compact.** This document established a colonial government deriving power from the consent of the governed. The previous year, Virginia had established its own **House of Burgesses,** elected representatives who helped govern the colony. In fact, colonial assemblies, patterned after the British Parliament, came to act as lawmaking bodies in charge of local problems throughout the colonies. Finally, because many people fled to the New World to escape religious persecution, a tradition of religious toleration also developed in many of the colonies.

THE SYSTEM OF MERCANTILISM

The American colonies grew in importance to Great Britain as their population and the value of their trade increased. Under **mercantilism,** trade between the Mother Country (*Great Britain*) and the colonies was regulated to benefit the Mother Country. The British sold costly manufactured goods to the colonists, while the colonists sold back cheaper raw materials, like tobacco, to the British. This system helped Great Britain to increase its wealth and power.

THE AMERICAN REVOLUTION, 1775–1783

By the mid-1700s, Britain and France had became rivals for overseas colonies. In North America, this struggle became known as the **French and Indian War** (1754–1763). Although English colonial assemblies, reluctant to give up power, refused to cooperate in the proposed **Albany** Plan of Union (1754), the French still lost the war. The British gained Canada, but also faced large debt.

"NO TAXATION WITHOUT REPRESENTATION"

The British Parliament wanted the colonies to help pay off the war debt and imposed new colonial taxes. In 1765, Parliament passed the **Stamp Act**, requiring all colonial newspapers, books, and documents to carry an official government stamp. The colonists objected to the tax, since they were not represented in Parliament. After a wave of colonial protests, Parliament repealed the stamp tax, but replaced it with taxes on paper, glass, and tea. The colonists again protested against taxes being imposed without their consent. Rioting broke out in several cities. The British repealed all the taxes but the duty on tea. In 1773, a group of protesters, disguised as Native Americans, threw tea off British ships into Boston harbor. As a result of the **Boston Tea Party,** the British government closed Boston harbor and banned public meetings until the tea was paid for.

THE IDEA OF INDEPENDENCE GROWS

Representatives from the colonies met in Philadelphia in 1774. In 1775, British soldiers exchanged gunfire with colonial volunteers in Massachusetts, marking the start of the American Revolution. A Second Continental Congress, held in Philadelphia,

Fighting breaks out between American colonists and British soldiers

Library of Congress

offered to negotiate with the British government. But **King George III** and Parliament refused. As fighting continued, many began to argue for independence from Great Britain. The colonists were further inflamed by the publication of **Thomas Paine's** pamphlet ***Common Sense.*** Paine wrote that it was ridiculous for the American colonies, occupying an entire continent, to be governed by a tiny far-off island like Great Britain. It was only "common sense" for the colonies to seek independence.

A DECLARATION OF INDEPENDENCE IS ISSUED

By mid-1776, a committee headed by **Thomas Jefferson** was set up to draft a Declaration of Independence. The Declaration was approved and formally adopted on July 4, 1776. Its main purpose was to explain and to justify to the world why the American colonists had decided to declare their independence from Great Britain. The key paragraph of the Declaration contained a statement of principles upon which the colonists believed all governments should be based:

> *We hold these truths to be self-evident, that all men are created equal, that they are endowed by their Creator with certain unalienable Rights, that among these are Life, Liberty and the pursuit of Happiness. That to secure these rights, Governments are instituted among Men, deriving their just powers from the consent of the governed. That whenever any Form of Government becomes destructive of these ends, it is the right of the People to alter or abolish it, and to institute new Government .....*

This paragraph was based on the following ideas:

★ **Natural Rights and the Equality of Mankind.** The Declaration stated that all people have **natural rights** (*"unalienable rights"*), which cannot be taken away. Among these basic human rights are "life, liberty and the pursuit of happiness." In this sense, "all men are created equal." Although it would take almost 200 years before full equality was extended to all Americans, the words of the Declaration were a powerful force in laying the foundation for true equality.

★ **The Social Contract.** The Declaration was based on the "Social Contract" theory of English philosopher **John Locke.** According to Locke, people form governments to protect their natural rights. If a government fails to protect its citizens and instead oppresses those it is designed to protect, its citizens have the right to overthrow the government and create a new one.

SIGNIFICANCE OF THE DECLARATION

The Declaration stated that the colonists' liberties had been violated and that they were justified in breaking their connection with Great Britain. The Declaration also encouraged foreign nations, like France, to support the colonists in their struggle for independence. The simple logic of the Declaration inspired subsequent revolutions — the French Revolution (1789) and later revolutions in Latin America, Asia, Africa, and the Middle East. The ideals of the Declaration also influenced many provisions of the U.S. Constitution.

OUR FIRST NATIONAL GOVERNMENT

The revolutionary army, commanded by General **George Washington,** eventually triumphed over the British. In 1783, Britain recognized the independence of the thirteen colonies. As a result, each colony became an independent state. Although each colony enacted a constitution establishing its own state government, Americans also recognized the need for some form of central government for all thirteen new states.

George Washington accepts the surrender of the British

U.S. Capital Historical Society

THE ARTICLES OF CONFEDERATION

After independence was declared, the Second Continental Congress began to work out a plan for a national government. An agreement, known as the **Articles of Confederation,** went into effect in 1781. The new confederation was a loose, weak association of independent states. Each state sent one representative to a Confederation Congress, where it had one vote. There was no national executive or national court. Under the Articles, individual state governments were more powerful than the new national government. The Confederation Congress could not levy taxes, raise its own army, regulate trade, or even enforce its own laws and treaties. It was up to the individual states to enforce and apply the acts of Congress.

THE CRITICAL PERIOD (1781–1786)

The Articles of Confederation successfully kept the nation together during the final years of the American Revolution. In addition, with the passage of the **Northwest Ordinance** in 1787, Congress provided a system for governing the western territories. Despite these successes, the period under the Articles is often called the "Critical Period" because of the serious problems that arose between 1781 and 1786. The major weakness of the Articles was that it gave little power to the National government. States taxed goods from other states, making commerce between states difficult. Each state printed its own money, increasing the problems of selling goods from one state to those in another. The states also refused to give the national Congress most of the tax money it requested. The new national government was powerless to do anything about these problems.

One of the most serious shortcomings of the national government was that it had no standing army. This weakness became apparent when a group of debtors and small farmers led by Daniel Shays rebelled in Massachusetts, demanding cheap money to pay off their debts. **Shays' Rebellion** was put down by state troops but created a wave of fear among many property-owners. If the rebellion had spread, the Confederation government would have been powerless to stop it.

THE ORIGINS OF THE U.S. CONSTITUTION

By 1786, merchants were unhappy that several states were obstructing trade. Property owners no longer felt safe. Many people feared that if a foreign country attacked the United States, the government would simply collapse. Several states called for a meeting to revise the Articles of Confederation.

THE CONSTITUTIONAL CONVENTION, 1787

Delegates from the states met in Philadelphia in 1787. The delegates quickly decided to abandon the Articles and to write a new **constitution** (*document outlining the basic form and rules of government*). The delegates at the Constitutional Convention agreed on the need for a strong national government with the power to tax, to maintain a national army, and to regulate commerce among the states. They also agreed on the need for a national executive, a national judiciary, and a national legislature. There were also important disagreements among the delegates, which were settled through a series of compromises.

THE GREAT COMPROMISE

Large states differed with small states on the best method of representation for the new legislature, known as Congress. To resolve the conflict, a **bicameral** (*two house*) legislature was created. In the **House of Representatives,** states would be represented according to the size of their population: larger states would have a greater number of representatives. In the **Senate,** each state would be represented equally by two Senators. This served to satisfy the smaller states.

In this room the compromises at the Constitutional Convention were worked out

Eastern National Park and Monument Assoc.

THE THREE-FIFTHS COMPROMISE

Delegates from the South wanted to count slaves as part of a state's population in order to increase the number of their representatives in the House of Representatives. A compromise was reached, allowing representation for three-fifths of the slave populations. In effect, every five slaves would be counted as three citizens, even though the slaves could not vote and had no rights.

THE SLAVE TRADE AND COMMERCE COMPROMISES

Northern and Southern states differed over both the slave trade and the taxing of exports. Two more compromises were reached: Congress would not pass any laws restricting the slave trade for another twenty years (*until 1808*), and the new government would have no power to tax exports.

THE DEBATE OVER RATIFICATION

The Constitutional Convention decided that a special convention should be held in each state to **ratify** (*approve*) the Constitution. Once nine state conventions had ratified the new Constitution, it would be put into effect.

FEDERALISTS SUPPORT RATIFICATION

The **Federalists** argued that the Articles of Confederation were a failure. They said that a stronger government was needed to protect citizens from rebellions and invasions, and to regulate trade among the states. A President was necessary to enforce the decisions of the national government. Citizens should not fear the power of this new government, Federalists claimed, because this power would be divided among three separate branches. These arguments were best expressed by Alexander Hamilton, James Madison, and John Jay in 85 essays published as *The Federalist Papers.*

ANTI-FEDERALISTS OPPOSE RATIFICATION

Anti-Federalists claimed the new Constitution would create a government that was too powerful. With control of the national army, government leaders might even make themselves dictators. Moreover, there was no **Bill of Rights** in the new Constitution to protect the life, liberty, and property of citizens, or to guarantee fair trials and free speech.

The Federalist position prevailed. Eleven state conventions ratified the Constitution by the end of 1788. In 1789, the first Congress assembled in New York City. The following month, George Washington was inaugurated as the nation's first President.

BASIC PRINCIPLES OF THE U.S. CONSTITUTION

In this section, you will review the basic principles of the system of government established by our Constitution.

POPULAR SOVEREIGNTY

The first and most basic principle of our Constitution is the belief that the final power in government rests with the people. This is reflected in the first words of the **Preamble;** "We the people …" Americans exercise this power by choosing their own representatives in elections.

FEDERALISM

Federalism is a system for sharing power between the national and state governments. The U.S. Constitution divides government power between the national (*or federal*) government and the state governments. The federal government deals with national concerns and relations among the states, while state governments deal with affairs within each state.

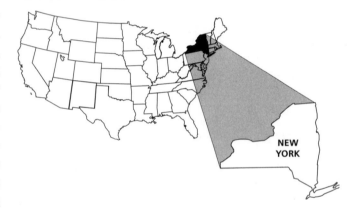

NEW
YORK

DELEGATED POWERS
(*Powers given to the national government*)

- declare war
- negotiate treaties
- issue money
- regulate interstate commerce and foreign trade

CONCURRENT POWERS
(*Powers held by both the federal and state governments*)

- levy taxes
- define crimes and punishments
- determine voting qualifications
- borrow money

RESERVED POWERS
(*Powers held exclusively by state governments*)

- regulate education
- grant licenses
- provide police protection
- regulate the sale of property within the state

SEPARATION OF POWERS

At the national level, power is further separated into three branches. This separation of powers makes it difficult for any one individual or group to gain control of the entire government.

Legislative Branch
Power to make
the laws

Executive Branch
Power to enforce
the laws

Judicial Branch
Power to interpret
the laws

LIMITED GOVERNMENT

The federal government and state governments cannot do just anything they want: their powers over our lives are strictly regulated and limited by the Constitution.

★ **Preamble.** The Preamble to the Constitution lists the purposes of the federal government — to establish justice, insure domestic peace, provide for the nation's defense, promote the general welfare, and secure the blessings of liberty. All federal government actions should be directed towards these goals.

★ **Delegated Powers.** The federal government has only those powers given to it by the Constitution. The Constitution also lists those powers specifically denied to either the federal or state governments.

Powers Denied to the Federal Government	Powers Denied to Both the Federal and State Governments	Powers Denied to State Governments
• To suspend the **writ of habeas corpus** except in times of war • To spend money without Congressional approval	• To pass **ex post facto** laws • To pass **bills of attainder** • To grant titles of nobility • To tax exports • To deny persons due process of law	• To coin money • To enter into treaties • To tax imports • To tax the federal government

★ **Implied Powers.** The **Elastic Clause** expands the powers of the federal government by giving it whatever additional powers are "necessary and proper" for carrying out those powers specifically listed in the Constitution. These additional powers are sometimes called the **implied powers.**

★ **The Bill of Rights.** The Bill of Rights and other later amendments also place limits on the powers of both our federal and state governments.

CHECKS AND BALANCES

To make sure that the national government does not become too strong or oppress its citizens, the Constitution gives each branch of the federal government several ways to stop or "**check**" the other branches. This system creates obstacles to government action, so that certain measures cannot be taken unless there is general agreement that they are needed.

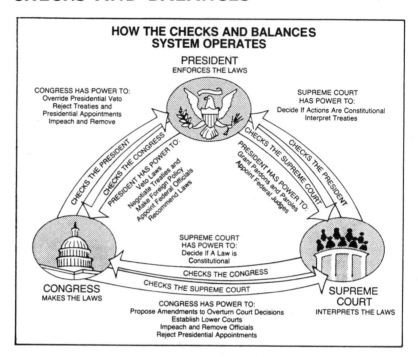

HOW THE CHECKS AND BALANCES SYSTEM OPERATES

PRESIDENT
ENFORCES THE LAWS

CONGRESS HAS POWER TO:
Override Presidential Veto
Reject Treaties and
Presidential Appointments
Impeach and Remove

SUPREME COURT
HAS POWER TO:
Decide If Actions Are Constitutional
Interpret Treaties

CHECKS THE PRESIDENT
CHECKS THE CONGRESS
PRESIDENT HAS POWER TO:
Veto Laws
Negotiate Treaties and
Make Foreign Policy
Appoint Federal Officials
Recommend Laws

PRESIDENT HAS POWER TO:
Grant Pardons and Paroles
Appoint Federal Judges
CHECKS THE SUPREME COURT
CHECKS THE PRESIDENT

SUPREME COURT
HAS POWER TO:
Decide If A Law is
Constitutional

CHECKS THE CONGRESS
CHECKS THE SUPREME COURT

CONGRESS
MAKES THE LAWS

SUPREME COURT
INTERPRETS THE LAWS

CONGRESS HAS POWER TO:
Propose Amendments to Overturn Court Decisions
Establish Lower Courts
Impeach and Remove Officials
Reject Presidential Appointments

FLEXIBILITY

The Constitution is still in use today because it has *flexibility*, the ability to adapt to changing situations through the amending process and new interpretations.

★ **The Amending Process.** Our Constitution serves as the nation's highest law. The Constitution can be changed by amendment, but the amending process was made more difficult and complicated than the passage of an ordinary law. This difficulty was created to ensure that an amendment has general support. Three-quarters of the states must approve any amendment.

★ **New Interpretations.** Much of the language in the Constitution is vague. The Supreme Court has the job of interpreting the Constitution. Its decisions often apply the Constitution to new circumstances. The elastic clause often permits the Court to justify the exercise of new powers by Congress. By finding new meaning, the Supreme Court helps to adapt the text to the needs of the times.

THE UNWRITTEN CONSTITUTION

The American government today relies on many practices that developed after the Constitution was put into effect. The practices became customary even though they were never formally incorporated into the Constitution. For this reason they are often referred to as our "**unwritten Constitution.**"

The Cabinet. The Constitution gave the President power to appoint people to assist him. Washington and later Presidents came to rely on these people — known as the Cabinet — for advice.	**Political Parties.** The Constitution does not specifically mention political parties, although these now play an important role in our system of government.

THE "UNWRITTEN CONSTITUTION"

Judicial Review. The Supreme Court has the power to review federal and state laws to determine if they are permissible under the U.S. Constitution.	**Congressional Committees.** These help Congress select the most important bills out of the thousands proposed. Committees hold hearings, discuss, and evaluate each bill.

THE FEDERAL GOVERNMENT: ITS STRUCTURE AND FUNCTIONS

Although there have been some important changes, our federal government still operates today under the same basic structure that the Constitution established over two hundred years ago. Federal power continues to be divided among three separate branches — the Congress, the President, and the Supreme Court.

CONGRESS: THE LEGISLATIVE BRANCH

STRUCTURE AND FUNCTIONS OF CONGRESS

The main task of Congress is to make our nation's laws. It is composed of two houses:

★ **The Senate.** Today, the Senate has 100 members, two from each state. Each Senator is elected for a six-year term by voters from his or her state. In addition to its law-making function, two-thirds of the Senate is needed to ratify treaties negotiated by the President. The Senate must also approve all Presidential appointments: federal judges, cabinet officers, and ambassadors.

★ **House of Representatives.** Today, the House has 435 members. Each Representative is elected for a two-year term by the voters of a single Congressional district. The number of Representatives of each state is determined by that state's population. Every ten years a national **census** (*population count*) is taken and the seats in the House of Representatives are redistributed.

	House of Representatives	Senate
Size	Based on the state's population: the more people, the more Representatives the state will have.	Two Senators from each state, no matter what the size of the state's population.
Qualifications for Membership	• must be 25 years of age • must be U.S. citizen for 7 years • must be a resident of state	• must be 30 years old • must be U.S. citizen for 9 years • must be a resident of state
Special Powers	• impeaches federal officials • introduces money bills • selects a President if the Electoral College fails to do so	• conducts impeachment trials • approves Presidential appointments • ratifies (*approves*) treaties

THE PRESIDENCY: THE EXECUTIVE BRANCH

The President must be a natural-born citizen who is at least 35 years old. The President is elected for a four-year term of office. Traditionally, Presidents only served two terms of office, until Franklin D. Roosevelt was elected four times. Several years later, the **Twenty-second Amendment** (1951) was ratified, limiting each President to two terms.

CHOOSING PRESIDENTIAL CANDIDATES

To become President today, a candidate must usually win the nomination of a major political party. To do this, candidates participate in state **primaries** — elections among rivals from the same party seeking the support of delegates to the party's **National Convention.** At the convention, the delegates choose their party's nominee. The delegates also draw up a party platform, stating their party's position on important issues in the campaign.

White House

Ronald Reagan at the Republican National Nominating Convention

After the conventions, the nominees of the two parties travel around the country, campaigning against each other. Occasionally, a person may run for President as an independent or third party candidate, as **Ross Perot** did in 1992 and 1996.

ELECTING A PRESIDENT: THE ELECTORAL COLLEGE

The members of the Constitutional Convention did not fully trust the common people to elect the President directly. Instead, they turned the selection of the President over to special electors who formed the **Electoral College.** To become President, a candidate needs to win a majority of the votes of the Electoral College. The number of electors each state has is equal to the number of its Senators and Representatives in Congress. The candidate with the most votes in a state wins *all* of the electors of that state. Sometimes, as in 2000, a candidate wins the popular vote but loses the electoral vote. If no candidate wins a majority (270) of the Electoral College, the election is decided in the House of Representatives. Each state gets one vote in the election, and a winner needs to receive a majority (26) of state votes.

THE MANY ROLES OF THE PRESIDENT

The Constitution defined and limited the powers of the Presidency. In spite of this, the powers of the President have expanded since the days when the U.S. Constitution was first adopted. Today, the President fills many roles:

As **Chief Executive**, the President enforces federal laws. The President is in charge of the federal government bureaucracy and submits an annual budget to Congress. The President nominates federal judges and can pardon, persons convicted of a federal crime.	As **Chief of State**, the President is the ceremonial head of the U.S. Government and represents the country in the world community.	As **Commander-in-Chief**, the President commands our armed forces and controls the use of our nuclear weapons.

THE MANY ROLES OF THE PRESIDENT

As **Foreign-Policy Chief**, the President conducts our nation's foreign relations, negotiates treaties with foreign countries, receives foreign ambassadors and diplomats, and appoints American ambassadors.	As **Chief Legislator**, the President can make recom-mendations to Congress which often become laws. In addition, the President can sign or veto bills passed by Congress.	As **Chief of a Political Party**, the President controls one of the two major national political parties: this gives the President influence over members of Congress from the same party.

Although these powers are impressive, the President must cooperate with Congress to perform many of these tasks. For example, although the President is the Commander-in-Chief of the armed forces, Congress determines just how much money is spent on them.

FEDERAL COURTS: THE JUDICIAL BRANCH

The **U.S. Supreme Court** is our highest federal court. The court has nine members, each chosen by the President and approved by the Senate. All federal judges hold office for a life term, to protect their decisions from political interference. Despite this fact, the Supreme Court is often influenced by public opinion and may

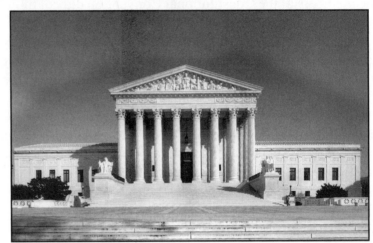

The U.S Supreme Court building

Collection of the U.S. Supreme Court

reverse its previous decisions. Below the Supreme Court are other federal courts that try cases involving federal law or disputes between citizens from different states. When a disagreement arises between different lower federal courts, the Supreme Court can review those decisions if they come before it on appeal. The Supreme Court can also review state court decisions involving federal law.

In reviewing cases, the Supreme Court not only decides whether the law has been applied correctly by the lower court, but also whether the law itself is within the power of the government according to the Constitution. The power of the Supreme Court to decide whether or not laws are constitutional is known as **Judicial Review.** The Supreme Court's use of judicial review has created much controversy over the proper role of the Court. Critics argue that the Court has sometimes overstepped its authority in declaring some laws to be unconstitutional.

John Marshall served as Chief Justice of the Supreme Court from 1801 to 1835. His interpretations of the Constitution and frequent use of judicial review laid the groundwork for establishing the importance of the federal judiciary and the supremacy of the national government over the states. His decisions gave a sense of unity to the nation by enormously expanding the power of the federal government.

Marbury v. Madison (1803). Secretary of State James Madison had refused to deliver a commission (*an official appointment*) to William Marbury, appointed by President Adams just before leaving office. Marbury asked the Supreme Court to require Madison to deliver his commission, based upon the Judiciary Act of 1789. The Court ruled that this part of the Judiciary Act was unconstitutional and that the Court couldn't deliver the commission. In so doing, the Court established the principle of **judicial review**, greatly strengthening the Supreme Court's authority as the final interpreter of the Constitution.

 KEY DECISIONS OF THE MARSHALL COURT

McCulloch v. Maryland (1819). Congress created the Bank of the United States, with a branch in Maryland. Maryland's legislature passed a law requiring the branch to pay a state tax. Bank officials refused to pay. The Court ruled that a state could not tax an agency of the national government, such as the bank. The Court further said that when a state law conflicts with a federal law, the federal law must be supreme. Finally, the Court held that the creation of the national bank was constitutional. Although the Constitution did not give Congress the expressed powers to create a bank, it was "necessary and proper" for Congress to do so to carry out its other powers.

Gibbons v. Ogden (1824). Ogden had been granted a monopoly by New York State to operate a steamboat between New York and New Jersey. Gibbons was granted a similar license by the federal government. Ogden sued to stop Gibbons. Gibbons appealed to the Supreme Court. The Court ruled that New York State had no right to grant the license. Only the federal government, according to the U.S. Constitution, could regulate **interstate commerce** (*trade between states*), including activities *affecting* interstate commerce. This established the federal government's right to regulate anything that involves or even affects interstate commerce.

CONSTITUTIONAL PROTECTION OF INDIVIDUAL LIBERTIES

The Bill of Rights were added to the U.S. Constitution to protect individual liberties from abuses by the federal government. The rights and liberties enjoyed by Americans today are not limited to the Bill of Rights. Other parts of the U.S. Constitution as well as subsequent Supreme Court decisions have helped to expand and ensure these protections.

PROTECTIONS FOUND IN THE BILL OF RIGHTS

The Bill of Rights was added to the Constitution in 1791. When first adopted, the Bill of Rights only protected individuals from actions by the federal government:

THE BILL OF RIGHTS

1. Guaranteed the freedoms of religion, speech, the press, and assembly.
2. Guaranteed the right to keep and bear arms.
3. Prohibited the forcible quartering of soldiers in one's home.
4. Prohibited unreasonable searches and seizures.
5. Guaranteed that no citizen could be deprived of life, liberty or property without **due process of law** (procedures according to established rules, such as a fair trial); also prohibited **double jeopardy** (being tried twice for the same crime) and **self-incrimination** (no person could be forced to give evidence against him or herself).
6. Guaranteed that those accused of a crime have the right to a speedy trial by jury, the right to confront accusers, and the right to be represented by a lawyer.
7. Guaranteed a jury trial in many civil cases.
8. Prohibited excessive bail and cruel and unusual punishment.
9. Stated that the listing of some rights in the Constitution did not mean that people did not also enjoy other rights.
10. Reserved for the states and the people those powers not delegated to the federal government, forming a basis for the reserved powers.

PROTECTIONS FOUND IN LATER AMENDMENTS

Several later amendments also contain important protections of individual rights. The Fourteenth Amendment was especially important because it extended federal law to protect individual rights from actions by state governments.

LATER AMENDMENTS PROTECTING INDIVIDUAL RIGHTS

13. Prohibited slavery. (1865)
14. Gave former slaves the right of citizenship, and guaranteed all citizens that they would enjoy "equal protection of the laws" and "due process of law" from state governments. (1868)
15. Guaranteed freed slaves the right to vote. (1870)
17. Changed the election of Senators from selection by state legislatures to direct election by voters. (1913)
19. Gave women the right to vote. (1920)
24. Prohibited poll taxes in federal elections. (1964)
26. Gave persons age 18 or over the right to vote. (1972)

SUMMARIZING YOUR UNDERSTANDING

KEY TERMS, CONCEPTS, AND PEOPLE

Create a vocabulary card for each of the following terms, concepts, and people.

Declaration of Independence   Bill of Rights   John Marshall
Articles of Confederation   Unwritten Constitution   *Marbury v. Madison*
The Federalist Papers   Judicial Review   *McCulloch v. Maryland*

COMPLETING A TABLE

Briefly describe the following documents associated with this period in history.

Document (date)	Describe the Document	Its Importance
Declaration of Independence ( )		
Articles of Confederation ( )		
U.S. Constitution ( )		
Bill of Rights ( )		

COMPLETING A GRAPHIC ORGANIZER

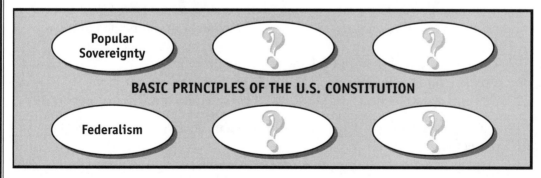

Briefly describe each basic principle of the U.S. Constitution.

TESTING YOUR UNDERSTANDING

MULTIPLE-CHOICE QUESTIONS

1   Which feature of government developed most fully during the colonial era?
1   separation of church and state   3   equality under the law
2   universal suffrage   4   representative assemblies

2   Which belief is expressed by the quotation: "we … will not hold ourselves bound by any Laws in which we have no voice, or Representation"?
1   the necessity of a separation of powers
2   government by the consent of the governed
3   freedom of press and assembly
4   the right to a writ of habeas corpus

3   The primary purpose of the Declaration of Independence was to
1   establish the basic laws of the United States
2   justify the revolt of the American colonists against Great Britain
3   provide a clear plan for a meaningful and effective political system
4   guarantee equal rights for all Americans

4   The Articles of Confederation created a
1   republic with a chief executive
2   strong central government
3   national government with legislative and judicial branches
4   loose association of free and independent states

5   At the Constitutional Convention of 1787, the "Great Compromise" concerned the issue of
1   representation in Congress   3   the powers of the Chief Executive
2   the future of slavery   4   control of interstate commerce

6   Which is an essential feature of democratic government?
1   a bicameral legislature   3   a written constitution
2   free and open elections   4   separate branches of government

7   The basic purpose of our constitutional system of checks and balances is to
1   protect states' rights
2   prevent one branch of the government from becoming too powerful
3   enable the federal government to run as efficiently as possible
4   provide a written guarantee of the rights of each citizen

Base your answer to question 8 on the table below and your knowledge of social studies.

POPULATION DATA, 1790

State	Total Population	Number of Enslaved Persons
Massachusetts	378,787	0
New Jersey	184,139	7,557
New York	340,120	10,088
Virginia	747,610	425,353

8 In terms of representation in the U.S. Congress, which state benefited most by agreeing to the "Three-Fifths Compromise" at the Constitutional Convention?
1 Massachusetts   3 New York
2 New Jersey   4 Virginia

---

9 The U.S. government is considered a federal system because
1 national laws must be passed by both houses of Congress
2 powers are divided between its national and state governments
3 the states are guaranteed a republican form of government
4 the President is selected by the Electoral College

10 Which feature of the Presidency is a result of a constitutional amendment?
1 two-term limit in office
2 power to appoint ambassadors
3 duty to act as Commander-in-Chief
4 responsibility to nominate justices to the U.S. Supreme Court

11 "The powers not delegated to the United States by the Constitution, nor prohibited to it by the states, are reserved to the states respectively, or the people."
— *U.S. Constitution, 10th Amendment*

Which principle of government is expressed in this amendment?
1 The states have only those powers that are listed in the Constitution.
2 Congress decides which powers the states can exercise.
3 Congress has the power to pass any law that it wishes.
4 The powers of the federal government are limited.

12 Which political development in the United States is considered part of the "unwritten constitution"?
1 the system of checks and balances   3 President's power to grant pardons
2 political parties   4 power of Congress to issue money

13 The decision of the Supreme Court in *Marbury v. Madison* was important because it
1   defined the meaning of the Bill of Rights
2   established the power of the Court to declare laws unconstitutional
3   freed enslaved people in the South
4   overturned the Commerce Clause of the U.S. Constitution

14 The idea that the U.S. Constitution establishes a central government of limited powers is best supported by the constitutional provision that
1   powers not delegated to the United States shall be reserved to the states
2   Congress shall make all laws "necessary and proper" to its functions
3   the President shall act as Commander-in-chief
4   the Supreme Court shall have both original and appellate jurisdiction

15 The section of the U.S. Constitution that grants Congress the power to "make all laws which shall be necessary and proper for carrying into execution the foregoing powers" has come to be known as the
1   Great Compromise
2   Supremacy Clause
3   Due Process Clause
4   Elastic Clause

16 Which concept from the U.S. Constitution provides the basis for the variety of laws that govern teenage driving in different parts of the United States?
1   checks and balances
2   judicial review
3   reserved powers
4   executive privilege

17 Which situation most clearly illustrates the principle of checks and balances?
1   Congress listens to the President's State of the Union address.
2   Congress votes on spending for cancer research.
3   The House of Representatives votes to impeach a federal judge.
4   A congressional committee revises the language of a bill.

18 The main reason that only a small number of amendments have been made to the U.S. Constitution is that the
1   executive branch has feared a loss of power
2   amending process was made extremely difficult
3   public has not objected to government's use of its powers
4   Constitution is clear in its intent and seldom needs to be amended

19 The U.S. President can influence the judicial branch of government by
1   removing members of the Supreme Court
2   choosing the chairperson of the Senate Judiciary Committee
3   nominating federal judges
4   requesting the Supreme Court to declare certain laws unconstitutional

20 The partial outline below concerns the U.S. Constitution.

> I. _____
>
> A. Checks and Balances
> B. Federalism
> C. Limited Government

Which entry would be most appropriate for line I?
1   The Balance of Power between the Federal Government and the States
2   Constitutional Flexibility
3   Basic Constitutional Principles
4   The Powers of the Chief Executive

21 The President of the United States can appoint new Justices to the Supreme Court
1   by first removing old members of the Supreme Court
2   with the approval of the chairperson of the Senate Judiciary Committee
3   with the approval of the U.S. Senate
4   with the approval of the Justices already on the court

22 Which governmental practice is a part of the unwritten constitution?
1   Presidential appointments need the consent of the Senate
2   popular election of U.S. Senators
3   holding political party conventions
4   limiting the President's period in office to two terms

23 Which Constitutional principle includes the concepts of reserved powers, delegated powers, and concurrent powers?
1   popular sovereighty   3   judicial review
2   federalism   4   separation of powers

24 The Supreme Court's power of judicial review is a result of
1   an order by the President
2   the Court's own interpretation of the Constitution
3   a provision in the Bill of Rights
4   the Court's decision to hear appeals regarding taxation

25 President Clinton nominated Ruth Ginsburg to the Supreme Court. Before she could take her seat on the Court, her appointment had to be approved by the
1   U.S. Senate   3   Supreme Court
2   Cabinet   4   House of Representatives

INTERPRETING DOCUMENTS

On the night of December 16, 1773, a band of Bostonians disguised as Native Americans boarded three British ships anchored in Boston harbor and threw overboard 342 chests of tea.

Library of Congress

A. Name the historical event taking place in the illustration.

_____

B. Describe the circumstances that led to this event. _____

THEMATIC ESSAY QUESTION

Directions: Write a well-organized essay that includes an introduction, several paragraphs addressing the task below, and a conclusion.

Theme: Political Systems

> The U.S. Constitution is based on a number of important principles aimed at preventing the abuse of power.

Task:

> Choose **two** principles from your study of U.S. history and government.
>
> For _each_ principle:
> - Describe the Constitutional principle.
> - Explain how that principle was designed to prevent an abuse of power.

You may use any principles from your study of United States history and government. Some suggestions you might wish to consider include: popular sovereignty, federalism, checks and balances, limited powers, and the separation of powers.

You are _not_ limited to these suggestions.

CHAPTER 7

THE CONSTITUTION TESTED

National Archives

The Civil War was the most tragic conflict in American history

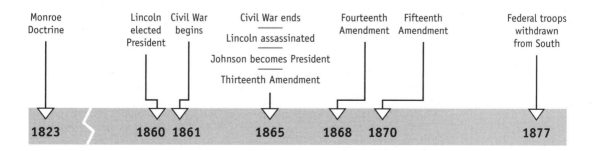

Monroe Doctrine	Lincoln elected President	Civil War begins	Civil War ends	Fourteenth Amendment	Fifteenth Amendment	Federal troops withdrawn from South
			Lincoln assassinated			
			Johnson becomes President			
			Thirteenth Amendment			
1823	**1860**	**1861**	**1865**	**1868**	**1870**	**1877**

79

WHAT YOU SHOULD FOCUS ON

In this chapter, you will learn how the new American nation endured its first great test after independence — the American Civil War. After five years of fighting, the South lost the war. The Union was preserved and slavery came to an end. During the Reconstruction Era, Southerners struggled with these changes and developed new ways of life. As you read this chapter, you will learn about:

Following the Civil War, many cities in the South lay in ruins

★ **The Young Republic.** After independence, early American leaders expanded democracy, steered a policy of cautious neutrality toward Europe, and promoted Westward expansion.

★ **The Civil War.** When Abraham Lincoln was elected President, Southern states seceded. The North's larger population, manufacturing facilities, and greater naval power enabled it to win the war. During the conflict, Lincoln freed Southern slaves in the Emancipation Proclamation.

★ **Reconstruction.** Southern states were only readmitted into the Union after they approved the Fourteenth Amendment, enabling the federal government to protect the rights of American citizens from the acts of state governments. Congress imposed military rule and Reconstruction governments on the South.

★ **The Aftermath of Reconstruction.** After the end of Reconstruction, Southern state governments introduced racial segregation and denied African Americans the right to vote and other rights.

In studying this period, you should focus on the following questions:

★ How well did early leaders achieve stability and democracy?
★ What were the goals of early American foreign policy?
★ What were the causes of the Civil War?
★ How did the South cope with the problems of Reconstruction?
★ How did African Americans lose their rights following Reconstruction?

LOOKING AT THE IMPACT OF GEOGRAPHY

he physical geography of the United States has had an important impact on the development of American history and culture. This section further explores the relationship between America's geography and history, so you will be prepared to answer questions on this subject.

LOCATION

Geographers often consider the location of a place **relative** to other places. The importance of such **relative location** may change over time as a result of changes in transportation and communications. Native Americans, for example, both benefited and suffered from a location that separated them from other civilizations. For centuries, the oceans protected these peoples, but also isolated them from the technological innovations of Asia, Europe, and Africa. Their location safeguarded Native Americans from many diseases but also prevented them from building up natural immunities. Because of improvements in ocean-going transportation, the Caribbean, the Atlantic coast of North America, and the Native American empires of Mexico and Peru eventually came within the reach of European explorers, conquerors, missionaries, and settlers. The greater population densities of Europe, their superior technology, and most important of all, a host of new micro-organisms like those causing measles and small pox, had a devastating impact on Native Americans.

PLACE

The characteristics of **place** — topography, natural resources, and climate — have had an equally important effect on the course of American development. Europeans found a continent of largely unexploited natural resources with a small population. These circumstances turned North America into a magnet for European colonization. Much of Europe's surplus population was willing to brave trans-Atlantic travel in order to share in the opportunities afforded by North America, where millions of acres of wilderness could be converted into farmland. These same geographical conditions further allowed the settlers to develop a society without a hereditary nobility, and encouraged greater individualism. They also permitted Europeans to bring millions of Africans to North America as enslaved laborers.

(continued)

Topography and climate also greatly affected patterns of settlement. The first areas to be settled were along the Atlantic Coastal Plain, stretching along the coastline, and extending inland to the Appalachian Mountains. By the time of the American Revolution, pioneers like Daniel Boone were crossing the Appalachians and entering the Ohio River Valley. Settlement around the Great Lakes was given further impetus by the opening of the Erie Canal in 1825. This event likewise transformed the relative location of New York City, turning it into the gateway to the West. Farmers around the Great Lakes region could ship their goods to Buffalo, east along the Erie Canal, and down the Hudson River to New York City, where they could be shipped to other states or across the Atlantic to Europe.

REGION

Already in colonial times, three distinct American **regions** had emerged: the North, the South, and the West. Differences among these three regions led directly to the sectionalism of the early 19th century and to the outbreak of the Civil War. Because of differences in topography and climate, different ways of life emerged in each of these three sections. This, in turn, attracted different types of people, reinforcing differences in physical geography. The closest thing to an American hereditary nobility, for example, developed among the planter class in the South, who owned large plantations worked by armies of slave laborers.

HUMAN-ENVIRONMENT INTERACTION

The rise of industry affected regional differences, and was affected by them, both before and after the Civil War. The location of key natural resources and important transportation routes dictated the location of cities and industries. Cities emerged at the hubs of several transportation routes, especially along the Atlantic, the Great Lakes, and great inland rivers. The rise of cities further transformed the landscape, from forests and rolling plains to farms, towns, and cities. The laying of railroad tracks in the North, and the greater development of Northern industry, played a crucial role in the North's triumph over the South. Later, Pennsylvania coal and the iron ore of the Mesabi range in Minnesota helped transform the Midwest into America's industrial heartland.

THE YOUNG REPUBLIC

LAUNCHING THE SHIP OF STATE

After the Constitution was ratified, George Washington was elected the nation's first President. Washington's Administration was especially significant because it laid the foundation for all later governments.

★ **The Cabinet.** To help carry out his duties, Washington appointed Secretaries of the Treasury, State, and War, and an Attorney General, and placed each of these at the head of a separate department. Together with the President and the Vice President, these officers formed the **Cabinet,** which met from time to time to consider the direction of national policy.

★ **Hamilton's Financial Plan.** The new nation faced a large debt from the Revolutionary War. As Secretary of the Treasury, **Alexander Hamilton** proposed a four-part program to establish the nation's finances on a solid basis.

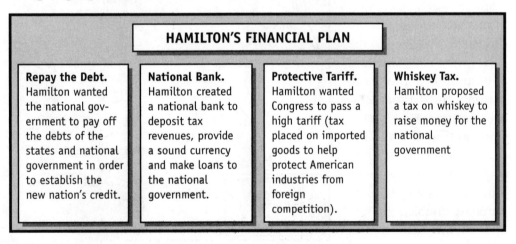

HAMILTON'S FINANCIAL PLAN			
Repay the Debt. Hamilton wanted the national government to pay off the debts of the states and national government in order to establish the new nation's credit.	**National Bank.** Hamilton created a national bank to deposit tax revenues, provide a sound currency and make loans to the national government.	**Protective Tariff.** Hamilton wanted Congress to pass a high tariff (tax placed on imported goods to help protect American industries from foreign competition).	**Whiskey Tax.** Hamilton proposed a tax on whiskey to raise money for the national government

★ **The Formation of Political Parties.** Thomas Jefferson, Washington's Secretary of State, opposed the plan because he though it favored rich bankers and investors at the expense of common farmers. Jefferson and his followers formed the nation's first political party, the **Democratic Republicans,** to oppose Hamilton's plan. Hamilton's supporters formed a different party, the **Federalists.** The Federalists were able to pass most of Hamilton's plan in Congress, except for the protective tariff. When some farmers west of the Appalachians took up arms against the new tax on whiskey, Washington used force to crush the so-called **Whiskey Rebellion.**

PRESERVING AMERICAN INDEPENDENCE

After independence, the U.S. remained militarily weak compared to the European monarchies. American leaders adopted a policy of **neutrality** to avoid becoming involved in European wars. At the same time, they pursued a vigorous policy of westward expansion.

WASHINGTON'S FAREWELL ADDRESS (1796)

Britain and France went to war in 1793 as a result of the French Revolution. The Federalists favored the British and the Democratic Republicans favored the French, but Washington steered the nation clear of involvement. In his final address as President, Washington cautioned against entering into a permanent alliance with any European country. Instead, Washington urged Americans to devote themselves to developing their own trade and assuming leadership of the Western Hemisphere.

THE LOUISIANA PURCHASE (1803)

In 1783, the U.S. only reached up to the Mississippi River. In 1803, France offered to sell the Louisiana Territory to the U.S. for $15 million. Although Jefferson, the nation's third President, was uncertain whether the Constitution allowed the federal government to do so, he went ahead with the purchase. The Louisiana Purchase doubled the size of the United States and gave Americans control of the Mississippi River.

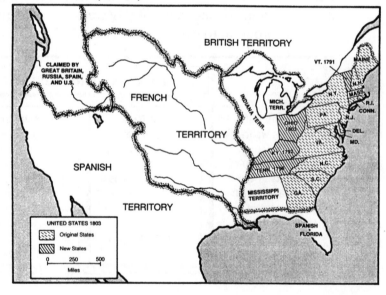

THE WAR OF 1812

Although attempting to stay of neutral, Americans could not avoid involvement in the wars between Britain and France. To prevent the British seizure of U.S. sailors in the Atlantic, to stop British support of Native American raids, and to seize Canada, Congress declared war on Britain in 1812. U.S. troops tried, unsuccessfully, to invade Canada. British troops occupied Washington D.C. and burned the White House. The war ended in a stalemate in 1815, coinciding with the end of the Napoleonic Wars in Europe.

THE MONROE DOCTRINE, 1823

Attempts by Spain to restore its authority at the end of the Napoleonic Wars triggered a series of independence movements in the Spanish colonies. The U.S. recognized the independence of these nations, but feared Spain might try to reconquer them. President Monroe announced the **Monroe Doctrine.** Monroe declared that the United States would oppose any attempt by European powers to establish new colonies in the Western Hemisphere or to reconquer former colonies that had achieved independence. In effect, Monroe told European nations to keep their hands off the Western Hemisphere. Monroe, however, agreed not interfere with European colonies already in existence, such as Canada or Cuba.

JACKSONIAN DEMOCRACY

One of the new nation's strongest leaders was President **Andrew Jackson.** A hero in the War of 1812, Jackson was elected President in 1828. A native of Tennessee, Jackson was the first President not born to wealth and not from an Eastern state. His main supporters were the common people, especially laborers and Western frontiersmen.

AN AGE OF REFORM

Jackson's two terms in office witnessed an expansion of American democracy.

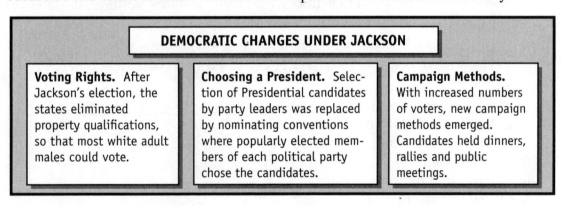

DEMOCRATIC CHANGES UNDER JACKSON

Voting Rights. After Jackson's election, the states eliminated property qualifications, so that most white adult males could vote.

Choosing a President. Selection of Presidential candidates by party leaders was replaced by nominating conventions where popularly elected members of each political party chose the candidates.

Campaign Methods. With increased numbers of voters, new campaign methods emerged. Candidates held dinners, rallies and public meetings.

THE SPOILS SYSTEM

Jackson believed the President should act as the voice of the common people. To make government more responsive to popular needs, Jackson used the "spoils system." Supporters who helped in his election were appointed to government posts in place of existing officials. Jackson believed in changing office-holders so that more people had experience in government. He felt circulating government posts was less likely to lead to corruption than permanent government officials.

JACKSON AND THE WAR ON THE BANK

Jackson disliked the National Bank believing it gave an unfair advantage to Eastern investors and bankers. Farmers resented the Bank because it made it hard to borrow money. The Bank's constitutionality was upheld by the Supreme Court, but Jackson weakened the Bank by removing federal deposits from it and putting them in state banks. In 1836, the Bank ended when Jackson refused to renew its charter.

JACKSON AND NATIVE AMERICAN INDIANS

Jackson believed Native American Indians were blocking the nation's westward expansion. Under Jackson, Congress moved all remaining Native American Indians to territories west of the Mississippi River. Jackson refused to help the Cherokees of Georgia even though the Supreme Court had declared their forcible removal unconstitutional.

JACKSON AND THE FEDERAL UNION

In 1832, South Carolina threatened to secede from the nation because it opposed federal tariffs on imports. Jackson threatened to use force and the crisis was avoided. Jackson became a symbol for national unity over sectional interests.

MANIFEST DESTINY

In the 1840s, Americans began to believe it was their "manifest destiny," or future, to extend the nation from the Atlantic to the Pacific Ocean.

THE IMPACT OF GEOGRAPHY ON AMERICAN HISTORY

The Erie Canal, completed in 1825, followed old Native American trails through the Mohawk Valley, connecting the Hudson River to Lake Erie. It was a natural connection between the Central Lowlands and the Atlantic Coastal Plain.

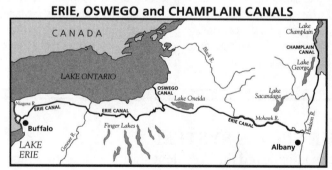

The canal made it possible to ship goods and people between the Great Lakes and New York City. The cost of shipping a ton of wheat fell from $100 to less than $5. Farmers in the Midwest were now able to ship their goods to Eastern markets. New York City became the fastest growing city in the nation.

ANNEXATION OF TEXAS, 1845

In the 1820s, Americans began settling in the Mexican province of Texas. These settlers declared their independence in 1835, when Mexico tried to prohibit further immigration from the United States. After being captured by Texan rebels, **General Santa Anna** of Mexico signed a treaty recognizing their independence. In 1845, Congress voted to annex Texas.

Reading of the Texas Declaration of Independence in 1835

The Institute of Texan Cultures

THE MEXICAN-AMERICAN WAR, 1846–1848

Shortly afterwards, a dispute broke out between the United States and Mexico over the southern border of Texas. U.S. President Polk sent troops into the contested area. In the war that followed, Mexico was quickly defeated and forced to give up California, Nevada, Utah, Arizona, and parts of Colorado and New Mexico. In the Treaty of **Guadalupe Hidalgo**, the United States paid the Mexican Government $15 million for these areas.

ADDITIONAL ACQUISITIONS

The United States had three more major territorial acquisitions on the North American mainland:

★ The **Gadsden Purchase (1853)** from Mexico (*now southern New Mexico and Arizona*) completed American expansion in the Southwest.

★ In an agreement with Great Britain in 1846, the line dividing Canada and the United States at the 49th parallel was extended westwards to the Pacific. This gave the United States part of the **Oregon Territory.**

★ In 1867, the United States purchased **Alaska** from Russia for $7.2 million. At first Secretary of State **William Seward's** purchase met with ridicule. But Alaska proved to be an important acquisition for its valuable natural resources. In 1959, Alaska became the 49th state.

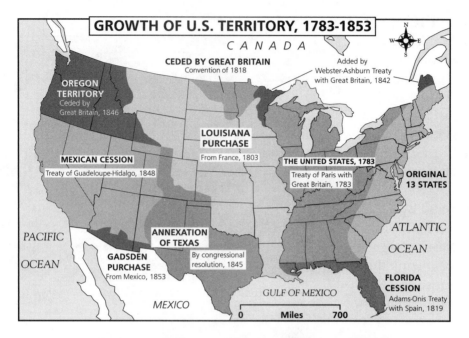

GROWTH OF U.S. TERRITORY, 1783-1853

THE CIVIL WAR, 1861–1865

The **Civil War** was the most divisive war in American history.

CAUSES OF THE CIVIL WAR

SECTIONALISM

In the early 19th century, as the United States expanded economically, each section of the country developed its own special characteristics.

The Northeast became a center of manufacturing, shipping, fishing, and small farms. This section witnessed the growth of a new class of factory workers. Factories and cities began to dramatically change traditional lifestyles.

The South's dominant institution was slavery. Although most Southerners never owned slaves, much of the region's economy was based on profits from the use of slave labor on large plantations, which grew crops such as cotton.

The Northwest (*now Wisconsin, Illinois, Indiana, Michigan, and Ohio*) became the nation's breadbasket. Its grain was shipped by river and canal to the Northeast and South. Small farmers predominated in this area.

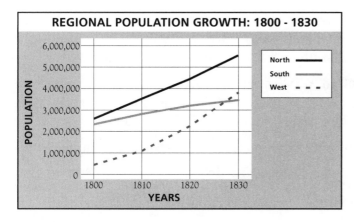

REGIONAL POPULATION GROWTH: 1800 - 1830

These regional differences led to the rise of **sectionalism** as early as the 1820s. Sectionalism referred to the greater loyalty many Americans felt towards their section (*North, South, or West*) than towards the country as a whole. Each section wanted the federal government to follow policies favorable to itself. These differences between sections made a clash appear almost inevitable.

SLAVERY

The most explosive issue facing the nation was the question of slavery. **Abolitionists** were reformers who wanted to end slavery. **William Lloyd Garrison's** publication, *The Liberator,* and **Harriet Beecher Stowe's** book, *Uncle Tom's Cabin,* helped spread a sense of moral outrage against slavery throughout the North. Former slaves, such as Frederick Douglass, Harriet Tubman, and Sojourner Truth, were leading abolitionists. Pro-slave Southerners argued that the slaves were better treated than northern factory workers.

LEADING ABOLITIONISTS

Harriet Tubman was a leading "conductor" of the Underground Railroad. The "railroad" was a network of sympathizers who hid fugitive slaves on the dangerous trip northward to freedom. Tubman personally helped more than 300 slaves escape.

Frederick Douglass published books and articles describing the horrors of slavery. A self-educated man who was born into slavery, Douglass became a gifted speaker. He traveled throughout the United States and England, inspiring crowds with anti-slavery speeches.

Frederick Douglass

National Archives

THE ISSUE OF SLAVERY IN THE NEW TERRITORIES

In the 1840s, the U.S. won control of new territories in Oregon and Mexico. These acquisitions posed the problem of whether slavery should be permitted there.

Southerners felt that only by extending slavery westward could they preserve the balance between slave and free states in Congress. Northerners opposed its spread. Congress preserved national unity by admitting new states in a series of compromises.

★ **Missouri Compromise of 1820.** Missouri was admitted as a slave state and Maine was admitted as a free state. Congress also decided to prohibit slavery in the lands of the Louisiana Purchase north of the 36° 30' latitude line.

★ **Compromise of 1850.** California was admitted as a free state. In return, a **Fugitive Slave Law** required Northern states to help return runaway slaves. The system of **popular sovereignty** was applied to other territories taken from Mexico. Under this system, settlers in new territories would decide for themselves if they wanted to allow slavery.

THE BREAKDOWN OF COMPROMISE

In the 1850s, the breakdown of these compromises made conflict between the North and South almost inevitable.

★ **Kansas-Nebraska Act, 1854.** Congress repealed the Missouri Compromise by introducing popular sovereignty in the Kansas and Nebraska Territories, where slavery had earlier been prohibited. In Kansas, pro- and anti-slavery forces tried to assure the outcome by bringing in their own supporters. Bloodshed on both sides followed, and federal troops were required to restore order.

★ **Dred Scott Decision, 1857.** The Supreme Court ruled that Congress could not prohibit slavery in any U.S. territory.

KEY COURT CASES: DRED SCOTT v. SANDFORD

Dred Scott, a slave, lived for a time in a Northern territory that prohibited slavery. Scott believed this made him free. When he was brought back to a slave state, Scott sued his owner for his freedom. The Supreme Court ruled that a slave was property and had no rights. Scott was not a citizen, and could not bring his case before the Court. The Court also stated that the prohibition of slavery in the Missouri Compromise had been unconstitutional, since slaves were property and Congress did not have the right to take away property.

Schomberg Collection

★ **John Brown's Raid (1859).** John Brown, a Northern abolitionist, sought to start a slave rebellion to free the slaves. Brown captured a federal arsenal in Virginia, but his tiny force was soon captured. Brown was hanged, but his attempt to stir the slaves created alarm and fear among Southerners.

STATES' RIGHTS

Southerners believed in **states' rights,** pointing out that the states had created the federal government as a *compact*, and that each state thus had the power to leave the Union if it desired. Northerners argued that the Constitution was the work of the American people, and that individual states could not leave the Union when they pleased.

THE ELECTION OF LINCOLN

The **Republican Party** was formed in 1854 to oppose the spread of slavery to new territories. When Republican presidential candidate **Abraham Lincoln** was elected in 1860, most Southern states **seceded** (*withdrew*) from the United States. The seceding states formed the **Confederate States of America.** Lincoln refused to recognize the secession and resolved to preserve the unity of the United States.

Abraham Lincoln

National Archives

HIGHLIGHTS OF THE CIVIL WAR

Fighting broke out in 1861, when **Fort Sumter,** a federal fort in South Carolina, was attacked by Confederate forces.

WHY THE NORTH WON

The Confederacy hoped to use experienced soldiers, like **Robert E. Lee,** to win a quick victory and force the North to accept their independence. Despite early successes, Southern armies were unable to capture Washington, D.C. The North possessed immense advantages: a larger population, more money, more railroad lines, greater manufacturing facilities, and superior naval power. The South depended on exporting cotton and other cash crops. Lincoln imposed a naval blockade on the South. A strong leader, he expanded his own powers in the wartime emergency. Despite its advantages, the North took four years to defeat the South.

Fort Sumter (note the Confederate flag flying over the fort)

National Archives

THE EMANCIPATION PROCLAMATION AND THE THIRTEENTH AMENDMENT

One of the most important events of the Civil War was the issuance of the **Emancipation Proclamation** in 1862. Lincoln announced that all slaves living in states still in rebellion on January 1, 1863 would be freed. The Proclamation gave a moral purpose to the war. It weakened the Confederacy by inciting slaves to rebel against their masters. Because the Proclamation only freed some slaves in the Confederate states, it also provided an incentive to the slave-holding border states to remain in the Union.

Many African Americans served in the Union Army

Library of Congress

Since it was unclear whether Lincoln had the constitutional power to free the slaves, Congress later proposed the **Thirteenth Amendment.** This amendment abolished slavery throughout the United States in 1865.

THE RECONSTRUCTION ERA, 1865–1877

The period immediately following the Civil War is known as the **Reconstruction Era.** It was a time in which Americans faced the task of reunifying the nation and rebuilding the South.

PLANS FOR RECONSTRUCTION

After the South surrendered in April 1865, the first major issue confronting the national government was how the Southern states were to be admitted back into the Union. A bitter power struggle followed between the President and Congress over which branch had the power to determine the conditions for admission.

THE PRESIDENTIAL PLAN

President Lincoln believed that in order to rebuild national unity, Southern states should be treated leniently. He proposed that in theory, the Southern States had never even left the Union. But in 1865, only a few days after the South surrendered, Lincoln was assassinated. The new President, **Andrew Johnson,** lacked Lincoln's authority. Nevertheless, he sought to follow Lincoln's plan of lenient treatment. Johnson recognized newly formed Southern state governments and pardoned

Four who conspired to assassinate Lincoln, are hanged

most rebel leaders. Many Southern states chose former Confederate leaders for seats in the new Congress.

THE BLACK CODES

The nation also faced the problem of how to deal with the millions of freed slaves, known as **freedmen.** Congress established the **Freedman's Bureau** to help the freed slaves. However, the Southern states were slow to extend voting rights to the freedmen. Some freedmen called for Congress to give them their own land and tools (*"forty acres and a mule"*), but the government failed to do so.

Southern landowners reclaimed their lands at the end of the Civil War, and refused to sell or rent land to freedmen. Southern states passed **Black Codes** to regulate the lives of the former slaves. The aim of these codes was to preserve traditional Southern society despite the abolition of slavery. For example, the "Black Codes" made it illegal for freedmen to hold public office, to travel freely, or to serve on juries.

THE CONGRESSIONAL PLAN FOR RECONSTRUCTION

Many Northerners were outraged at the election of rebel leaders in the South and the passage of the new Black Codes. Congress refused to recognize the new Southern governments. The **Radical Republicans,** a group of Northern Congressmen, wanted the freedmen to be granted political equality. They passed a **Civil Rights Bill** guaranteeing freedmen's rights, and restored military rule over the South. To ensure that this legislation would not be held unconstitutional by the Supreme Court, they rewrote the Civil Rights Bill as the **Fourteenth Amendment**. This amendment granted U.S. citizenship to all former slaves. It also prohibited state governments from denying any citizen the right to a fair trial or the equal protection of the laws. In effect, the Fourteenth Amendment allowed federal courts to protect individual rights from acts by state governments. Before being re-admitted into the Union, Southern states were forced to ratify the amendment.

A Thomas Nast cartoon depicts Southern opposition to Reconstruction

Library of Congress

THE POLITICS OF RECONSTRUCTION

President Johnson opposed the Congressional program, believing that only the President had the power to determine the conditions for the return of Southern states. The **Radical Republicans** in Congress believed Congress alone had the constitutional power to admit states back to the Union. They also suspected Johnson, a Southerner from Tennessee, of being overly sympathetic towards the South.

THE IMPEACHMENT OF PRESIDENT JOHNSON

To enforce its program, Congress passed the **Tenure of Office Act,** limiting the President's power to dismiss his own Cabinet members. Johnson refused to obey this law, which he believed was unconstitutional. When Johnson dismissed his Secretary of War, Congressional leaders attempted to remove Johnson from office through the process of **impeachment.** Johnson was impeached by the House of Representatives, but the Radical Republicans fell one vote short in the Senate of removing Johnson from office.

THE GRANT PRESIDENCY, 1869–1877

Shortly after the attempt to remove Johnson from office, **Ulysses S. Grant,** a general in the Civil War and the Radical Republican candidate, was elected President. Although Grant had been a brilliant general, his administration was characterized by weak leadership and widespread corruption at the national and local levels.

THE RECONSTRUCTION GOVERNMENTS

The Fourteenth Amendment made freedmen into citizens while excluding Confederate leaders from government offices. The **Fifteenth Amendment** gave freedmen the right to vote. As a result of these amendments, a new political leadership emerged in the South: **carpetbaggers** were Northerners who went South to help the freedmen or to profit from Reconstruction; **scalawags** were Southern whites who had opposed the Confederacy; **freed-**

The first African Americans to serve in Reconstruction government

men themselves also actively participated in running Southern governments in this period. During Reconstruction, over 600 African Americans served as state legislators and sixteen were elected to the U.S. Congress.

ACCOMPLISHMENTS AND WEAKNESSES

Among the greatest accomplishments of the Reconstruction governments were new public schools, laws banning racial discrimination, and the rebuilding of public roads, buildings, and railroads.

Reconstruction governments, nevertheless, faced great financial difficulties. Many were guilty of corruption and extravagance. White Southerners resented Northern interference and did not recognize their former slaves as equals. Without changing Southern attitudes, Reconstruction policies were ultimately doomed to failure.

THE END OF RECONSTRUCTION

In 1877, Reconstruction ended when the last remaining Northern troops were withdrawn from the South. Home rule was restored to Southern state governments. Former Confederate leaders could now serve in office. State legislatures quickly moved to bar African Americans from the political process. Most white Southerners resented their treatment at the hands of the Radical Republicans. As a result, the South gave its political support almost entirely to the Democratic Party for decades to come, becoming known as the "**Solid South.**"

THE AFTERMATH OF RECONSTRUCTION

Wartime destruction and the abolition of slavery brought permanent change to the South after the Civil War.

THE ECONOMIC EFFECTS: THE NEW SOUTH

Without slave labor, the old plantation system could not be restored.

SHARE-CROPPING AND TENANT FARMING

Many plantation owners entered into **share-cropping** arrangements with their former slaves. The landowner provided a cabin, a mule, tools, and land to the sharecropper. The sharecropper, in turn, gave a large share of his crop to the landowner as a form of rent. Other freedmen became **tenant farmers,** renting the land but providing their own tools and provisions. Few freedmen were able to become landowners themselves.

Library of Congress

After the Civil War, freedom did not always bring improved economic conditions

AGRICULTURAL PROGRESS AND INDUSTRIAL GROWTH

After the war, the introduction of new farming methods increased the yield per acre. New crops, like fruits and vegetables, were added to old staples like cotton, tobacco, rice, and sugar. With financial backing from the North, railroads, cotton mills, and steel furnaces were built. With industrial expansion, people began moving from farms into Southern cities looking for jobs. This encouraged the growth of Atlanta and several other large cities.

A LEADING AGRICULTURALIST

George Washington Carver was an African-American scientist who trained at the Tuskegee Institute. His discoveries helped revolutionize Southern agriculture by teaching farmers about scientific farming, such as rotating crops to prevent soil erosion. Carver taught them to plant peanuts, sweet potatoes, and other crops to replenish nitrates in the soil. He is credited with developing hundreds of new products and helping to end the South's dependence on cotton.

Library of Congress

THE SOCIAL EFFECTS: THE SEGREGATED SOUTH

The social system that developed in the aftermath of Reconstruction was one of racial segregation and white supremacy, depriving African Americans of their political and civil rights.

THE FAILURE TO ACHIEVE EQUALITY

There were several reasons why Reconstruction failed to achieve true equality:

★ **Economic Dependence.** The failure to give freedmen their own land after the Civil War meant that African Americans in the South remained dependent on their former masters. Most freedmen were uneducated, weakening their ability to compete with whites on equal terms. To protect their livelihoods, African Americans were often afraid to assert their political rights.

★ **White Terrorism.** Starting in 1866, some whites created secret organizations to hold blacks down by using terrorist tactics. The most important of these organizations was the **Ku Klux Klan.** The Klan terrorized African Americans with violence against those who asserted their rights. Faced with such intimidation, most African Americans were afraid to challenge the Klan.

New members being inducted into the Klan

★ **Loss of Northern Interest.** After Reconstruction ended, most Northerners lost interest in what was happening in the South. Instead, Republicans focused on industrial expansion while Northern reformers turned their attention to correcting the abuses of big business.

AFRICAN AMERICANS LOSE THE RIGHT TO VOTE

In the years after Reconstruction, Southern state governments systematically stripped African Americans of their rights. Based on their own racial prejudices and the need to satisfy poor whites, Southern legislators passed new laws in the 1890s to prohibit African Americans from voting.

★ **Literacy Tests** were introduced as a requirement for voting. Most freedmen lacked a formal education and were unable to pass this test. Often reading passages were made more difficult for African Americans than for whites.

★ **Poll Taxes** were registration fees for voting. These poll taxes were imposed on poor African Americans who could least afford to pay them.

A laundry sign indicates the extent of racial segregation in the South as late as the 1950s

★ **Grandfather Clauses** were state laws that allowed those whose ancestors qualified to vote in 1867 to vote without passing a literacy test or paying a poll tax. These clauses exempted poor whites but not poor African Americans, since few African Americans were qualified to vote in 1867.

RACIAL SEGREGATION: THE JIM CROW LAWS

In the 1880s and afterward, Southern legislatures passed laws **segregating** (*separating*) African Americans from whites. African Americans were not permitted to ride in the same train cars, attend the same schools, or use many of the same public facilities as whites. These laws became known as "Jim Crow" laws. In 1896, the Supreme Court upheld racial segregation in *Plessy v. Ferguson.*

KEY COURT CASES: PLESSY v. FERGUSON, 1896

Plessy, a racially mixed man, sat in a railroad car where only whites were permitted. He was arrested for violating a state law that provided "separate but equal" facilities for non-whites. Plessy said this law violated his "equal protection" rights under the 14th Amendment. The Supreme Court held that so long as a state provided "equal" facilities, it could legally separate African Americans from whites. The decision allowed the continuation of "separate but equal" facilities — resulting in whites and African Americans attending different schools, using different water fountains, and bathing in different public beaches.

THE AFRICAN-AMERICAN RESPONSE

African Americans responded to these unfair conditions in a variety of ways. Many developed strong community and church ties and evolved their own unique, robust culture. Others left the South when they had the opportunity. Close to two million African Americans moved to Northern cities from 1910 to 1930. African-American leaders also offered alternative responses to the dilemmas facing African Americans.

A mother and son head North seeking work

Library of Congress

BOOKER T. WASHINGTON

Booker T. Washington was born into slavery in 1856. In 1881, he founded the Tuskegee Institute in Alabama. In 1901, he wrote *Up From Slavery,* an autobiography. Washington believed that African Americans should first concentrate their efforts on trying to achieve economic independence before seeking full social equality. He believed economic prosperity could best be achieved by vocational training and practical, job-related education. As a result, Washington wanted young African Americans to develop skills and attitudes that would help them to survive in an environment of increasing violence and discrimination.

National Archives

W.E.B. DUBOIS

W.E.B. DuBois was the first African American to obtain a Ph.D. from Harvard University and became a notable historian and writer. Unlike Booker T. Washington, DuBois urged the next generation of African Americans to move in a new direction. DuBois believed African Americans should agitate for full social and political equality immediately and not rest content with an inferior social and economic status. In his writings, DuBois encouraged African Americans not to define themselves as whites saw them, but to take pride in their dual heritages — as both Africans and Americans. In 1909, DuBois helped form the **National Association for the Advancement of Colored People.**

Schomburg Center for Research in Black Culture

N.A.A.C.P. leaders believed in working through the courts to win rights for African Americans and to end racial injustice. As director of the N.A.A.C.P., DuBois edited its official journal, *The Crisis.*

SUMMARIZING YOUR UNDERSTANDING

KEY TERMS, CONCEPTS, AND PEOPLE

Make a vocabulary card for each of the following terms, concepts, and people.

Alexander Hamilton	Sectionalism	*Plessy v. Ferguson*
Andrew Jackson	Black Codes	Booker T. Washington
Abolitionists	Fourteenth Amendment	W.E.B. DuBois

COMPLETING A GRAPHIC ORGANIZER

Briefly describe each cause of the Civil War.

COMPLETING A TABLE

Briefly describe the following important legislation enacted during this period.

Legislation (date)	Major Provisions	Importance in American History
Missouri Compromise of 1820		
Compromise of 1850		
Kansas-Nebraska Act (1854)		
Emancipation Proclamation (1863)		
"Black Codes" (1866)		
"Jim Crow Laws" (1880s)		

TESTING YOUR UNDERSTANDING

1 A fundamental reason for issuing the Monroe Doctrine (1823) was to
   1   halt the slave trade from Africa to the United States
   2   prevent European intervention in the Western Hemisphere
   3   prevent the start of the Civil War
   4   protect American trading interests in China and Japan

2 The term "abolitionist" is used to describe a person who
   1   believed in free trade   3   desired to end slavery
   2   opposed foreign alliances   4   supported colonial rule

3 • "Compromise Enables Maine and Missouri to Enter Union"
   • "California Admitted to Union as a Free State"
   • "Kansas-Nebraska Act Establishes Popular Sovereignty"

   Which public issue was reflected in these headlines?
   1   enactment of protective tariffs   3   extension of slavery
   2   voting rights for minorities   4   universal public education

Base your answer to question 4 on the poster and on your knowledge of social studies.

4 This poster was most likely promoted by
   1   slave traders   3   abolitionists
   2   bounty hunters   4   confederates

> **Negroes for Sale.**
> *A Cargo of very fine ftout Men and Women, in good order and fit for immediate fervice, juft imported from the Windward Coaft of Africa, in the Ship Two Brothers.—* Conditions are one half Cafh or Produce, the other half payable the firft of Jaruary next, giving Bond and Security if required.
> The Sale to be opened at 10 o'Clock each Day, in Mr. Bourdeaux's Yard, at No, 48, on the Bay.
> May 19, 1784.   JOHN MITCHELL.
>
> **Thirty Seafoned Negroes**
> *To be Sold for Credit, at Private Sale.*
> AMONGST which is a Carpenter, none of whom are known to be difhoneft.
> Alfo, to be fold for Cafh, a regular bred young Negroe Man-Cook, born in this Country, who ferved feveral Years under an exceeding good French Cook abroad, and his Wife a middle aged Wather-Woman, (both very honeft) and their two Children. Likewife, a young Man a Carpenter. For Terms apply to the Printer.

National Archives

5 Which best describes President Lincoln's reason for undertaking the Civil War?
   1   As an abolitionist, Lincoln wanted to end slavery.
   2   Lincoln wanted to keep the South dependent on the industrial North.
   3   Lincoln believed it was his duty to defend and preserve the Union.
   4   Lincoln wanted to protect the freedom of the seas.

6 Which was a major result of the Civil War?
   1   Slavery was ended.   3   States secured the right to secede.
   2   The colonies won independence.   4   Women gained the right to vote.

7   The decision of *Dred Scott v. Sandford* (1857) was important because it
  1   strengthened the determination of abolitionists to achieve their goals
  2   triggered the immediate outbreak of the Civil War
  3   ended the importation of slaves into the United States
  4   increased the power of Congress to exclude slavery from new territories

8   A person speaking about Black Codes, carpetbaggers, and Radical Republicans is most likely discussing the
  1   American Revolution   3   Reconstruction period
  2   Civil War   4   Emancipation Proclamation

Base your answers to questions 9 and 10 on the statements of the Speakers and on your knowledge of social studies.

> **Speaker A:** Since the states were the ones to create the Union, they have a right to leave it.
>
> **Speaker B:** The Constitution is the work of the American people as a whole. No state has the right to secede individually.
>
> **Speaker C:** Let the people be the judge as to whether slavery should be introduced into a new territory. If not, I fear we will surely lose our political power in Congress.
>
> **Speaker D:** Although the different sections of the nation have disagreements, we must try to resolve our differences.

9   Which two speakers would support the position taken by the South on the eve of the Civil War?
  1   A and B   3   B and C
  2   A and C   4   C and D

10 Speaker C would probably be most worried about
  1   abolitionists being elected to the U.S. Congress
  2   carpetbaggers becoming judges in the South
  3   anti-federalists forming a new political party
  4   an alliance between Britain and the Northern states

11 A major reason the Radical Republicans in Congress opposed President Lincoln's Reconstruction plan was that it
  1   demanded payments from the South that would damage its economy
  2   postponed readmission of Southern states into the Union for many years
  3   granted too many rights to formerly enslaved people
  4   offered amnesty to Confederates who pledged loyalty to the Union

12 President Lincoln's plan for the reconstruction of the South was based on the theory that the former Confederate states
   1   should be treated as conquered territories
   2   could be re-admitted to the Union only by Congress
   3   had never actually left the Union
   4   must grant full equality to all people

13 How were African Americans in the South affected by the end of Reconstruction?
   1   A constitutional amendment prevented segregation.
   2   The Freedmen's Bureau helped them become independent farm owners.
   3   "Jim Crow" laws placed major restrictions on their civil rights.
   4   Southern landowners offered them training, new opportunities, and freedom.

THEMATIC ESSAY QUESTION

Directions: Write a well-organized essay that includes an introduction, several paragraphs addressing the task below, and a conclusion.

Theme: Change

> Throughout U.S. history, individuals and groups have disagreed about certain controversial issues.

Task:

> Choose **two** controversies from your study of United States history and government.
>
> For *each* controversy:
> - Describe the circumstances that gave rise to the controversy
> - Explain how that controversy was resolved

You may use any example from your study of United States history and government. Some suggestions you might wish to consider include: larger states vs. smaller states at the Constitutional Convention, Thomas Jefferson vs. Alexander Hamilton over the interpretation of the U.S. Constitution, Northern states vs. Southern states over the issue of slavery, Andrew Johnson vs. the Radical Republicans over plans for Reconstruction, and Booker T. Washington vs. W.E.B. DuBois over the best strategy for African Americans.

You are *not* limited to these suggestions.

DOCUMENT-BASED ESSAY QUESTION

Before you answer your first question, let's quickly review the "L•A•W" approach.

REVIEWING THE "L•A•W" APPROACH

"L"— LOOK AT THE TASK

Start by looking at the "Historical Context" and the "Task." Focus on (**1**) the "action word," and (**2**) the topic of the question.

"A" — ANALYZE THE DOCUMENTS

As you read each document, think about: (**1**) who wrote it; (**2**) the time period in which it was written; (**3**) the purpose for which it was written; and (**4**) what it says. After you carefully answer the question following each document, create your own Analysis Box.

> **Note:** Two keys to writing document-based essays are: (1) linking information in the documents to the **Task**; and (2) using your own words instead of copying from the document. Questions following each document will help identify relevant information.

In the Analysis Box, show how information in each document relates to the **Task**. Use note-taking form rather than full sentences. Add relevant information at the bottom of the box. Remember, the instructions will ask for information not in the documents.

"W" — WRITE THE ESSAY

In writing your essay answer, the key parts to include are as follows:

★ **Opening Paragraph.** Your opening sentences state the historical context and set the time and place. The next sentence is your thesis statement, which you can obtain from the question. Then write a transition sentence to lead into your supporting paragraphs.

★ **Supporting Paragraphs.** These paragraphs provide evidence to support your thesis statement. They must include references to the documents, using your own words (*not just quoting the documents*), as well as additional related information from your knowledge of the topic.

★ **Closing Paragraph.** Your closing paragraph should restate your thesis statement and summarize your ideas. You may include your views on the general topic in the "historical context" section of the question.

A SAMPLE DOCUMENT-BASED ESSAY QUESTION

Directions: Read the documents in Part A and answer the questions after each document. Then read the directions for Part B and write your essay.

Historical Context:

Soon after the Civil War, amendments were passed to provide African Americans with freedom and equality. However, during the century that followed, African Americans still lacked real equality.

Task:

Discuss the treatment of African Americans in the South in the century following the Civil War.

This task is based on the accompanying documents (1–5). Some of these documents have been edited for the purposes of this task. This task is designed to test your ability to work with historical documents. As you analyze the documents, take into account both the source of each document and the author's point of view.

DOCUMENT 1

"Neither slavery nor involuntary servitude, except as a punishment for crime …. shall exist within the United States, or any place subject to their jurisdiction."
— 13th Amendment (1865)

"All persons born or naturalized in the United States, and subject to the jurisdiction thereof, are citizens of the United States and of the state wherein they reside. No state shall make or enforce any law which shall abridge the privileges and immunities of citizens of the United States, nor shall any state deprive any person of life, liberty, or property without due process of law."
— 14th Amendment, Section 1 (1868)

"The right of the citizens of the United States to vote shall not be denied or abridged by the United States or by any state, on account of race, color, or previous condition of servitude."
— 15th Amendment, Section 1 (1870)

1. What rights did African Americans gain, based on these amendments? _____

DOCUMENT 2

Barrier	Description
Poll Tax	A voting tax that discriminated against poor people by requiring a voter to pay a fee in order to vote.
Property Tax	A requirement that a person must own a certain amount of property to vote; a requirement few poor Americans could meet.
Literacy Test	A requirement that a man must be able to read to vote; white registrars decided who passed the test.
Grandfather Clause	These waived literacy and property tests only for those whose grandfather had been eligible to vote *before* the Civil War.
Primary Elections	African Americans were banned from these primaries, since such elections were not covered by the 15th Amendment.

2a. What impact did these barriers have on African Americans? _____

b. How did the passage of Grandfather Clauses help benefit poor white

Southerners? _____

DOCUMENT 3

SELECTED JIM CROW LAWS, 1870–1965

Date	State	Purpose of Law	Date	State	Purpose of Law
1870	Georgia	separate schools	1915	South Carolina	unequal spending for education
1900	South Carolina	separate railroad cars	1922	Mississippi	separate taxicabs
1905	Georgia	separate parks	1935	Oklahoma	no boating or fishing together
1906	Alabama	separate streetcars	1937	Arkansas	segregation at race tracks
1915	Oklahoma	separate phone booths	1965	Louisiana	no money for integrated schools

3. What impact did Jim Crows laws have on Southern society? _____

DOCUMENT 4

"Here I am, a member of your honorable body, and yet, when I leave my home to come to the capital to make laws for this great Republic, I am treated not as an American citizen, but as a brute. Forced to occupy a filthy smoking-car, with drunkards, gamblers, and criminals; and for what? Simply because I have a darker complexion. If this treatment was confined to persons of our own sex we could possibly endure it. But our wives, daughters, sisters, and mothers are subjected to the same insults and uncivilized treatment. The only time I ever question my loyalty to my government is when I read of outrages committed upon innocent colored people or when I leave my home to go traveling."

— John Lynch, Rep. from Mississippi, House of Representatives (1870–1876)

4. Why did John Lynch feel that he was being treated "as a brute?" _____

DOCUMENT 5

5a. What was the "colored balcony' referred to on the awning?

_____

b. What does this photograph tell us about society in the South in the early 1900s?

_____

_____

Library of Congress

PART B - ESSAY

Directions: Write a well-organized essay that includes an introduction, several paragraphs, and a conclusion. Use evidence from at least **four** documents in the body of the essay. Support your response with relevant facts, examples, and details. Include additional outside information.

Using information from the documents and your knowledge of American history and government, write an essay in which you:

Discuss the treatment of African Americans in the South in the century following the Civil War.

ANALYZE THE DOCUMENTS

Use your answers to the document questions to help you complete the Analysis Box. Information about the first document and some related outside information have both been provided for you. Complete the rest of the Analysis Box for the other documents. Remember, when analyzing a document — relate it to the essay Task.

Document	What the document says about the treatment of African Americans following the Civil War
Document 1: Civil War Amendments	*The Civil War Amendments promised African Americans freedom from slavery, the right to vote, and all the rights and privileges of U.S. Citizens.*
Document 2: Barriers to voting	***You should complete.***
Document 3: Jim Crow laws	***You should complete.***
Document 4: Member of Congress	***You should complete.***
Document 5 Photograph	***You should complete.***

Related outside information:

• *After the Civil War, many freedmen became sharecroppers or tenant farmers on white-owned lands.*

• *In 1896, the Supreme Court upheld racial segregation in Plessy v. Ferguson.*

• _____ ***You should complete.*** _____

• _____ ***You should complete.*** _____

WRITE THE ANSWER

Now that you have looked at the question and analyzed the documents, you are ready to write your essay. Use the following page to write your answer. The opening sentences and the first part of the essay have been written for you. Complete the rest of the essay using information in your Analysis Box as a guide.

Introduction

Just after the Civil War, as Document 1 indicates, the Civil War Amendments — the Thirteenth, Fourteenth, and Fifteenth Amendments — were passed to provide African Americans with freedom and equality. However, during the century that followed the passage of these amendments, African Americans found that they had achieved freedom without real equality. Following the end of Reconstruction, white Southerners started to place limits on African Americans in order to preserve their control over Southern society.

Document 2 is explored

Southern states quickly passed a variety of laws to prevent African Americans from voting, as shown in Document 2. Since many African Americans could not pass the literacy tests or pay the poll taxes, they could not vote. This helped ensure white control. African Americans were given the message that, despite the Civil War Amendments, they were not full citizens. Without political or economic power, African Americans had no ability to improve their conditions or to promote change.

Body further discusses the treatment of African Americans in the South

Conclusion

Therefore, although the Civil War Amendments promised African Americans freedom and equality, the century following the passage of these amendments saw African Americans in the South achieve only limited freedom without real equality.

NOTE: To further help you practice answering document-based essay questions, you will find other document-based essay questions in Chapters 9, 11, and 15.

THE RISE OF INDUSTRY

CHAPTER 8

Library of Congress

This period saw the transformation of America into one of the world's leading industrial powers

TIMELINE OF IMPORTANT EVENTS

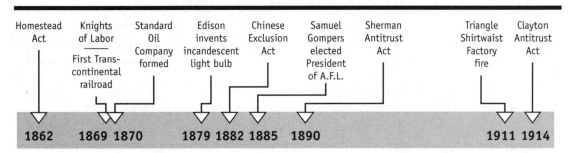

Homestead Act	Knights of Labor	Standard Oil Company formed	Edison invents incandescent light bulb	Chinese Exclusion Act	Samuel Gompers elected President of A.F.L.	Sherman Antitrust Act	Triangle Shirtwaist Factory fire	Clayton Antitrust Act
	First Trans-continental railroad							

| 1862 | 1869 | 1870 | 1879 | 1882 | 1885 | 1890 | 1911 | 1914 |

WHAT YOU SHOULD FOCUS ON

In this chapter, you will learn how the United States became one of the world's leading industrial powers in the decades following the Civil War. Industrialization touched almost every aspect of American life. It is easiest to think of these changes as occurring in the following four areas:

In these years, immigrants entered the United States in ever-increasing numbers

★ **The Rise of American Industry.** The development of new machines led to the rise of factories and mass production. Population growth, immigration, and the expansion of the railroad led to the rise of a national market. Entrepreneurs like Vanderbilt, Carnegie, and Rockefeller spearheaded these changes.

★ **The Rise of Labor.** Often ill-treated and poorly paid, industrial workers eventually organized into unions to obtain better working conditions. At first, public opinion opposed unions, but attitudes changed in the early 20th century.

★ **The Growth of Cities.** People flooded into cities in search of employment and a better way of life. Immigrants were also attracted to city life. Cities grew so rapidly they could not deal with the problems of congestion and insufficient public services.

★ **Westward Expansion.** The completion of transcontinental railroads allowed settlers to occupy the Great Plains and Far West. Native American tribes were forced off their traditional lands and onto reservations.

In studying this period, you should focus on the following questions:
    ★ What forces enabled the United States to emerge as a world power?
    ★ How were workers affected by the rise of industry?
    ★ How did cities cope with new problems?
    ★ What factors led to increasing immigration to the United States?

LOOKING AT ECONOMIC CHANGE

he Industrial Revolution began a period of growth and change unique in history. To better understand the influence of these economic changes on American life, let's look briefly at what an economy is, how a market economy works, and the causes and effects of economic change.

HOW SOCIETIES MEET THEIR ECONOMIC NEEDS

We all have wants and needs. Unfortunately, our wants are unlimited and can never be fully satisfied because we have limited resources at our disposal. As a result, every society makes choices in answering three basic economic questions:

What should be produced?

How should it be produced?

Who gets what is produced?

Economics is the study of how societies use their limited resources to satisfy these unlimited wants.

TYPES OF ECONOMIC SYSTEMS

Societies have answered these basic economic questions in three different ways, each of which is referred to as an **economic system.** In a **traditional economy,** the basic economic questions are answered by doing what has traditionally been done in the past. In a **command economy,** all important economic decisions are made by government leaders. In a **market economy,** people are free to produce whatever they wish and to consume whatever they can afford; the decisions of producers and consumers, taken together, determine the answers to the three basic economic questions.

HOW THE FREE MARKET WORKS

In a market economy, the **profit motive** acts as an incentive for people, while competition and the laws of supply and demand determine how much will be produced and at what price. Producers who charge too much will lose customers to more efficient producers. The government provides stable conditions and a system of laws so that people can conduct business. The government also acts to police the marketplace, insuring that persons and businesses treat each other fairly.

(continued)

THE FACTORS INFLUENCING ECONOMIC CHANGE

Economists have identified several important causes of economic change.

TECHNOLOGICAL INNOVATION

Each generation builds on the technological achievements of the past. The Industrial Revolution was one of the great turning points in the development of technology. People learned to use new sources of energy to replace human and animal power. Factories and machines replaced hand-produced goods.

CAPITAL INVESTMENTS AND PRODUCTIVITY

When a society invests labor and resources to build schools, factories, and machinery, its workers and businesses become more productive. As technology improves, each worker can produce more in the same amount of time.

NEW FORMS OF BUSINESS ORGANIZATION

The development of new forms of business organization has made it possible to bring together labor and resources in large quantities to mass-produce goods to meet business and consumer needs. For example, the rise of corporations in 19th-century America allowed a greater pooling of private resources.

POPULATION CHANGES

Although populations usually expand, they sometimes decline because of famine or war. Populations can also change in terms of age or location. For example, large numbers of people may move from the countryside to the city, or from the east to the west. Such shifts can affect the demand for goods and services.

Philadelphia, 1897 — industrialization often led to urban congestion

CONTACTS WITH OTHER SOCIETIES

Contacts with others may introduce new products, markets, or ways of producing things. However, contact with other societies can also lead to disputes with significant economic consequences.

NATURAL RESOURCES

Natural resources provide sources of energy and raw materials for agriculture and manufacturing. The development of new ways to use existing resources can stimulate economic change. For example, in the early stages of the Industrial Revolution, cheap energy sources, such as coal and water power, helped speed industrialization.

GOVERNMENT POLICY

Government policy can also greatly affect a nation's economy. Even in a free market system, the government sets the rules, provides the money supply, regulates trade, and purchases public goods and services.

THE IMPACT OF ECONOMIC CHANGE

The political, social, and cultural life of a nation is always closely tied to its economic life. As technology develops and a nation's economy is transformed, other aspects of national life also change. Here are some of the ways in which economic change can affect the rest of society:

Changes in Standards of Living. Economic improvements generally raise standards of living. Economic catastrophes, like wars or depressions, often lead to a decline in standards of living.

Greater Opportunities. The opportunities available to people are greatly affected by the economic system in which they live. In a traditional economy, people follow the occupations of their parents; in advanced economies, individuals have greater career choices.

HOW ECONOMIC CHANGES AFFECT A SOCIETY

Beliefs, Arts, and Culture. Economic change can affect art styles, fashions, and even what people believe. For example, the plight of workers during early industrialization led to the rise of Socialism and Communism.

Family Life. Before industrialization, most people lived under one roof in extended families, with grandparents, parents and children. After industrialization, people moved to cities and began living in smaller families consisting of parents and their children.

Relationships with Other Societies. New forms of production may require raw materials found elsewhere, leading to both greater competition and interdependence among societies.

THE RISE OF AMERICAN INDUSTRY

The Industrial Revolution began in Great Britain in the mid-1700s, and soon afterwards spread to the United States. New inventions and ideas introduced new ways of making goods and meeting people's needs. Instead of producing goods by hand at home, workers were placed in factories. Water power or the newly invented steam engine powered the machines in these factories, allowing manufacturers to produce more goods for less money. As goods became cheaper, demand increased, leading to more jobs. Cities grew up around factories, as workers moved closer to where they worked.

Ford Motor Corporation

As industry grew, scenes like this at a Ford factory became typical throughout the nation

THE FOUNDATIONS OF ECONOMIC GROWTH

Much of the foundation for America's rapid economic growth was already in place by the end of the Civil War.

AN ABUNDANCE OF NATURAL RESOURCES

The United States possessed fertile soil, swift-flowing streams and rivers, vast quantities of timber, and rich deposits of coal, iron ore, copper, and oil.

THE FREE ENTERPRISE SYSTEM

Americans enjoyed the benefits of the "free enterprise" or **capitalist** system. Under this system, **capital** (*wealth*) is privately owned and invested. Producers who stay in business are those who are able to compete effectively. American culture further stressed individualism, thrift, and hard work. Americans believed that individual efforts would be rewarded with material success.

THE CONTRIBUTION OF GOVERNMENT

The 19th-century American government officially followed a "hands-off" or **laissez-faire** policy towards the economy. Government policies nevertheless promoted industrialization in several important ways.

Federal and state laws protected property and contracts. In the late 1800s and early 1900s, Congress also passed **protective tariffs,** to protect American manufacturers from competition with cheaper foreign-made goods. A **tariff** is a tax on foreign imports, making them more costly for U.S. consumers. This encouraged consumers to buy goods made in the United States. Finally, a system of **patents** encouraged new inventions by giving inventors exclusive use of their ideas for a limited time.

THE MODERN INDUSTRIAL ECONOMY EMERGES

American industrialization proceeded at a rapid pace after the end of the Civil War.

THE EXPANSION OF RAILROADS

One key to the rise of the industrial economy in the United States was the expansion of the railroads. The first transcontinental railroad, linking the east and west coasts, was completed in 1869. The amount of railroad track increased fivefold in the next 25 years. Railroads affected just about every aspect of American life. Railroads connected raw

Linking of the transcontinental railroad at Promontory Point, Utah (1869)

Library of Congress

materials to factories and factories to consumers throughout the nation. Construction of the railroads stimulated the iron, steel, and coal industries.

The railroads also promoted the settlement of the frontier. They brought settlers to the Great Plains with the promise of cheap farm land. Then they linked the farms on the plains to urban markets. Railroad companies promoted immigration by advertising in Europe for settlers. They also used Irish and Chinese immigrants as a cheap labor force for building their new transcontinental lines.

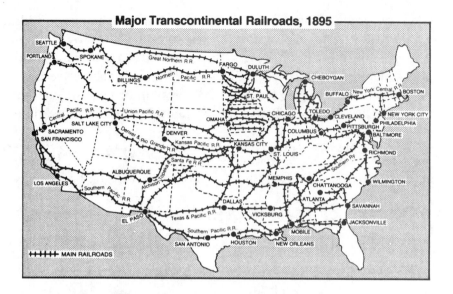

Major Transcontinental Railroads, 1895

THE GROWTH OF POPULATION

Between 1860 and 1900, the population of the United States more than doubled. This population increase was partly fueled by a constant stream of European immigrants. Population growth created favorable conditions for business expansion — a steadily rising demand for goods and a source of cheap labor.

DEVELOPMENT OF A NATIONAL MARKET

The high investment costs of mass production required a large market to remain profitable. In the late 19th century, a national market emerged as a result of a number of factors. Railroads, telegraphs, and telephones linked together different parts of the country. National producers could make and ship goods more cheaply than local producers, since they could take advantage of more machinery and economies of scale. New methods of selling were developed, such as department stores, chain stores, and mail order houses.

TECHNOLOGICAL PROGRESS

New inventions and technologies helped fuel the economic expansion of the late 19th century. The **Bessemer process** made the production of steel more economical. By 1900, electricity was being used to power an increasing number of machines, including electric streetcars and subway trains. The first oil well was drilled in Pennsylvania in 1859. Improvements in refining allowed petroleum products to be used in lighting and machine lubrication. The internal combustion engine, developed at the end of the 19th century, was used to run cars and the first airplanes. Each of these major new inventions had a dramatic effect on the American economy.

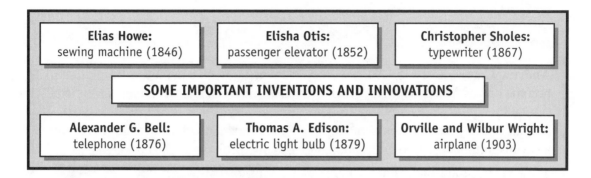

Elias Howe: sewing machine (1846)	**Elisha Otis:** passenger elevator (1852)	**Christopher Sholes:** typewriter (1867)
	SOME IMPORTANT INVENTIONS AND INNOVATIONS	
Alexander G. Bell: telephone (1876)	**Thomas A. Edison:** electric light bulb (1879)	**Orville and Wilbur Wright:** airplane (1903)

BUSINESS ORGANIZATION: THE CORPORATION

Before the Civil War, most businesses were owned by individuals or partnerships. Following the Civil War, the corporate form of business became much more popular. A **corporation** is a company chartered by a state and recognized in law as a separate "person." A corporation issues shares to investors, making each **stockholder** one of its partial owners. Stockholders share in the corporation's profits in the form of dividends. Corporations enjoyed many advantages because of the large amounts of money they could raise. During the period from 1865 to 1900, many Americans became involved in the pursuit of material wealth and luxuries.

THE GREAT ENTREPRENEURS:
ROBBER BARONS OR CAPTAINS OF INDUSTRY?

Because of the lavish lifestyle of those who became rich from industry, this period became known as the **Gilded Age.** Business entrepreneurs began to exercise a dominant influence on American life. Some observers thought of these entrepreneurs as **captains of industry** because they helped forge the modern industrial economy. Through the efficiencies of large-scale production, these industrialists lowered the prices of many goods, making them more affordable. Based on the ideas of **Social Darwinism,** these leaders thought they had become rich and powerful because they were superior in talent and energy. Critics called them **robber barons** because of the ruthless tactics they used to destroy competition and to keep down their workers' wages.

Andrew Carnegie, magnate of the steel industry

CAPTAINS OF INDUSTRY

Andrew Carnegie (1835–1919) worked his way up from a penniless immigrant to become one of America's richest and most powerful men. His steel mills undercut all competition. His workers put in 12-hour shifts at very low wages. Carnegie crushed any attempts by his workers to unionize. Carnegie spent much of his later life giving away his fortune to support education, libraries, medical research, and world peace.

John D. Rockefeller (1839–1937) formed the Standard Oil Company in 1870. He forced railroad companies to give him special, secret rates for shipping his oil, while charging competitors higher prices. By 1900, he controlled almost 90% of all oil refining in the nation. Like Carnegie, he gave millions to education and science.

Original stock certificate for Standard Oil

Jarrett Archives

BIG BUSINESS CONSOLIDATION

Beginning with the Depression of 1873, many large producers like Carnegie and Rockefeller began driving smaller companies out of business and acquiring their companies. In other cases, rival companies reached agreements to **consolidate** (*join together*) in the form of a **trust**. Many producers hoped to eliminate competition by establishing a **monopoly** (*complete control over a product*). Monopoly power allowed them to dictate their own prices to consumers.

THE DEMAND FOR REFORM

At first, the government did very little in response to the abuses of big business. Government leaders strongly believed in the operation of the free market. They also questioned whether the Constitution gave them the power to regulate business. However, some of the abuses of big business were so glaring that reformers called for federal legislation to remedy them. Although the first laws passed by Congress were weak, they established the right of Congress to regulate business.

★ **Interstate Commerce Act** (1887) was enacted when the Supreme Court overruled state laws regulating railroads. The new federal law prohibited unfair practices by railroads such as charging more for shorter routes. A special regulatory commission, the **Interstate Commerce Commission,** was established to enforce the act.

★ **Sherman Antitrust Act** (1890) made unfair monopoly practices illegal. The act marked a significant change in the attitude of Congress toward the abuses of big business. However, in *U.S.* v. *E.C. Knight* (1895), the Supreme Court refused to apply the act to manufacturing.

THE IMPACT OF GEOGRAPHY ON AMERICAN HISTORY

The backbone of American industry was iron and steel, needed for locomotives, railroad tracks, and construction. By the late 1850s, the coal resources of western Pennsylvania made possible the construction of larger furnaces. The new Bessemer process for making steel was introduced in the late 1860s. The iron ore of the Upper Peninsula of Michigan and Minnesota's Mesabi Range was shipped across the Great Lakes to Ohio and Western Pennsylvania, where it was smelted, refined, and rolled in large steel mills. Andrew Carnegie constructed his first

Pittsburgh, 1886 — making steel using the Bessemer process

steel mill just outside of Pittsburgh, at the focal point of these natural resources. For nearly a century, the region from Chicago to Pittsburgh remained America's industrial heartland.

THE RISE OF ORGANIZED LABOR

One factor in America's rapid economic growth was an increasing exploitation of workers. Gains in productivity were often achieved at a terrible human cost.

INDUSTRIAL WORKERS FACE NEW PROBLEMS

UNFAVORABLE WORKING CONDITIONS

Industrial working conditions in the late 19th century were often extremely hazardous. Safeguards around machinery were inadequate. Thousands of workers were injured or killed in industrial accidents each year.

★ **Long Hours and Low Wages.** Hours were incredibly long by today's standards. Workers faced a six-day work week of 10 to 14 hours per day. Employers hired the least expensive laborers. Pay averaged from $3 to $12 weekly, but immigrants were often willing to work for far less. Women and children were also frequently used as low-paid workers.

★ **Impersonal Conditions and Boring, Repetitive Tasks.** As factories and work places grew larger, workers lost all personal contact with their employers. Jobs were offered on a take-it or leave-it basis. Usually a worker had no choice but to accept. As industrialists sought to achieve greater speed and efficiency, each worker became nothing more than a human cog in a vast machine. Work became less skilled, more repetitive, monotonous, and boring.

CHILD LABOR

Textile mills and coal mines made use of child labor to perform special tasks. About one-fifth of all American children under 15 were working in 1910. These children missed sunshine, fresh air, play, and the chance to improve their lives by attending school.

Entire families often toiled in sweatshop tenements for a few dollars a day

Library of Congress

LACK OF SECURITY

Industrial workers could be fired at any time for any reason. In bad economic times, manufacturers simply halted production and fired their employees. Workers lacked the benefits of workers today: there was no unemployment insurance, no worker's compensation for injuries on the job, no health insurance, no old-age pensions, and no paid sick days. In some company towns, the company even controlled housing, town officials and the police, making it impossible for workers to complain or organize.

RISE OF LABOR UNIONS

With the rise of big business, individual workers lost all bargaining power against their employers.

Since most work was unskilled, the workers could easily be replaced. Many workers realized that some form of labor organization was needed to protect their interests. Some workers formed **unions** so that they could act as a group instead of as individuals. Unions organized strikes and other forms of protest to obtain better working conditions. Industrialists like Carnegie used immigrant workers or closed down factories rather than negotiate with unions.

WORKERS SEEK A NATIONAL VOICE

The **Knights of Labor,** begun in 1869, hoped to form one large national union joining together all skilled and unskilled workers. After 1881, even women workers were admitted. The Knights demanded an 8-hour work day, higher wages, and safety codes in factories. They opposed child labor and supported equal pay for women. They supported restrictions on immigration,

Workers often labored long hours for low wages

since they saw immigrants as competitors for their jobs. Under the leadership of **Terrence Powderly,** the Knights grew rapidly in the 1880s. But the Knights proved to be too loosely organized. Skilled workers resented being in the same union as the unskilled. After losing several important strikes, the Knights of Labor fell apart.

The American Federation of Labor (AFL) was formed in 1881 by a Jewish cigar-maker, **Samuel Gompers.** Gompers hoped to create a powerful union by uniting workers with similar economic interests. Unlike the Knights of Labor, the AFL consisted of separate unions of skilled workers joined together into a federation. The participating craft unions limited their membership to skilled workers such as carpenters and cigar-makers. Gompers' approach was known as "bread and butter" unionism because he limited his goals to winning economic improvements for his workers.

Samuel Gompers

Gompers focused on obtaining higher pay, an 8-hour work day, and better working conditions. Gompers fought hard to improve members' job security by seeking **closed shops** (*places where only union members were hired*). The AFL quickly emerged as the principal voice of organized labor. By 1900, it had half a million members. But the AFL was weakened in its early years by excluding unskilled workers, who made up the bulk of the labor force. As late as 1910, less than 5% of American workers were unionized.

GOVERNMENT'S ATTITUDE TOWARD UNIONS

The attitudes of government leaders were critical to the fortunes of the early labor movement. In the late 19th century, most government leaders favored business and opposed unions. There were several reasons for this attitude.

THE GREATER INFLUENCE OF BUSINESS

In general, unions lacked political strength, while business leaders contributed heavily to political campaign funds. Moreover, business leaders and politicians often shared the same outlook. They believed that successful businesses were chiefly responsible for American prosperity.

PROTECTOR OF THE ECONOMY

More than 20,000 strikes involving more than six million workers took place between 1880 and 1900. Government leaders feared the disruptive effect of strikes on the economy. In 1895, the Supreme Court supported the use of the Sherman Antitrust Act against unions, ruling that strikes were an illegal interference with interstate commerce. State governors and the President used troops to put down strikes and to restore order.

Strikers, such as these cloakmakers, were often viewed with hostility

PUBLIC OPINION

Public opinion supported *laissez-faire* policies, since many Americans believed businesses should have the right to hire and fire employees as they pleased. People were hostile to unions because their wage demands led to higher prices.

Union activities were often associated with violence and radical ideas. In the **Haymarket Affair** of 1886, labor leaders were blamed when a bomb exploded at a demonstration of striking workers at Haymarket Square in Chicago. Seven policemen were killed and 67 others were severely wounded. In 1892, the **Homestead Strike** at Carnegie's steel works collapsed when new workers were brought in to replace the strikers.

A SHIFT IN GOVERNMENT ATTITUDE

In the early 20th century, the attitude of the government and public towards unions began to change. One event that led to this change was a fire in New York City at the **Triangle Shirtwaist Factory** in 1911, which killed 146 garment workers. Public sympathy for the workers grew when it was learned that the factory doors had been bolted shut from the outside, and that the building lacked a sprinkler system and had only one inadequate fire escape. Soon after, Congress passed legislation sympathetic to unions.

★ **Department of Labor** (1913). Congress created a separate cabinet post to study the problems of labor, collect statistics, and enforce federal labor laws.

★ **Clayton Antitrust Act** (1914). Congress passed a law preventing the application of antitrust laws to unions. The act also banned the use of federal **injunctions** (*court orders*) to prohibit strikes in labor disputes.

CHANGING AMERICAN LIFESTYLES

The nation's industrialization led to a significant change in American lifestyles. This section examines the impact of industrialization on city life and immigration.

URBANIZATION

One of the most important results of industrialization was the rapid expansion of American cities. In 1865, most Americans lived in the countryside. By 1920, half of all Americans lived in cities. The movement of people from the countryside to cities is known as **urbanization.**

An increased use of farm machinery reduced the number of farm jobs, forcing many farmers, farm laborers, and their families to seek work in towns and cities. At the same time, the rise of industry created new job opportunities in factories and sweat shops. Immigrants from Europe flooded American cities in search of work and places to live. In the largest American cities, European immigrants often outnumbered native-born Americans. Still others were attracted by the cultural opportunities, entertainments, and rich variety of city life.

CITIES FACE NEW PROBLEMS

American cities mushroomed so quickly that municipal authorities were unable to deal adequately with their problems.

OVERCROWDING AND CONGESTION

As cities grew, whole families crowded into **tenements** — single-room apartment buildings often without adequate heat or lighting. Many families shared a single toilet. Horse-drawn cars crowded the streets, making movement almost impossible. As cities grew, they often developed haphazardly. Streets were frequently not wide enough for the increased traffic.

New York State Archives

A crowded tenement street in New York City

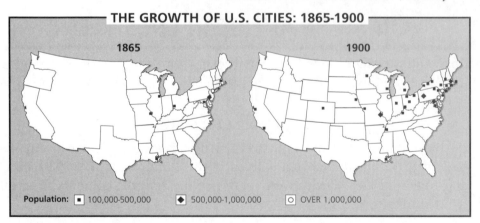

THE GROWTH OF U.S. CITIES: 1865-1900

1865   1900

Population: ■ 100,000-500,000   ◆ 500,000-1,000,000   ○ OVER 1,000,000

Factories polluted the air, and sewage sometimes contaminated drinking water. Cities lacked the ability to deliver enough of many essential services, such as police, schools, fire departments, and garbage collection.

POLITICAL CORRUPTION

Cities were often run by corrupt "**political machines.**" Political bosses provided jobs and services for immigrants and the poor in exchange for their votes. These bosses then used their control of city hall to make illegal profits by overcharging on city contracts.

IMMIGRATION

Late 19th-century America was equally affected by a sudden flood of immigrants.

WHY THE IMMIGRANTS CAME

Immigrants have been attracted to America throughout its history. The decision to come to America has often been the product of several factors.

> **Push Factors.** Conditions in immigrants' native lands often propelled or "pushed" them to leave. Immigrants came to escape conditions of poverty or religious and political persecution.

FACTORS EXPLAINING WHY IMMIGRANTS CAME

> **Pull Factors.** Conditions in the U.S. also attracted or "pulled" many immigrants to come. Many newcomers heard about the greater political freedom, higher standards of living, and availability of jobs in America. News of these benefits was spread by letters from relatives, steamship advertisements, and industrialists seeking to recruit laborers.

SHIFTING PATTERNS OF IMMIGRATION

Between 1607 and 1880, most immigrants came from Northern Europe, especially Great Britain, Ireland, and Germany. In general, these immigrants were Protestant, except for large numbers of Irish Catholics. Most of these early immigrants also spoke English. These immigrants came looking for cheap farmland available in the West, and many settled on the western frontier. No laws limited the number of these immigrants.

An immigrant awaits processing at Ellis Island, 1905

THE NEW IMMIGRANTS, 1880–1920

Existing patterns of immigration changed in the 1880s. The construction of railroads and larger steamships made the voyage to America more afford-able for many Europeans. Most of the **"New Immigrants"** came from Southern and Eastern Europe, especially Poland, Italy, Austria-Hungary, Greece, and Russia. They were Catholic and Jewish, rather than Protestant.

The **New Immigrants** were poor, spoke no English, and dressed differently from Northern Europeans. A trickle of Asian immigrants also arrived. This immigration was quickly limited by new laws.

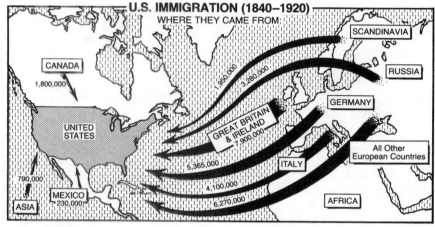

U.S. IMMIGRATION (1840–1920)
WHERE THEY CAME FROM:

CANADA 1,800,000

SCANDINAVIA
RUSSIA
GERMANY
All Other European Countries

UNITED STATES

GREAT BRITAIN & IRELAND — 7,900,000

1,950,000
3,280,000

5,365,000
ITALY
4,100,000
6,270,000
AFRICA

ASIA 790,000
MEXICO 230,000

THE PROCESS OF BECOMING AMERICANIZED

Immigrants in the 19th century usually faced great hardships in making the passage to America. They traveled in steamships in the cheapest compartments, often with their life's belongings in a single bag. On arrival, they had to be processed at the vast government center at Ellis Island in New York harbor. Those with tuberculosis or other diseases were sent back.

Immigrants being inspected at Ellis Island

National Archives

Becoming **"Americanized"** — learning to act, speak, and behave like other Americans — was a gradual process. Often it was their children, not the immigrants themselves, who became fully Americanized.

★ **Initial Hardships.** The New Immigrants arriving after 1880 were poor and often settled in cities. Most spoke no English and were unfamiliar with American customs. They lived in crowded, unsanitary apartments and worked at unskilled jobs for long hours at low pay. They faced hostility and discrimination, both from native-born Americans and from other ethnic groups.

★ **Ethnic Ghettos.** To cope with these problems, many immigrants settled with others of the same nationality in neighborhoods known as **ghettos.** The immigrants felt more comfortable around those who spoke the same language and who followed the same customs. Here they could speak their native language, attend familiar churches and synagogues, and be among friends from the "Old Country." However, living in such ethnic ghettos isolated them from mainstream American life, making it harder for them to become **acculturated** (*learning the language and culture of their adopted land*).

★ **The Process of Assimilation.** While some immigrants attended night school to learn English, most were too busy working or caring for families to spend much time learning a new language or culture. It was left to their children to learn English and to become familiar with American customs. In this way, immigrant children were eventually

Immigrant children learn English while attending school

assimilated (*made similar to other Americans*). American public schools greatly assisted in the process. Often assimilation was accompanied by bitter conflict between generations. For example, immigrant parents might insist on an arranged marriage for their children, while their children would insist on finding their own marriage partners according to the American custom.

THE RISE OF NATIVISM

As the flood of immigrants grew at the end of the 19th century, nativist hostility mounted. As early as the 1840s, nativists known as the **Know-Nothings** had attacked Irish Catholics. Later nativists wanted immigration to be restricted. They argued that New Immigrants were inferior to "true" Americans — white, Anglo-Saxon, and Protestant. **Nativists** believed people of other races, religions, and nationalities were physically and culturally inferior. They feared the New Immigrants would never be absorbed into society, since they lived in ghettos and spoke their own languages. Many Nativists also feared that the immigrants, who worked for low wages, would take jobs from Americans.

EARLY RESTRICTIONS ON IMMIGRATION

Throughout the nineteenth century, immigration to the United States was generally unrestrained. Anyone who was healthy and could afford to come was permitted to emigrate. In the late 1800s, the first laws restricting immigration were passed. These laws reflected the racial prejudices of the time, and were directed solely against Asians. The **Chinese Exclusion Act** (1882) was passed to satisfy anti-Chinese feelings in California against the flood of Chinese workers; all future Chinese immigration was banned. In the **Gentlemen's Agreement** (1907), the Japanese government promised to limit future Japanese immigration to the United States. Restrictions on European immigration were not introduced until after World War I, and are dealt with in Chapter 10.

THE LAST AMERICAN FRONTIER

Just as life in American cities was affected by the rapid pace of industrial change, life on the last frontier was also transformed by America's industrial development. The American

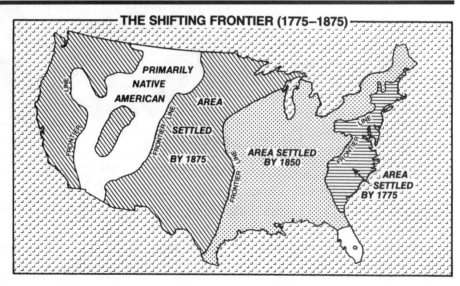

frontier has generally been defined as the line separating areas of settlement from "unsettled" wilderness territory. From another point of view, the American frontier marked the dividing line between areas where Native American Indians lived and those areas where people originally from Europe and Asia had settled.

THE SETTLEMENT OF THE FRONTIER

Since the arrival of the first colonists, the American frontier had been moving slowly westwards. By the end of the Civil War, American settlers occupied the Midwestern prairies and had settled along the Pacific coast. Between these two lines was a vast expanse of territory.

Much of this last frontier consisted of the Great Plains, home to millions of buffalo and the Native Americans who lived off their food and hides. From about 1860 to 1890, these herds of buffalo were destroyed, and the Native Americans were forced onto reservations. The Great Plains were divided into farms and ranches.

A buffalo hide yard, 1878, with 40,000 hides from killed buffalo

By 1890, the U.S. government declared the last frontier was settled. Several factors contributed to closing of the frontier.

THE DISCOVERY OF PRECIOUS METALS

Gold and silver had been discovered in California, the Rocky Mountains, and the Black Hills of South Dakota from 1848 onwards. Thousands of prospectors and adventurers moved to these areas in the hope of striking it rich. Rough-and-ready mining towns sprang up overnight. Often they collapsed just as fast as they had arisen.

THE ROLE OF THE RAILROADS

The extension of the railroads was one of the principal factors behind the settlement of the Great Plains. With the completion of the first transcontinental railroad in 1869, the journey from one coast to another was cut from several months to a few weeks. Sharp-shooters on the railroads killed off many of the buffalo.

The railroads pushed Native American Indians off their tribal lands

Railroads made it possible for ranchers and farmers to ship their cattle and grain to eastern markets.

THE IMPACT OF GEOGRAPHY ON AMERICAN HISTORY

Stewart Millstein, Photographer

To reach California in 1848, those struck by gold fever had either to sail around South America, cross Central America or take a horse-drawn coach or wagon across the United States. Americans soon realized the need for a transcontinental railroad, but were divided on the route. Southerners proposed a route through New Mexico. After the Civil War, a more northern route was chosen. The choice of the route had an important impact on the geographical environment. Completion of the transcontinental railroad made it possible to cross the continent in a matter of weeks, instead of months. It opened the Great Plains to settlement and made it possible for farmers and ranchers to ship their crops and livestock back east.

THE AVAILABILITY OF CHEAP LAND

Immigrants from Europe and farmers from the East and Midwest of United States were attracted by the prospect of cheap land under the terms of the **Homestead Act.**

KEY LEGISLATION

The Homestead Act of 1862 gave federal land away to anyone who settled it. Anyone over twenty years old could claim a 160-acre lot. In order to obtain ownership, a person only needed to farm the land for five years. After paying a small fee, the land then became the homesteader's.

THE FATE OF THE NATIVE AMERICAN INDIANS

Native American Indians once occupied all of the United States. The Native Americans were composed of many different groups, or tribes, speaking hundreds of languages. The advancing line of settlement, and diseases from Europe like smallpox, had severely reduced Native American populations and pushed them westwards.

EARLY GOVERNMENT POLICY

From 1830 to 1890, the government systematically followed a policy of pushing Native American Indians from their historic lands onto government reservations in the West.

Forced Removal. In 1830, Congress ordered the removal of all Native American Indians to west of the Mississippi. Nearly one-quarter of the Cherokees perished on the journey westward, known as the **Trail of Tears**.

Flood of Settlers. large numbers of settlers overwhelmed the Native Americans. In 1869, the transcontinental railroad was completed. Along with the Homestead Act, the continuation of railroad lines made Native American lands even more desirable.

FACTORS ERODING NATIVE AMERICAN CONTROL OF THE WEST

Warfare. The technological superiority of the U.S. government made resistance futile. The **"Indian Wars,"** which pitted settlers and federal troops against Native American Indians, lasted from 1860 to 1890.

Destruction of Natural Environment. Competition between settlers, miners, and farmers for the land led to the destruction of the natural environment on which Native Americans depended for their livelihood.

THE RESERVATION

Once a Native American tribe submitted to federal authority, its members were settled on **reservations**. Reservation lands were smaller than the lands from which the tribe was removed and often consisted of undesirable land. The federal government promised food,

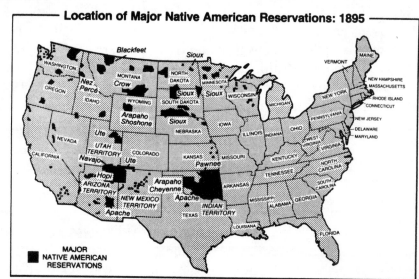

Location of Major Native American Reservations: 1895

MAJOR NATIVE AMERICAN RESERVATIONS

blankets, and seed, but this policy clashed with tribal customs, since Native Americans were traditionally hunters, not farmers.

REFORMERS URGE AMERICANIZATION

In the 19th century, prejudice against Native American Indians was widespread. Nonetheless, some reformers protested against their mistreatment. The most famous of these was **Helen Hunt Jackson.** Her book, *A Century of Dishonor* (1881), harshly criticized the government for repeatedly breaking its promises to Native American Indians. In her novel *Ramona,* she told of the plight of Native Americans as the frontier disappeared.

THE DAWES ACT, 1887

Some reformers urged that the Native American Indians undergo **"Americanization,"** — adopting the mainstream culture. The **Dawes Act** sought to hasten Americanization. The act abolished Native American tribes. Each family was given 160

Shoshone on the reservation at Ft. Washahie, Wyoming (1892)

National Archives

acres of reservation land as its own private property. Private property was expected to replace tribal ownership, as each Native American Indian became a farmer. Those who adopted this way of life were given U.S. citizenship. In 1924, all Native American Indians were made citizens. Although well intentioned, the act was a failure.

Threatened Tribal Ways. Assimilation threatened Native American culture. The act encouraged individual farm ownership, opposing the tradition of sharing tribal lands.	**Hunters, Not Farmers.** Many Native American Indian tribes had never farmed the land, since they were hunters by lifestyle and tradition.

SHORTCOMINGS OF THE DAWES ACT

Infertile Lands. The lands given to Native American Indians were often infertile. The government also never provided farm equipment or assistance in learning how to farm.	**Reservation Life.** Many suffered from malnutrition, poverty, and untreated health problems. Reservation schools provided an inferior education.

SUMMARIZING YOUR UNDERSTANDING

KEY TERMS, CONCEPTS, AND PEOPLE

Make a vocabulary card for each of the following terms, concepts, and people.

Free Enterprise System	Samuel Gompers	Nativism
Gilded Age	Urbanization	Assimilation
Andrew Carnegie	New Immigrants	Reservations
Knights of Labor	Gentlemen's Agreement	Helen Hunt Jackson

COMPLETING A TABLE

Briefly describe the following legislation associated with this period.

Legislation	Major Provisions	Intent of this Legislation
Homestead Act (1862)		
Chinese Exclusion Act (1882)		
Dawes Act (1887)		
Interstate Commerce Act (1887)		
Sherman Antitrust Act (1890)		
Clayton Antitrust Act (1914)		

COMPLETING A GRAPHIC ORGANIZER

Briefly describe the following developments described in this chapter.

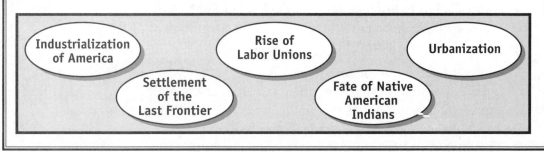

- Industrialization of America
- Rise of Labor Unions
- Urbanization
- Settlement of the Last Frontier
- Fate of Native American Indians

TESTING YOUR UNDERSTANDING

MULTIPLE-CHOICE QUESTIONS

1   Which term best describes the economic system found in the United States?
1   mercantilism   3   Communism
2   free enterprise   4   balance of trade

Base your answer to questions 2 and 3 on the speakers' statements below and on your knowledge of social studies.

> **Speaker A:** Consumers in the marketplace must be allowed to choose which goods they want to buy. Consumer demand for those goods will establish a fair and reasonable price.
>
> **Speaker B:** Our nation's factories and workshops are dangerous places to work, and wages are lower than they should be. Only labor unions can convince managers to improve both wages and working conditions.
>
> **Speaker C:** Our economy is now far too complex to remain unregulated. Businesses have grown large and powerful. Too many monopolies and too many companies ignore the public good.
>
> **Speaker D:** Our government has fostered economic growth through its willingness to allow businesses to compete with one another. Government regulation would discourage economic growth.

2   The common topic of all these speakers is the
1   free enterprise system   3   effects of foreign competition
2   growing power of unions   4   safety of consumer products

3   Which individual held ideas similar to those of Speaker B?
1   Andrew Carnegie   3   Thomas Edison
2   John D. Rockefeller   4   Samuel Gompers

4   A major cause of industrialization in the United States was the
1   Fourteenth Amendment   3   development of labor unions
2   Sherman Antitrust Act   4   expansion of railroads

5   Which statement about the Sherman Antitrust Act (1890) is most accurate?
1   It gave states the power to regulate interstate railways.
2   It prohibited monopolies that unfairly restricted interstate commerce.
3   It established the Federal Trade Commission.
4   The Supreme Court ruled that it was unconstitutional.

6 The term "robber barons" is frequently used to describe the industrialists of the late nineteenth century because they
1   made large charitable donations to worthy causes
2   sought greater profits by eliminating competition and exploiting workers
3   attempted to stimulate the economy by keeping prices as low as possible
4   opposed the entry of uneducated immigrants into the United States

7 The term "Gilded Age" suggests that in the latter part of the nineteenth century, Americans were primarily concerned with
1   materialistic goals   3   overseas expansion
2   social equality   4   artistic achievement

8 In the nineteenth century, the industrialization of the United States became concentrated in the Northeast largely because
1   this region had the greatest supply of capital and labor
2   the climate of the South was not suitable for industrial development
3   other regions lacked good water transportation
4   the West and South had few natural resources

9 What was the greatest problem facing American industrial workers in the late nineteenth century?
1   shortage of farm crops   3   decreased rates charged by railroads
2   inability to vote in elections   4   harsh working conditions

10 Which was a major reason for the failure of nineteenth-century labor unions in the United States?
1   public disapproval of unions
2   Congressional measures outlawing unions
3   an abundance of technical workers
4   workers were generally satisfied with working conditions

11 Which belief was shared by both the Knights of Labor and the American Federation of Labor?
1   Unions must limit their membership to become strong.
2   Unskilled workers should be excluded from union membership.
3   Workers should support socialist candidates.
4   Labor requires a national voice.

12 Which act occurred last?
1   Clayton Antitrust Act   3   Sherman Antitrust Act
2   Homestead Act   4   Chinese Exclusion Act

13 Which statement is an opinion rather than a fact?
1   The Knights of Labor was organized in 1869.
2   Thomas Edison invented the incandescent light bulb.
3   The main reason for early business mergers was to limit competition.
4   Early craft unions limited their membership to skilled workers.

14 Which statement about immigration to the United States is most accurate?
1   Industrialization reduced the demand for cheap immigrant labor.
2   A diverse immigrant population helped to create a pluralistic society.
3   Organized labor generally favored unrestricted immigration.
4   Most immigration legislation was passed to encourage immigration.

15 Which was a common complaint of nativist groups in the United States during the late 19th and early 20th centuries?
1   Congress failed to protect domestic industries.
2   Many immigrants brought customs and beliefs that were "un-American."
3   Too many elected officials came from immigrant backgrounds.
4   Native American Indians should be given back their ancestral lands.

16 An experience shared by most immigrants to the United States during the period 1880 to 1920 was that they
1   met with local prejudice
2   settled in rural areas
3   were rapidly assimilated into mainstream lifestyles
4   joined radical political parties to bring about reform

17 Which would be a *primary* source of information about immigrants coming to the United States in 1880?
1   a textbook chapter on immigration policy
2   a biography of a famous immigrant
3   a news account about the re-opening of Ellis Island as a museum
4   a diary of an immigrant who passed through Ellis Island

18 The influx of people from the country to the cities in the later nineteenth century resulted in
1   decreased literacy
2   crowded slums and unsanitary conditions
3   a decline in economic growth
4   unused farmland

Base your answer to question 19 on the graph below and on your knowledge of social studies.

19 Which generalization concerning population trends during the nineteenth century is most clearly supported by the information provided by the graph?
1 Jobs attracted about 60% of the population to urban areas.
2 Most immigrants moved to rural areas.
3 Family size was greater in rural areas than in urban areas.
4 The percentage of the population in urban areas grew.

Percentage of United States Population
Urban and Rural: 1800 – 1900

KEY
Rural
Urban

1800   1850   1900

20 During the second half of the nineteenth century, the federal government encouraged the westward settlement of the United States by
1 making low-interest loans to settlers
2 paying Western farmers to grow certain crops
3 giving free land to homesteaders
4 honoring Native American Indian territorial claims

21 A landless settler heading west in the 1860s would most likely have supported the passage of the
1 Dawes Act   3 Sherman Antitrust Act
2 Homestead Act   4 "Jim Crow" laws

22 After the Civil War, the policy of the U.S. government toward Native American Indians was mainly one of
1 moving Native American Indians from ancestral lands onto reservations
2 encouraging Native American Indians to retain their customs and traditions
3 educating society about the cultural heritage of Native American Indians
4 shifting responsibility for Native American Indian affairs to state governments

23 The main purpose of antitrust legislation was to
1 promote mergers   3 preserve business competition
2 restrict foreign trade   4 reduce union membership

INTERPRETING DOCUMENTS

What is the main idea of this cartoon?

_____

_____

_____

_____

_____

_____

The trust giants' point of view

Library of Congress

THEMATIC ESSAY QUESTION

Directions: Write a well-organized essay that includes an introduction, several paragraphs addressing the task below, and a conclusion.

Theme: Change

> Throughout American history, certain groups in American society have been profoundly influenced by economic changes.

Task:

> Choose **two** groups from your study of U.S. history and government.
>
> For *each* group:
> • Describe the characteristics of that group.
> • Explain the impact of an economic change on that group.

You may use any example from your study of American history. Some suggestions you might wish to consider include: Native Americans, workers, entrepreneurs, immigrants, farmers, and city-dwellers.

You are *not* limited to these suggestions.

CHAPTER 9

THE PROGRESSIVE ERA: PROTEST, REFORM, AND EMPIRE

Library of Congress

Women parade down Broadway in New York City demanding the right to vote (May 1912)

TIMELINE OF IMPORTANT EVENTS

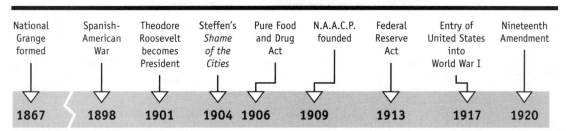

National Grange formed	Spanish-American War	Theodore Roosevelt becomes President	Steffen's *Shame of the Cities*	Pure Food and Drug Act	N.A.A.C.P. founded	Federal Reserve Act	Entry of United States into World War I	Nineteenth Amendment
1867	1898	1901	1904	1906	1909	1913	1917	1920

WHAT YOU SHOULD FOCUS ON

In this chapter, you will learn how Americans adopted important reforms to meet the new problems posed by industrialization and urbanization. American industrial power also enabled the United States to become a world power. As the nation became more assertive in the Pacific and the Caribbean, it acquired its first overseas colonies. In this chapter you should be aware of the following:

Women became more insistent on their right to vote

Library of Congress

★ **Agrarian Reform and Populism.** In the late 1800s, farmers were hit by falling food prices while their expenses remained high. To protect themselves, American farmers organized to demand change.

★ **Progressive Movement.** Progressive reformers sought to end political corruption, to curb big business, and to remedy the social problems caused by industrialization. Presidents Theodore Roosevelt and Woodrow Wilson introduced Progressive reforms at the national level.

★ **Struggle for Women's Rights.** American women organized to achieve equal rights with men.

★ **American Foreign Policy, 1898–1920.** Americans went to war with Spain in 1898 to halt atrocities in Cuba. After the war, the United States acquired a colonial empire. To protect freedom of the seas, the United States was drawn into World War I in Europe in 1917. American involvement led to Allied victory and the end of Progressivism in the United States.

In studying this period, you should focus on the following questions:

★ What were the problems of farmers and how did they try to overcome them?
★ What changes were brought about by the Progressives?
★ What changes took place in the lives of American women?
★ What factors led to America's becoming a colonial power?
★ Why did the United States become involved in World War I?

LOOKING AT THE ARTS

any people have an inner drive to express their deepest beliefs, feelings, and desires. The arts — such as literature, painting, architecture, photography, dance, and music — are forms that this inner drive for self-expression can take. Forms of artistic expression almost always also reflect something about the society and time in which they were produced. One art critic summed it up best by stating:

"A painting is ... a projection of the personality of the individual who painted it, and a statement of the philosophy of the age that produced it ...."

INTERPRETING ART

On some Regents Examination questions, you may be asked how a form of art is a reflection of the times. The question could be presented in two different formats:

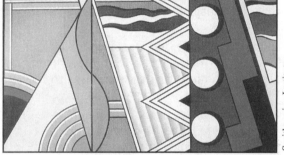

A modern painting by American artist Roy Lichtenstein

Smithsonian Institute

★ **Multiple Choice Questions.** You might be given a work of art — such as a painting, photograph of a building, or literary passage. The question will then ask you either (a) to interpret the artwork; or (b) to indicate how it reflects the time in which it was produced. To answer such questions, ask yourself the following:

◆ In what time period was the artwork created?
◆ What is the theme or message of the artwork?
◆ How does the theme of the artwork or its features reflect the time in which it was produced?

★ **Essay Questions.** You could also be asked about artworks on a thematic or document-based essay question. In this type of question, you could be asked to discuss the major artistic achievements of several different artists. To help you answer such questions, you should have some knowledge of the major writers and artists in American history.

(continued)

AUTHORS

Certain writers and commentators have had an especially important impact on American society. Some of these writers and their major works include:

Author	Major Work	Impact
Thomas Paine (1776)	In *Common Sense*, Paine urged colonists to break away from Great Britain. He ridiculed the idea of an island ruling a continent.	This pamphlet helped convince colonists to revolt against Britain and to fight for independence.
Alexander Hamilton (1787)	Hamilton, Jay, and Madison wrote *The Federalist*, explaining the new Constitution and the advantages of adopting it.	This group of 85 essays was very influential in persuading Americans to ratify the new U.S. Constitution.
Harriet Beecher Stowe (1852)	In *Uncle Tom's Cabin*, Stowe described the horrors of slavery as they existed in the deep South.	The book stirred Northern sentiment to end slavery. It gave increased vigor to the abolitionist cause.
Helen Hunt Jackson (1881)	In *A Century of Dishonor*, Jackson criticized the federal government's policy of broken promises to the Native American Indians.	Hunt's book awakened the nation to the plight of Native Americans, and led to legislation to help the Native American Indians.
Frederick Jackson Turner (1893)	Turner's essay, *The Significance of the Frontier in American History*, explained the key role of the frontier in America.	Turner alerted historians and social scientists to the key role of the frontier in shaping the development of the United States.
Upton Sinclair (1906)	Sinclair's novel, *The Jungle*, described the unsanitary conditions in the meat-packing industry.	The book shocked the nation, prompting legislation that regulated the food and drug industries.
Rachel Carson (1962)	Her book, *Silent Spring*, sounded a warning alarm to Americans about the harmful effects of insecticides and pesticides.	The book led to a greater public awareness of the need for greater environmental protections and safeguards against insecticides.
Betty Friedan (1963)	In her book, *The Feminine Mystique*, Friedan attacked the belief that women were happy at home being housewives.	Friedan's book became the rallying point that sparked the Women's Liberation Movement of the 1960s.
Ralph Nader (1965)	In *Unsafe at Any Speed*, Nader attacked auto makers for being more concerned with profits than with building safe cars.	Congress passed legislation forcing auto makers to build safer cars.

ARTISTS

Artists often portray scenes and lifestyles that later generations would otherwise be unable to see.

Artist	Achievements
Gilbert Stuart (1755–1828)	Stuart concentrated on painting portraits of famous people. His best known portrait of George Washington appears on the face of the one dollar bill.
George Catlin (1796–1872)	Catlin focused on frontier life, making the frontier come alive for people in the East. His paintings featured Native American Indians hunting, riding, and performing ceremonial rituals.
Frederic Remington (1861–1909)	Remington's paintings, drawings and sculptures depicted scenes of action and excitement associated with life in the West — cowboys roping a calf or a cavalry charge against Native American Indians.
Winslow Homer (1836–1910)	Homer achieved attention when his paintings depicting the horrors of the Civil War appeared in *Harper's Weekly*. It was the sea that truly inspired Homer. His best known works featured seascapes in rich watercolors, such as *Breaking Storm*, and *The Hurricane*.
Mary Cassatt (1844–1926)	Although Cassatt spent much of her life in France, she is one of America's best known female artists. Her favorite themes were motherhood and children. Her paintings were known for their simplicity and use of pastel colors. Her best known works include *Mother and Child*, *Lady at the Tea-Table* and *Modern Women*.
Thomas Eakins (1844–1916)	Eakins' works depicted everyday life in America. One of his best known works, *The Gross Clinic*, showed a surgeon during an operation. The painting created a sensation by showing surgical instruments and the blood normally associated with surgery.
Jackson Pollock (1912–1956)	Pollock became the symbol of abstract modern art by breaking with traditional-looking paintings. His abstract paintings created a controversy in the art world because they showed splashes and drips of brightly colored paint criss-crossing a canvas.
Andy Warhol (1922–1987)	Warhol was one of the nation's best known modern "pop" artists. His art featured everyday objects like Campbell's soup cans. He believed that painting such everyday objects showed that the real art was in the object and not in the version depicted by the artist.

ARCHITECTS

Earlier in American history, buildings reflected European architectural styles. As Americans moved from a rural to an industrial society, it was not surprising that their architecture reflected this development.

Architect	Achievements
Louis Sullivan (1856–1924)	Sullivan was the architect behind the skyscraper. Believing "form follows function," he designed the first modern skyscraper in 1890, using a steel framework to create a ten-story building. His designs permanently changed the skyline of America's cities.
Frank Lloyd Wright (1869–1959)	Wright harmonized a building's architecture with its landscape. For example, a building he constructed overlooking a waterfall reflected that feature. One of his most famous designs was the Guggenheim Museum in New York City.
I.M. Pei (1917–)	Pei carefully integrated his structures with their surrounding environment. Some of his best known works include the Kennedy Memorial Library at Harvard, the Payne Mellon Arts Center, and the Mile High Center in Denver, Colorado.

PHOTOGRAPHERS

Photographs are historical documents that allow us to travel back in time almost as though we were there when the photograph was taken.

Architect	Achievements
Matthew Brady (1799–1826)	Brady created a photographic history of the Civil War. His photographs documented the people and events of that time. His pictures have allowed later generations to view the suffering and devastation of that tragic conflict.
Dorothea Lange (1895–1965)	Hired during the New Deal, Lange traveled throughout the nation taking pictures of life in rural America. Her photographs are famous for depicting the suffering of people in the Great Depression. The photographs on pps. 183 and 184 are two of Lange's most famous pictures.
Ansel Adams (1902–1984)	Adams is best known for his regional landscape photographs, especially those of the American Southwest. His photographs emphasize conservation, nature, national parks, and monuments.

THE AGRARIAN MOVEMENT

THE UNITED STATES: A NATION OF FARMERS

Today, less than 2% of Americans live on farms. Lifestyles were quite different in the 1870s, when a majority of Americans still lived on farms.

THE PROBLEMS OF FARMERS, 1870–1900

In the late nineteenth century, farmers experienced increasing difficulties as food prices began to drop, while their own expenses remained high.

Agricultural Overproduction. The opening of the West greatly increased the amount of land cultivated. Machinery and improved farming techniques increased productivity per acre. As farmers produced more crops, food prices fell.

High Costs. Farmers had to ship their crops to market and were forced to pay whatever railroads charged. Railroads often took advantage of the lack of competition on local routes by charging higher rates for shorter distances.

REASONS FOR FARMERS' ECONOMIC PROBLEMS

Farmer Indebtedness. Farmers often borrowed to make improvements or to buy machinery. During a poor harvest, farmers also borrowed, using their farms as security. Banks saw farmers as poor credit risks and charged them high interest rates.

Periodic Natural Disasters. Farmers were subject to droughts, insect invasions, and floods. One bad year could wipe out a family's savings from many good years.

THE IMPACT OF GEOGRAPHY ON AMERICAN HISTORY

When farmers moved to the Great Plains, they found a physical environment quite unlike the Atlantic Coastal Plain. A scarcity of trees made it hard to build houses or fences. Lack of water posed an even more serious problem. The fertile soil of the plains was covered by thick sod created by the dense roots of prairie grasses. To overcome these problems, farmers had to devise new farming techniques. Heavy plows broke up the dense sod. Bricks of sod were used to make settlers' homes, with walls several feet thick. Barbed wire was used instead of wooden fences. Windmills pumped water from deep underground wells to water crops.

THE GRANGE MOVEMENT

With the rise of industrial society, farmers began to see themselves as a special interest group. In 1867, the **Grange Movement** was formed to reduce the isolation of farmers and to spread information about new farming techniques. Within ten years, the Grangers had 1.5 million members and began urging economic and political reform.

GRANGER COOPERATIVES

Grangers tried to eliminate middlemen by forming cooperatives to buy machinery, fertilizers, and manufactured goods in large numbers at a discount. The cooperatives sold their crops directly to city markets. Lacking experience, most Granger cooperatives failed.

THE GRANGER LAWS

Most farmers blamed the railroads for many of their difficulties. In several Midwestern states, Grangers elected candidates to state legislatures who promised to regulate the railroads. These states passed laws regulating railroad and grain storage rates. Railroad companies protested the new Granger laws. In *Munn v. Illinois*, the Supreme Court initially supported state government attempts to regulate railroads.

KEY COURT CASES: MUNN v. ILLINOIS (1877)

Farmers in the Midwest felt they were being overcharged by railroads and grain storage warehouses. Illinois passed a law regulating the maximum rate a railroad or grain warehouse could charge. Railroad owners argued that Illinois was depriving them of "due process" of law as guaranteed in the Constitution. The Supreme Court upheld the right of a state to regulate businesses that affect the public interest within state lines.

However, farmers were discouraged nine years later when the Supreme Court ruled against them.

KEY COURT CASES: WABASH v. ILLINOIS (1886)

Illinois passed a law penalizing railroads if they charged the same or more for shipping freight for shorter distances than for longer distances. The Wabash Railroad claimed Illinois had no right to regulate prices on trips that were not limited to within the state's border. The Supreme Court ruled against Illinois, stating that only Congress could regulate rates on interstate commerce.

The *Wabash* decision ended state regulation of railroads. The Grangers then turned to Congress for help. In 1887, Congress passed the **Interstate Commerce Act,** which prohibited railroads from charging different rates to customers shipping goods the same distance. It also banned the charging of more for short hauls than for long hauls over the same route. The **Interstate Commerce Commission,** created to investigate complaints and to enforce the act, marked the first step towards having the federal government regulate unfair business practices. The "I.C.C." became the first of many regulatory agencies created to regulate business activities that might harm the public.

THE POPULIST PARTY: 1891–1896

Despite the successes of the Grange Movement, farmers continued to experience problems. In 1892, farmers gave their support to the **Populist Party**, a new national political party representing laborers, farmers, and industrial workers in the struggle against banking and railroad interests. Women played a prominent role in the Populist Movement as speakers and organizers.

THE POPULIST PLATFORM

Populists were convinced that rich industrialists and bankers had a stranglehold on government. Like the Grangers before them, the Populists wanted government to take greater responsibility in ending oppression, injustice, and poverty. In 1892, the Populists held a convention at Omaha, Nebraska, where they chose a Presidential candidate. They also drew up a party platform with several innovative proposals:

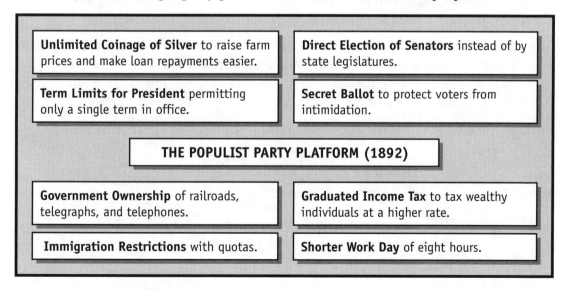

Unlimited Coinage of Silver to raise farm prices and make loan repayments easier.

Direct Election of Senators instead of by state legislatures.

Term Limits for President permitting only a single term in office.

Secret Ballot to protect voters from intimidation.

THE POPULIST PARTY PLATFORM (1892)

Government Ownership of railroads, telegraphs, and telephones.

Graduated Income Tax to tax wealthy individuals at a higher rate.

Immigration Restrictions with quotas.

Shorter Work Day of eight hours.

ELECTION CAMPAIGNS

With strong support in the South, Northwest, and Mountain states, the Populists turned their attention to getting candidates elected to office.

A political cartoon attacks Bryan for his Cross of Gold speech

★ **Election of 1892.** In 1892, Populists elected five Senators and received over a million votes for their Presidential candidate. Soon afterwards, the economy collapsed in the Depression of 1893. Populists blamed the depression on the scarcity of currency, due to the gold standard.

★ **Election of 1896.** In 1896, the Democratic Party nominated **William Jennings Bryan** for President after he delivered a speech at the convention. His **"Cross of Gold" Speech** praised farmers and denounced bankers for "crucifying mankind on a cross of gold." The Populists supported Bryan instead of nominating their own candidate. But Bryan's moral outrage frightened many voters, and he lost the election to Republican William McKinley.

★ **Election of 1900.** This election again pitted Bryan against McKinley. McKinley's second victory marked the end of the Populist Party. In subsequent years, new gold discoveries, higher farm prices, and rural migration to the cities weakened interest in a separate farmer's party.

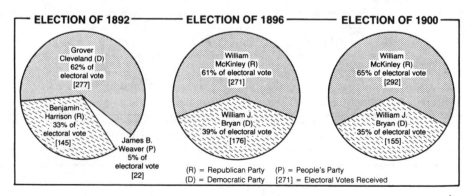

THE LEGACY OF POPULISM: THE ROLE OF THIRD PARTIES

Many Populist proposals, such as the graduated income tax and the direct election of Senators, were later enacted by other political parties. The Populists thus illustrate the role often played by third parties in American politics — providing an outlet for minorities to voice grievances, generate new ideas, and advocate new solutions. If a third party gains wide public support, one or both of the major parties will often adopt its ideas. The best evidence of the influence of third parties is that many of their proposals have eventually passed into law.

THE PROGRESSIVE MOVEMENT: 1900–1920

The **Progressive Movement** flourished between 1900 and the start of World War I. Although the Progressives borrowed ideas from the Populists and the labor movement, they differed in important ways. Progressives were mainly middle-class city dwellers, rather than farmers and workers. Their activities reflected the rising influence of the middle class. Progressives believed society could be studied scientifically and that impartial experts could assist politicians in creating better laws and regulations. The scientific investigation of problems could point the way towards new solutions. Progressives placed their confidence in progress, science, and technology.

EMERGENCE OF THE PROGRESSIVE MOVEMENT

Progressives believed that people could shape their own environment, permitting social improvement. The primary goal of the Progressives was to correct the political and economic injustices that had resulted from America's industrialization. Progressives were appalled at the increasing inequalities between the wealthy and the poor. They feared that monopolies were stifling competition. Progressives did not oppose industrialization, but they wanted to use the power of government to correct its evils so that all Americans, not just the wealthy, could enjoy better lives. To achieve this, the Progressives felt they also had to reform government itself — which had been corrupted by big business and political "bosses."

National Archives

Eliminating child labor in factories was a main focus of Progressive reformers

PRESSURES FOR REFORM

The demand for reform has been a continuing theme throughout American history. Reform movements, such as during the Jacksonian period, are usually based on the belief that society can be made better. The Progressives provided one of the best examples of Americans' attempting to overcome problems by calling for reform.

★ **Problems Created by Industrialization.** The rise of industry had brought many new social problems: brutal working conditions, child labor, political corruption, urban overcrowding, misuse of the environment, extreme inequalities of wealth, and the abuse of consumers.

★ **Middle Class Fears.** Progressive support came mainly from members of the middle-class who felt threatened by the rise of big business, labor unions, and political machines.

This cartoon shows Americans' concern with the growing influence of business in government

★ **The Social Gospel Movement.** Progressives often acted out of a sense of moral responsibility derived from religion. Many Protestant ministers in the **Social Gospel Movement** were especially concerned with the needs of the poor. Instead of blindly accepting poverty as God's will, these clergymen called for social reform — including the abolition of child labor and safer working conditions. The Salvation Army, the YMCA and the YWCA were further attempts by Protestant churches to help the poor and provide services to urban youth. These efforts helped set an example for the Progressives.

The abuses of industrial capitalism even led some critics to demand an end to capitalism itself. *Socialists* believed that government should take over basic industries, while *Communists* believed that workers should forcibly seize control and abolish all private property. Most Progressives rejected these extremes, but argued that some reform was necessary if social revolution was to be avoided.

THE ACHIEVEMENTS OF THE EARLY PROGRESSIVES

The Progressive Movement operated at many levels of society and government.

THE MUCKRAKERS

The most influential of the early Progressives were investigative reporters, writers, and social scientists who exposed the abuses of industrial society and corruption in government. These writers became known as **muckrakers** because they "raked" up the muck or dirt of American life. They examined the rise of industry and the abuses that had often led to the accumulation of large fortunes. They also examined business practices affecting consumers, and the lives of the very poor.

Jacob Riis photographed conditions of the urban poor in *How The Other Half Lives*. His book examined the conditions of the poor in America's cities.

Ida Tarbell, in her *History of the Standard Oil Company* (1902), showed how John D. Rockefeller's rise was based on ruthless business practices.

Lincoln Steffens exposed corruption in city and state governments in his book, *The Shame of the Cities* (1904).

FAMOUS MUCKRAKERS

Frank Norris wrote *The Octopus*, a fictional work that depicted the stranglehold of railroads over California farmers.

Upton Sinclair, in his novel *The Jungle* (1906), described the unsanitary practices of the meatpacking industry.

THE SOCIAL REFORMERS

Some Progressives were so stirred at the abuses of industrial society that they made individual efforts at social reform. **Settlement houses** were started in slum neighborhoods by Progressives like **Jane Addams.** These houses provided immigrants with services such as child care, nursing the sick, and English lessons. Other Progressives formed associations to promote social change and professional responsibility, such as the **N.A.A.C.P.** and the **Anti-Defamation League** (*a Jewish organization opposing religious prejudice*).

Corbis-Bettman Archives

Jane Addams

MUNICIPAL REFORM

Other Progressives focused on correcting abuses at the municipal (*town or city*) level of government. Some cities had grown so fast in the late 19th century that city services were inadequate. Adding to this problem, city governments were often controlled by "political machines" run by political bosses. Political machines provided immigrants and the working poor with jobs, housing, loans, and help in obtaining citizenship. In exchange, these residents voted for candidates recommended by the boss. The machine used its control of city government to steal from the public treasury through bribes. Progressives replaced the rule of "bosses" with public-minded mayors. They expanded city services to deal with overcrowding, fire hazards, and the lack of public services. In some cities, Progressives even introduced new forms of municipal government to discourage corruption.

A crowded Broadway in 1897

Library of Congress

THE REFORM OF STATE GOVERNMENT

At the state level, Progressive governors like **Robert LaFollette** in Wisconsin and **Theodore Roosevelt** in New York took steps to free their state governments from corruption and make them more democratic. Many of the measures Progressives introduced to state governments were later adopted at the federal level.

Secret Ballot. Voters were less subject to pressure and intimidation, when they could vote in secret.	**Initiatives.** Voters could directly introduce bills in the state legislature and could vote on whether they wanted a bill passed.	**Referendum.** Voters could compel legislators to place a bill on the ballot for approval.

PROGRESSIVE POLITICAL REFORMS

Recall. Elected officials could be removed by voters in a special election.	**Direct Party Primaries.** Special elections were held to determine whom party members wanted to represent them as candidates in the general election.	**Direct Election of Senators.** Senators were elected directly by the people (17th Amendment) instead of being chosen by state legislatures.

States also enacted laws to deal with the worst effects of industrialization. These laws regulated conditions in urban housing and forbade the employment of young children. They regulated safety and health conditions in factories, limiting the number of hours women could work and forcing employers to give compensation to workers injured on the job. Other state laws were passed to conserve natural resources and to create wildlife preserves.

REFORM OF THE FEDERAL GOVERNMENT

Throughout much of the late 19th century, corruption was also widespread in the federal government. Much of this corruption could be traced to the effects of the **"spoils system,"** in which government jobs were used to reward people who made contributions to politicians or who helped in their campaigns. In 1883, Congress passed the **Pendleton Act,** creating a Civil Service Commission which gave competitive exams and selected appointees to permanent posts on the **merit system.**

THE PROGRESSIVE PRESIDENTS

Between 1901 and 1919, two strong-willed Presidents, Theodore Roosevelt and Woodrow Wilson, launched a series of Progressive reforms from the White House.

THEODORE ROOSEVELT AND THE SQUARE DEAL, 1901–1909

In the late 19th century, the Presidency had been relatively weak, leaving direction of the country's affairs mainly to Congress. Theodore Roosevelt reversed this trend when he became President after McKinley's assassination. Roosevelt believed that the President was the single official who represented all Americans, and that the President should therefore exercise vigorous leadership in their interest. In Roosevelt's view, the President acted as the "steward," or manager, of the people's interests. Roosevelt put his theory to the test when the **Coal Miners' Strike of 1902**

Roosevelt (center) with other naturalists in front of a California redwood

threatened the nation with a winter without coal. Roosevelt brought representatives to the White House from both sides of the dispute. When mine-owners refused to negotiate, Roosevelt threatened to use troops to run the mines. This convinced the owners to compromise.

★ **Roosevelt as Trust-Buster.** Roosevelt revived the use of the Sherman Antitrust Act against big business monopolies and consolidations, known as **trusts.** For example, he launched the breakup of Rockefeller's Standard Oil Company. Roosevelt did not attack all trusts, but distinguished "good trusts" from "bad trusts" which acted against the public interest.

"Good trusts and bad trusts"

Library of Congress

★ **Roosevelt's Square Deal.** Roosevelt promised Americans a **"Square Deal."** He launched new laws to protect consumer health, to regulate some industries, and to conserve the nation's natural resources.

Protecting the Public Health. Upton Sinclair's account of the meat-packing industry shocked the nation. Congress passed the **Meat Inspection Act** (1906), providing for government inspection of meat. The **Pure Food and Drug Act** (1906), regulated the preparation of foods and the sale of medicines.

SQUARE DEAL LEGISLATION

Regulating Transportation and Communication.
Roosevelt increased the power of the Interstate Commerce Commission to regulate railroads, and gave it authority over the telegraph and telephone.

Conserving the Nation's Resources.
Roosevelt drew attention to the need to conserve forests, wildlife, and natural resources. He stopped the practice of selling public lands for development and added millions of acres to the national forests and parks. He formed the National Conservation Commission to protect the nation's natural resources.

WILSON AND THE NEW FREEDOM, 1913–1921

Roosevelt was a Progressive Republican. In 1908, Roosevelt refused to run for office again and helped his friend **William Taft** win the Presidency.

In 1912, Taft was nominated again by the Republican Party. By then, Roosevelt had grown unhappy with Taft and decided to accept the nomination of a new third party, known as the **Bull Moose Party.** This division of the Republican Party helped the Democratic nominee, **Woodrow Wilson,** win the election.

★ **Wilson's "New Freedom".** While Roosevelt was emotional and enthusiastic, Wilson was cool and logical. Wilson nevertheless shared Roosevelt's belief in a strong President who would use all the powers at his disposal. In the campaign of 1912, Wilson promised Americans a **"New Freedom,"** taming big business, allowing greater competition, and eliminating special privileges. Wilson especially focused his attention on attacking the tariff, the banking system, and trusts, and pushed several major reforms through Congress.

Woodrow Wilson

Underwood Tariff (1913). Wilson believed that high tariffs benefited rich monopolists but hurt average Americans. He enacted a law lowering tariffs by 25%. To make up for the lost revenue, he introduced the nation's first income tax.

Graduated Income Tax (1913). In a graduated income tax, rich taxpayers are taxed at a higher rate than less well-off taxpayers. The original Constitution did not permit Congress to tax individuals on their income. The **Sixteenth Amendment**, ratified in 1913, gave Congress the power to tax personal income.

WILSON'S LEGISLATIVE RECORD

The Federal Reserve Act (1913). The act reformed the banking industry by establishing 12 regional Federal Reserve Banks to serve as "banker's banks." The act further allowed the Federal Reserve to regulate the money in circulation by controlling the amount of money that banks could lend.

Antitrust Legislation. In 1914, Congress passed the **Clayton Antitrust Act** increasing the federal government's power to prevent unfair business practices. In addition, the **Federal Trade Commission Act** was created to further protect consumers against unfair business practices by corporations.

THE WOMEN'S RIGHTS MOVEMENT, 1865–1920

The Progressive Movement was accompanied by significant gains in women's rights, for which women had been fighting for over half a century.

THE TRADITIONAL ROLE OF WOMEN

In the early 19th century, the United States was a *patriarchal* society — men held positions of authority and women were considered to be inferior. Women were not supposed to be capable of acting rationally or of controlling their emotions. Women lacked the right to vote, to serve on juries, or to hold public office. They were excluded from public life and were left in charge of the home and children. In most states, once a woman married she lost control of her property and wages to her husband. Women received little schooling. In the early 19th century, no American college would accept women. Working-class women often had to work outside the home, usually for low wages as servants, laundresses, cooks, and factory workers.

THE SENECA FALLS CONVENTION, 1848

By the mid-19th century, some women began to challenge male supremacy. The abolitionist movement helped trigger the movement for women's rights. Women had been extremely active in the Abolitionist Movement, and had even formed their own anti-slavery societies. In 1848, two abolitionists, **Elizabeth Cady Stanton** and **Lucretia Mott,** organized a Women's Rights Convention in Seneca Falls, New York. This event is often seen as the start of the **Women's Rights Movement** in the United States. The convention passed a resolution paraphrasing the Declaration of Independence, proclaiming that women were equal to men and deserved the right to vote: "all men and women are created equal; that they are endowed by their Creator with certain unalienable rights."

Susan B. Anthony (left) and Elizabeth Cady Stanton

Library of Congress

In the years following the Seneca Falls Convention, the issue of women's rights was put aside as Americans debated the future of slavery. The Northern victory in the Civil War and the emancipation of the slaves filled women reformers with the hope that freed slaves and women would be given the vote at the same time. Women reformers were bitterly disappointed when the Fourteenth and Fifteenth Amendments gave citizenship and the vote to male freedmen, but not to women. In 1874, the Supreme Court ruled that although women were citizens, they could not vote.

THE SUFFRAGE MOVEMENT

The focus of the Women's Rights Movement became securing **suffrage** (*the right to vote*). The fact that women did not have the right to vote was seen as symbolic of their inferior status and a violation of basic democratic principles. One leading reformer, **Susan B. Anthony,** traveled throughout the country delivering lectures and attending conventions in favor of giving women the right to vote. Anthony and other women reformers were able to obtain suffrage in a number of Western states, but they could not succeed in introducing a constitutional amendment requiring all states to give women the vote. By 1890, the failure to achieve women's suffrage led several women's groups to merge into the National American Woman Suffrage Association, under the leadership of Elizabeth Cady Stanton and Susan B. Anthony.

THE TRADITIONAL ROLE OF WOMEN CHANGES, 1870–1914

Meanwhile, industrialization was bringing important changes to the traditional role of women. Free public schools became open to both boys and girls. A few special colleges opened for women. Inventions such as the sewing machine, typewriter, and telephone added new job opportunities for women. By 1919, one in five American workers was female. Industrialization led many families to move to cities in search of jobs. City

More and more women entered the workforce — these women are trimming currency at the U.S. Treasury

National Archives

life exposed women to new products and new ideas. New labor-saving devices — electric irons, washing machines, and vacuum cleaners — helped reduce housework and provided women with more leisure time.

WORLD WAR I AND THE 19TH AMENDMENT

When men went off to fight in World War I in 1917, millions of women took their places in factories, mills, and mines. The contribution of women to the war effort was the final argument in favor of women's suffrage. Moreover, it seemed odd to fight for democracy abroad and to oppose it at home. An amendment was introduced into Congress during the war, establishing that no state could deny a citizen the right to vote on the basis of sex. This was ratified as the **Nineteenth Amendment** in 1920. Although women's suffrage was a significant advance, the amendment did not result in some of the changes its supporters had hoped for and its opponents had feared. Women did not sweep men out of public office, and social and economic inequalities between men and women persisted for many decades.

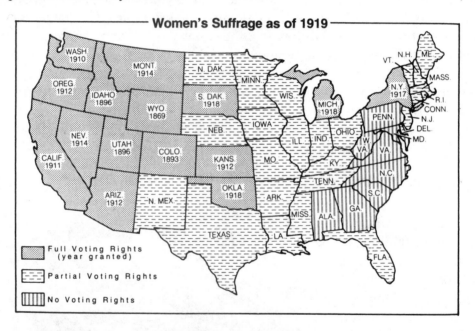

AMERICAN FOREIGN POLICY, 1898–1920

The Progressive Era coincided with a period of greater American involvement in foreign affairs. Many Americans believed that the United States, as one of the world's leading industrial nations, should play a greater role on the world stage.

THE SPANISH-AMERICAN WAR, 1898

The **Spanish-American War** marked a major turning point in American foreign relations, changing the United States from a nation without colonies to one in possession of an overseas empire.

ORIGINS OF THE SPANISH-AMERICAN WAR

By the 1890s, Spain's New World empire had been reduced to a few islands in the Caribbean. In 1894, Cuban sugar workers rebelled from Spain seeking their independence. A Spanish army was sent to Cuba to crush the rebellion with brutal force. To isolate the rebels, entire villages were forced into special camps, where many died of disease and starvation. These atrocities eventually led to American intervention in the conflict.

Humanitarian Concerns. Americans felt they had a moral obligation to help the Cuban people in their struggle for independence from Spain.

Yellow Journalism. Publishers like **William Randolph Hearst** and **Joseph Pulitzer** sensationalized news events to sell more newspapers. Their newspapers deliberately distorted the news from Cuba with exaggerated stories of atrocities.

CAUSES OF THE SPANISH-AMERICAN WAR

Economic Interests. The American government sought to protect American investments in Cuba and to block any interruption of U.S. trade with Cuba.

De Lôme Letter. The Spanish Ambassador, De Lôme, called President McKinley "weak" in a private letter that was published in the press. De Lôme's letter inflamed Americans against Spain.

Sinking the *Maine*. The battleship *U.S.S. Maine* was blown up in Havana harbor, killing 250 American sailors. Even though the explosion was probably caused by an accidental fire, the press blamed the explosion on Spanish sabotage. The public was outraged.

U.S.S. Maine at its launch

Wreckage of the U.S.S. Maine

RESULTS OF THE SPANISH-AMERICAN WAR

Finding it hard to resist the public outcry, **President McKinley** asked Congress for a declaration of war against Spain shortly after the explosion of the *Maine*. The Spanish-American War lasted less than four months. American forces quickly overcame the Spanish navy in the Philippines and Spanish troops on Cuba. As a result of the war, the United States acquired the Philippines, Puerto Rico, and Guam. Cuba became independent in name but fell under the indirect control of the United States. The United States thus emerged from the war with its own far-reaching colonial empire.

AMERICA BUILDS A COLONIAL EMPIRE

The United States itself had once been a British colony, and even as late as the 1890s, many Americans felt uneasy about forcing colonial rule on others. Opponents of colonialism felt it violated the democratic principles of self-government on which America was founded. However, after the Spanish-American War, American leaders reversed the nation's traditional policy by becoming imperialist. **Imperialism** refers to the control of one country by another. There were several reasons behind this transition:

Need For Raw Materials and Markets.
The United States was now an industrial power. Colonies could provide needed raw materials for factories, a guaranteed market for manufacturers, and a place for farmers to sell surplus crops.

Strategic Reasons.
Some Americans believed colonies would promote American naval strength. With naval bases throughout the world, future expansion would be assured.

REASONS FOR COLONIAL EXPANSION

Nationalism.
Some saw colonial expansion as a means of showing that the United States was a great and powerful nation. They argued that the European powers were gathering colonies in Africa, Asia, and the Pacific, and that the United States should grab some colonies before nothing was left.

Attitudes towards other Peoples.
Many Americans believed in Anglo-Saxon superiority — that Americans were a superior race that should rule others. **Social Darwinists** thought that Americans were more powerful because of their superior nature. Progressives wanted to help other peoples, believing that by spreading American institutions, they could help less fortunate peoples.

THE IMPACT OF GEOGRAPHY ON HISTORY

Admiral **Alfred Thayer Mahan,** President of the Naval War College, became America's leading advocate of imperial expansion. In *The Influence of Sea Power Upon History,* Mahan argued that the examples of Greece, Rome, and Great Britain showed that naval power was the key to national greatness. To achieve world power, a country needed a powerful navy, a large merchant marine, colonies, and naval bases. Because other nations would compete for naval supremacy and world markets, Mahan believed it essential for Americans to seize control of the Pacific trade routes, to construct a canal through Central America, and to dominate the Caribbean region. Geographically, Americans would control the sea lanes from the Caribbean Sea across the Pacific as far as China and Japan. Theodore Roosevelt, convinced by Mahan, put many of his ideas into practice.

Library of Congress

AMERICAN INVOLVEMENT IN THE PACIFIC

After the Spanish-American War, the United States acquired a colonial empire in the Pacific consisting of the Philippine Islands, Guam, Hawaii, Samoa, and Midway.

★ **The Philippines.** Filipinos were disappointed when Americans decided to annex the Philippines at the end of the Spanish-American War instead of granting the Filipinos their independence. Filipino rebels fought against their new colonial rulers until they were finally defeated by the U.S. in 1902. Philippine independence was later granted in 1946, after World War II.

★ **Hawaii.** The Hawaiian islands provided a refueling station for American ships traveling to Asia. In the mid-19th century, American settlers built sugar and pineapple plantations on Hawaii. In the 1890s, **Queen Liliuokalani** tried to assert her authority over American landowners. In response, the landowners overthrew her in 1893. A provisional government, formed by resident Americans, asked to be annexed by the United States. At first, Congress refused. After the outbreak of the Spanish-American War, Congress voted for annexation in 1898. Hawaii later became the nation's 50th state in 1959.

★ **Other Pacific Islands: Guam, Samoa, and Midway.** Midway had been an American possession since 1867. Guam was taken from Spain during the Spanish-American War. Samoa came under the joint control of Britain, Germany and the United States in 1889. In 1899, it was divided outright between Germany and the United States. These Pacific islands provided valuable naval bases and refueling stations for American ships traveling to Asia.

U.S. POSSESSIONS IN THE PACIFIC

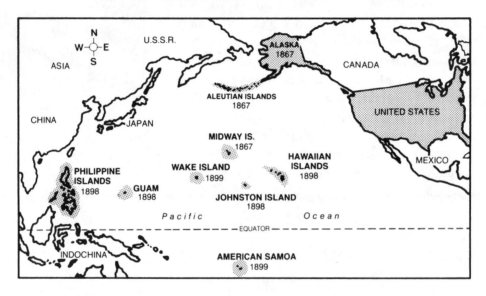

AMERICAN INVOLVEMENT IN EAST ASIA

Americans were in an advantageous position for trade with East Asia, since they were separated from this region only by the Pacific Ocean. After 1898, control of the Philippines, Midway, Hawaii, Guam, and Samoa made the United States an important power in the Pacific. This increased American opportunities for trade with both China and Japan, leading to American political involvement in these countries.

★ **China.** In China, European powers had established "spheres of influence," threatening to cut off Americans from trade. Secretary of State **John Hay** announced the **"Open Door Policy,"** favoring equal trading rights for all foreign nations in China. In 1900, a rebellion was started by a group of Chinese nationalists, known as **Boxers,** who opposed the growing Western influence in China. The **Boxer Rebellion** threatened foreigners living in China. An international army, with U.S. participation, crushed the rebellion. Afterwards the United States announced it opposed any attempt by other nations to use the rebellion as an excuse to dismember China.

★ **Japan.** The United States opened an isolationist Japan to Western trade and influence when **Commodore Matthew Perry** landed there with American gunships in 1853. By the 1890s, Japan had adopted many Western ways and had become an industrial power. Japan even adopted imperialist policies. In 1894–1895, Japanese forces drove China out of Korea and Taiwan, and incorporated Taiwan into the Japanese empire. In 1905, Japan surprised the West by defeating Russia in the Russo-Japanese War. Americans feared seeing either Japan or Russia becoming dominant in the Far East. President Theodore Roosevelt brought both sides to a peace settlement in the **Treaty of Portsmouth** (1905), winning the Nobel Peace Prize for his efforts.

President Roosevelt meets with the Japanese and Russian delegates

U.S. IMPERIALISM IN THE CARIBBEAN

The Spanish-American War gave Americans direct control of Puerto Rico and indirect control of Cuba, leading to increased American interest in the Caribbean region.

Hemispheric Security. The United States sought to keep foreign powers out of the Caribbean because they might pose a threat to U.S. security.

Economic Interests. The Caribbean region was an important supplier of agricultural products, like sugar, and provided a valuable market for American goods and investment.

REASONS FOR U.S. INTEREST IN THE CARIBBEAN

Importance of the Canal. The United States needed easy access by water between the Atlantic and the Pacific Oceans. The most likely way to achieve this was by building a canal in Central America.

★ **Cuba.** Cuba is the largest island in the Caribbean. After the Spanish-American War, Cuba became a **protectorate** under American control. U.S. forces remained on

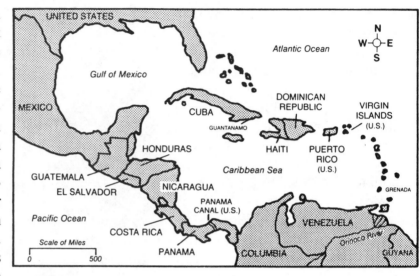

the island, and American businesses invested heavily in Cuba. Cubans were forced to agree to the **Platt Amendment,** which gave the United States the right to intervene in Cuban affairs at any time. The Platt Amendment was later repealed in the 1930s.

★ **Panama Canal.** The Spanish-American War highlighted the need for a canal, so that the U.S. navy could send ships between the Atlantic and Pacific Oceans without circling South America. By 1903, Americans decided to build the canal across Panama. Panama was then still a part of Colombia. The government of Colombia could not agree to terms with the United States, while Panamanian rebels wished to establish their independence. Roosevelt made a deal with the rebels, who declared their independence. Roosevelt ordered U.S. warships in the area to protect them.

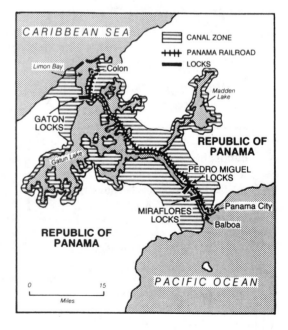

Roosevelt next recognized Panamanian independence. In return, the new government of Panama gave the United States complete control of a 10-mile strip of jungle through the center of Panama, known as the **Panama Canal Zone.** Construction of the Panama Canal was a monumental effort, using complex locks to overcome differences in elevation. It took 10 years (1904–1914) to complete and cost thousands of lives.

U.S. INTERVENTION IN THE CARIBBEAN

In the late 19th and early 20th centuries, American governments extended the Monroe Doctrine by intervening in the Caribbean to protect American economic interests. In 1904, President Roosevelt barred European countries from using force to collect debts owed by the Dominican Republic. Roosevelt declared that the United States would intervene to collect the debt itself, acting as an "international police power." This "Roosevelt Corollary to the Monroe Doctrine" also became known as the **Big Stick Policy**, since Roosevelt boasted he would "walk softly but carry a big stick." The corollary was often used to justify sending troops to the West Indies and Central America. Repeated interventions in Haiti, Nicaragua, Honduras, and the Dominican Republic were deeply resented by many Latin Americans.

WILSON'S LATIN AMERICAN POLICY

Several important developments in Latin American affairs occurred during the Presidency of Wilson. Seeking additional bases in the Caribbean, Wilson bought the Virgin Islands from Denmark in 1917. Wilson sent troops to Haiti, Nicaragua,

Pancho Villa and his band of rebels

Library of Congress

and the Dominican Republic to protect American interests. Wilson also became involved in Mexico, then in the throes of civil war. Troops of the rebel leader **Pancho Villa** murdered Americans both in Mexico and across the border. Wilson reacted by sending troops to Mexico. Nevertheless, Villa eluded capture. Wilson finally withdrew the troops in 1917, when America faced involvement in World War I.

THE UNITED STATES IN WORLD WAR I

Since winning independence from Britain in 1783, American leaders had avoided "entanglements" with Europe. However, following the Spanish-American War, Americans acquired an overseas empire. Another turning point was reached in 1917 when Americans entered World War I.

EUROPEAN CAUSES OF THE WAR

The outbreak of **World War I** in Europe in 1914 had several causes:

Nationalism. Nationalism led to rivalries among France, Germany, Austria-Hungary and Russia. Several nationalities in Austria-Hungary wanted to form their own national states.

CAUSES OF WORLD WAR I

Economic Rivalries and Imperialism. The European powers had competing economic interests. For example, Russian interests in the Balkans threatened Austria-Hungary. Competing colonial claims added to these tensions.

The Alliance System. By the 1890s, Europe was divided into two alliances. On one side stood Germany and Austria; on the other side Russia, France and Great Britain. Any dispute involving two of these nations threatened to involve all of them.

EUROPE AT THE START OF WORLD WAR I

THE SPARK THAT IGNITED WORLD WAR I

The assassination of **Archduke Francis Ferdinand** by Slavic nationalists in 1914 was the immediate cause of

German infantry on the attack

National Archives

the war. Austria invaded Serbia to avenge the assassination. Existing alliances quickly brought Russia, Germany, Britain and France into the war. What might have been a minor regional crisis quickly escalated into a major European war. New weapons — the machine gun, poison gas, airplanes, and submarines — prevented either side from winning a quick victory.

REASONS FOR UNITED STATES INTERVENTION

When the war first broke out in Europe, President Wilson attempted to follow the traditional American policy of neutrality. Despite his efforts, the United States eventually became involved in the conflict for several reasons.

★ **Closer Ties with the Allies.** Many Americans traced their ancestry to Britain. A common language and history tied Americans to the British. The United States, Britain, and France all shared the same democratic political system.

★ **German Actions and Allied Propaganda.** Americans were shocked at the German invasion of neutral Belgium. The **Zimmerman Telegram,** a secret message from the German Foreign Minister, promised to return U.S. territories to Mexico if Mexico acted against the United States. The American public was enraged when the telegram appeared in the press.

★ **Violation of Freedom of the Seas.** The main reason for American entry into World War I was German submarine warfare.

◆ **The British Blockade.** A British naval blockade prevented food and arms from being shipped to Germany. Meanwhile, the United States became the main source for Allied arms, supplies, food, and loans. The German navy was too weak to break the British blockade. By using submarines, Germany could retaliate by sinking ships delivering goods to Great Britain. However, unlike battleships, submarines had no room to pick up survivors.

◆ **Sinking the *Lusitania*.** In 1915, a German submarine sank the British passenger ship *Lusitania,* killing over 1,000 passengers, including 128 Americans.

◆ **Sussex Pledge.** After a German submarine attacked a French passenger ship in 1916, Wilson threatened to break off relations with Germany. Germany pledged not to sink any ships without warning or helping passengers.

◆ **Germany Uses Submarine Warfare.** Suffering from near-starvation, the Germans announced they would sink ships in the blockaded areas. This was a violation of the "freedom of the seas" — the right of neutral ships to ship non-war goods to nations at war. When German submarines attacked merchant vessels, Wilson asked Congress to declare war on Germany in 1917.

AMERICA AT WAR, 1917–1918

As an idealist and a Progressive, Wilson tried to broaden American involvement from defense of "freedom of the seas" to a crusade for democracy and world peace. Wilson announced that "the world must be made safe for democracy." Americans found it inspiring to endure the war for such high-minded ideals. To fight the war, Wilson was given sweeping powers by Congress. He established agencies to regulate the economy during the war. Railroads came under direct government control. Congress passed the **Selective Service Act** (1917) and millions of Americans registered for the draft. Almost two million American troops eventually reached Europe, while women and African Americans filled their jobs at home. The cost of the war, about $30 billion, was paid for by higher taxes and war bonds. Civil liberties were curtailed to meet wartime needs. Espionage acts made it a crime to criticize the war. The Supreme Court upheld these restrictions on free speech in *Schenck v. U.S.*

A poster encourages Americans to buy war bonds

National Archives

KEY COURT CASES: SCHENCK v. U.S. (1919)

During World War I, Schenck was convicted for distributing literature that encouraged men to resist the draft. Schenck claimed his First Amendment rights to freedom of speech and of the press had been violated. The Supreme Court ruled that there were limits to free speech. The Court said that free speech could not be used to protect someone from falsely shouting "fire" in a crowded theater. Inflammatory speech could not be allowed in the face of a "clear and present danger." The decision became a guide for measuring the limits of free speech.

THE PEACE SETTLEMENT

American troops broke the deadlock in Europe, causing Germany to surrender in November 1918. Wilson had already announced America's war aims in the **Fourteen Points.** These points reflected American idealism and Wilson's view that the war should be a crusade for democracy and lasting peace. The Fourteen Points stated that each major European nationality should have its own country and government. It called for freedom of the seas, reduced armaments, and an end to secret diplomacy. Wilson felt the most important point he proposed was the creation of a **League of Nations.** He hoped to create a world of peaceful nations in which future wars could be avoided.

The Versailles Treaty. Wilson traveled to Europe to help negotiate the peace treaties. He made a crucial mistake in not inviting influential Senators to accompany him, since the Senate would eventually have to ratify the treaty. Almost immediately, Wilson came into conflict with Allied leaders who wanted to impose a harsh treaty on Germany. Wilson had to

Allied leaders meet with President Wilson at Versailles

make many concessions in order to get their support for the formation of the League of Nations. The final terms of the Treaty of Versailles and the other peace treaties were extremely harsh on Germany and the other defeated powers.

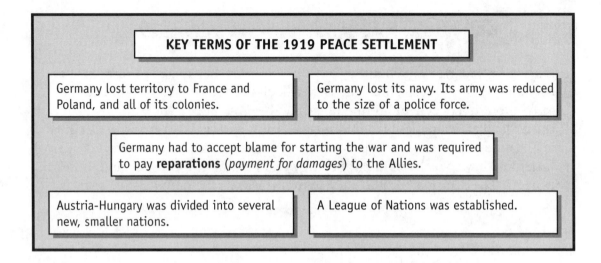

KEY TERMS OF THE 1919 PEACE SETTLEMENT

Germany lost territory to France and Poland, and all of its colonies.

Germany lost its navy. Its army was reduced to the size of a police force.

Germany had to accept blame for starting the war and was required to pay **reparations** (*payment for damages*) to the Allies.

Austria-Hungary was divided into several new, smaller nations.

A League of Nations was established.

THE U.S. SENATE REJECTS THE TREATY

Wilson hoped the League of Nations would discourage future wars, but his opponents believed it would drag America into unnecessary military commitments. The League failed, in part, because many major powers, including the United States, never became members. Wilson needed two-thirds of the Senate to ratify the Versailles Treaty, yet he rejected any compromises proposed by the Senate. Instead, he appealed directly to American voters for support by going on a national speaking tour. Wilson failed to gauge the feelings of most Americans, who were disappointed with the peace treaty and disillusioned with world affairs. During his tour, Wilson suffered a stroke. Later, the Senate rejected the treaty, and the United States never joined the League.

AMERICA RETREATS INTO ISOLATION

Most Americans were dissatisfied with the huge costs and limited benefits the United States had achieved from its involvement in the war. Americans once again heeded George Washington's advice to avoid European entanglements, and turned their attention to their material well-being at home. This move marked a return to a policy of **isolationism** — refusing to become involved in other countries' affairs.

THE PROGRESSIVE MOVEMENT COMES TO AN END

Women's suffrage and the prohibition of alcohol were passed at the end of the war — becoming the final reforms of the Progressive Era. By 1919, the force of the Progressive Movement was spent. Americans had met many of the challenges posed by industrialization and once again focused on economic growth.

SUMMARIZING YOUR UNDERSTANDING

KEY TERMS, CONCEPTS, AND PEOPLE

Make a vocabulary card for each of the following terms, concepts, and people.

Granger Movement	Muckrakers	Imperialism
"Cross of Gold" Speech	Square Deal	Open Door Policy
Populist Party	Theodore Roosevelt	Fourteen Points
Progressive Movement	Woodrow Wilson	League of Nations

COMPLETING A TABLE

Briefly describe the following legislation associated with this period.

Legislation	Major Provisions	Intent of this Legislation
Interstate Commerce Act (1887)		
Pure Food and Drug Act (1906)		
Graduated Income Tax (1913)		
Federal Reserve Act (1913)		

COMPLETING A GRAPHIC ORGANIZER

Briefly describe the following key events taking place during this period.

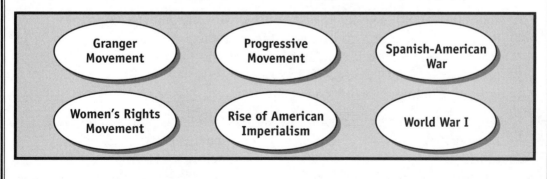

TESTING YOUR UNDERSTANDING

MULTIPLE-CHOICE QUESTIONS

1 A supporter of the Grange Movement would most likely also have supported
   1   government regulation of railroads   3   laissez-faire capitalism
   2   abolishing private property   4   women's suffrage

Base your answers to questions 2 and 3 on the chart and on your knowledge of social studies.

UNITED STATES CROP PRICES, 1878–1897			
Years	**Wheat** (*per bushel*)	**Corn** (*per bushel*)	**Cotton** (*per pound*)
1878–1881	$1.00	$.43	$.09
1882–1885	$.80	$.39	$.09
1886–1889	$.74	$.35	$.08
1890–1893	$.70	$.41	$.07
1894–1897	$.63	$.29	$.05

2 Which factor was most likely a major cause of the trend shown by the chart?
   1   a series of major droughts   3   widespread crop failures
   2   prices set by government regulations 4   overproduction

3 To protect themselves from the trend shown by the chart, American farmers wanted the federal government to
   1   reduce regulation of the railroads   3   pay for increased crop yields
   2   increase the money supply   4   raise tariffs on foreign goods

4 A major aim of both the Grange and Populist Movements was
   1   the establishment of a gold standard for currency
   2   mandatory government policies to curb inflation
   3   the passage of laws to regulate monopolies
   4   unlimited immigration of Asians

5 The Granger Laws were an attempt by various state legislatures to regulate
   1   farmers   3   manufacturers
   2   railroads   4   factories

6 Which contributed to the birth of the Progressive Movement?
1 the influence of muckrakers, Populists, and social reformers
2 the Stock Market Crash of 1929
3 racial conflict in the New South
4 the migration of population from cities to the countryside

7 The muckrakers of the Progressive Era and the investigative reporters of the present day are most similar in that both have
1 sought to document corruption in American life
2 advocated fewer government controls on the economy
3 focused their efforts on increasing patriotism
4 called for increased aid to developing nations

8 A study of the Progressive Movement would indicate that the Progressives
1 wished to ease immigration requirements
2 sought to correct the abuses of industrial society
3 opposed most of the Populist platform
4 were mainly supported by big business

Base your answers to questions 9 and 10 on the speakers' statements and on your knowledge of social studies.

Speaker A: Our job is to report the graft and corruption in our society to the public. Unless these deeds are brought to light by crusading journalists like myself, present abuses will continue.

Speaker B: Government control must be shifted from the hands of the power brokers and political bosses to the people. The people know what is best.

Speaker C: Our national government must learn to keep its hands out of the affairs of business. If the government continues to regulate business, future economic opportunities will be threatened.

Speaker D: I'm concerned about the number of children working in factories. A factory is no place for a child. We need laws to prevent our children from working long hours at an early age.

---

9 Which speaker would most likely support laissez-faire capitalism?
1 A   3 C
2 B   4 D

10 Which speaker best expresses beliefs held by Robert La Follette?
   1 A   3 C
   2 B   4 D

11 Many of Theodore Roosevelt's actions demonstrated his belief that the role of the President was to
1   act vigorously in the public interest
2   follow the lead of Congress
3   remain free from politics
4   free business from burdensome government regulation

12 Theodore Roosevelt's Square Deal and Woodrow Wilson's New Freedom were primarily designed to
1   increase the power and influence of the United States in foreign affairs
2   reduce the role of government in the economy
3   help Americans cope with the problems caused by industrialization
4   protect the constitutional rights of religious and racial minorities

13 The Federal Reserve System was established to
1   serve as a source for farm loans   3   balance the federal budget
2   reform the practices of big business   4   regulate the circulation of money

14 The Women's Rights Movement of the late 19th century primarily focused its efforts on securing
1   Cabinet positions for women   3   equal rights for all minorities
2   the reform of prisons   4   suffrage for women

15 Which headline best illustrates the concept of imperialism?
1   "The Supreme Court Bans Segregation in Public Schools"
2   "United Nations is Founded in San Francisco"
3   "President McKinley Announces U.S. Annexation of the Philippines"
4   "President Roosevelt Meets Japanese and Russian Leaders at Portsmouth"

16 The primary reason for the construction of the Panama Canal was the need to
1   increase the security and power of the United States
2   spread the American way of life to less developed nations
3   encourage the economic development of Central America
4   stop the spread of Communism in the Western Hemisphere

Base your answer to question 17 on the following cartoon and on your knowledge of social studies.

17 Which U.S. foreign policy does the cartoon to the right depict?
1 Open Door Policy
2 isolationism
3 Big Stick Policy
4 neutrality

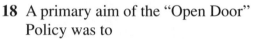

Library of Congress

18 A primary aim of the "Open Door" Policy was to
1 encourage Chinese citizens to emigrate to other nations
2 preserve American trade with China
3 develop China's industrial capacity
4 introduce democratic government into China

19 In *Schenck v. United States,* the Supreme Court decided that a "clear and present danger" to the United States permitted
1 an expansion of Presidential power
2 restrictions on 1st Amendment rights
3 establishment of a peacetime draft
4 limitations on the right to vote

20 Which was a major result of World War I?
1 American troops occupied Japan.
2 The Austro-Hungarian empire was divided into smaller nations.
3 The Soviet Union gained control of Eastern Europe.
4 Britain and France lost their colonies.

21 A major reason why some members of the U.S. Senate objected to joining the League of Nations was their opposition to
1 lower tariffs
2 freedom of the seas
3 potential military commitments
4 German membership in the League

22 The refusal of the United States to join the League of Nations illustrates the policy known as
1 Manifest Destiny
2 imperialism
3 neutrality
4 isolationism

INTERPRETING DOCUMENTS

This World War I poster was created by
James Montgomery Flagg.

National Archives

1. What is the main idea of this poster?

    _____

    _____

2. How does Flagg communicate this idea

    in his poster? _____

    _____

THEMATIC ESSAY QUESTION

Directions: Write a well-organized essay that includes an introduction, several paragraphs addressing the task below, and a conclusion.

Theme: Culture and Intellectual Life

> Throughout American history, important works of literature and art have addressed concerns or problems facing American society.

Task:

> Choose **two** works of literature or art from your study of American history.
>
> For *each* work of literature or art:
> • Describe the work of literature or art.
> • Explain how that work addressed a problem facing Americans.

You may use any example from your study of American history. Some suggestions you might wish to consider include: Thomas Paine's *Common Sense*, *The Federalist Papers*, Harriet Beecher Stowe's *Uncle Tom's Cabin*, Matthew Brady's photographs of the Civil War, and Upton Sinclair's *The Jungle*.

You are *not* limited to these suggestions.

DOCUMENT-BASED ESSAY QUESTION

Directions: Read the documents in Part A and answer the questions after each document. Then read the directions for Part B and write your essay.

Historical Context:

The decison to go to war is among the gravest choices made by any nation. Throughout their history, Americans have made this choice for a variety of reasons.

Task:

Compare and contrast the various reasons why Americans have become involved in wars.

Part A: Short Answers

Directions: Analyze the documents and answer the questions that follow each document.

DOCUMENT 1

"Whenever any form of government becomes destructive [of the people's rights] it is the right of the people to alter or abolish it.... The history of the present King of Great Britain is the history of repeated injuries .... all having in direct object the establishment of an absolute tyranny over these states. He has obstructed the administration of justice. He has kept among us ... standing armies, without the consent of our legislatures."
— Declaration of Independence, July 4, 1776

1. According to the Declaration, why were Americans justified in fighting Britain?

DOCUMENT 2

"My [main] object in this struggle is to save the Union, and is not either to save or destroy slavery. If I could save the Union without freeing any slave, I would do it; if I could save it by freeing all the slaves, I would do it; and if I could do it by freeing some and leaving others alone, I would also do that."
— Abraham Lincoln's reply to the New York Tribune, August 22, 1862

2. What does Lincoln argue was his main reason for involvement in the Civil War?

DOCUMENT 3

"Slavery was of less importance to the seceding States than the recognition of the federal principle. The conflict was a conflict between those who were for maintaining the federal character of the government, and those who were for centralizing all power in the federal head. It was a conflict between the supporters of the Union established by the Constitution, and those who wanted to overthrow this union of states and to erect a national consolidation in its place."

— *Alexander H. Stephens, former Confederate Vice-President*

3. What did Confederates see as the main cause of the conflict between the states?

DOCUMENT 4

"The horrors of the barbarous struggle for the extermination of the native population are witnessed in all parts of the country. Blood on the roadsides, blood in the fields, blood on the door-steps, blood, blood, blood! The old, the young, the weak, the crippled, all are butchered without mercy."

— Article in Pulitzer's *New York World* describing Spanish atrocities in Cuba, 1896

4. How did articles like these contribute to the outbreak of the Spanish-American War?

DOCUMENT 5

5a. What does the tombstone refer to?

_____

_____

_____

b. What is the main idea of the political cartoon?

_____

_____

_____

"The Spanish Brute"

Library of Congress

DOCUMENT 6

6. How did the policy announced in this proclamation eventually bring the United States into World War I?

_____

_____

_____

_____

_____

_____

_____

ADMIRALTY PROCLAMATION

The waters surrounding Great Britain and Iceland including the whole English Channel are hereby declared to be within the war zone and all enemy merchant vessels found in those waters after the eighteenth of February, 1915 will be destroyed. In addition, it may not always be possible to save crews and passengers...

Danger to neutral vessels within this zone of war cannot be avoided and neutral vessels may suffer from attacks intended to strike enemy ships

— *German Admiralty, February 4, 1915*

DOCUMENT 7

The *New York Times* reports the sinking of the British passenger ship *Lusitania*.

The New York Times

VOL. LXIV   *NEW YORK, SATURDAY, MAY 8, 1915*   *One Cent*

LUSITANIA SUNK BY A SUBMARINE,
Twice Torpedoed Off Irish Coast

Probably 1,260 Dead, 128 Are Americans;
Washington Sees a Crisis at Hand

7. How did this newspaper headline serve to inflame American public opinion?

_____

DOCUMENT 8

"We intend to begin unrestricted submarine warfare in February [1917]. We shall [seek] to keep the United States neutral. In the event of our not succeeding, we [offer to] Mexico a proposal on the following basis: Make war together, make peace together, generous financial support, and an understanding that Mexico [will be given] the lost territories of Texas, New Mexico, and Arizona. Inform the President of Mexico of the above most secretly as soon as the outbreak of war with the United States is certain ... ."

— Telegram sent by German Foreign Secretary Zimmerman to the German Ambassador in Mexico, intercepted and published in American newspapers.

8. Why did many Americans call for war against Germany shortly after this telegram was made public? _____

PART B - ESSAY

Directions: Write a well-organized essay that includes an introduction, several paragraphs, and a conclusion. Use evidence from at least **four** documents in the body of the essay. Support your response with relevant facts, examples, and details. Include additional outside information.

Historical Context:

> The decision to go to war is among the gravest choices made by any nation. Throughout their history, Americans have made this choice for a variety of reasons.

Task:

> Using information from the documents and your knowledge of United States history and government, write an essay in which you:

- Compare and contrast the various reasons why Americans have become involved in war.

CHAPTER 10

PROSPERITY AND DEPRESSION

A mother holds her child in front of their "home" during the Great Depression

Library of Congress

TIMELINE OF IMPORTANT EVENTS

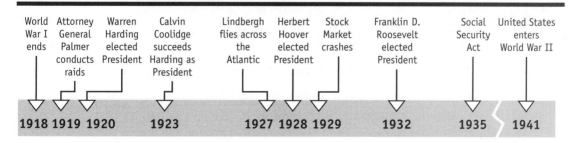

World War I ends	Attorney General Palmer conducts raids	Warren Harding elected President	Calvin Coolidge succeeds Harding as President	Lindbergh flies across the Atlantic	Herbert Hoover elected President	Stock Market crashes	Franklin D. Roosevelt elected President	Social Security Act	United States enters World War II
1918	1919	1920	1923	1927	1928	1929	1932	1935	1941

WHAT YOU SHOULD FOCUS ON

In this chapter, you will learn how the nation entered a new age of prosperity in the 1920s. Automobiles, telephones, and electricity made life more convenient than ever before. Unfortunately this prosperity was cut short by the Great Depression — the worst economic crisis in American history. President Herbert Hoover proved unable to restore economic growth. Under President Franklin D. Roosevelt and his New Deal, the federal government intervened in the economy on a massive scale to restore employment. In this chapter you will learn about the following:

A photograph taken by Dorothea Lange during the Great Depression

★ **The Roaring Twenties.** In the 1920s, the spread of the automobile and other new technologies contributed to growing prosperity, as did Republican policies that were favorable to business. Mass consumption also led to new cultural values, such as new roles for women. However, farmers and minorities failed to share in the economic benefits of the decade.

★ **The Great Depression.** Overproduction, speculation, and the lack of buying power among many groups set the stage for the Great Depression. When the New York Stock Market crashed in 1929, banks failed, markets vanished, and businesses went bankrupt. Soon millions were out of work.

★ **The New Deal.** President Franklin D. Roosevelt introduced policies of relief, recovery, and reform to revive the economy, including the Social Security Act and the Wagner Act. The New Deal greatly increased the size, power, and responsibilities of the federal government.

In studying this period, you should focus on the following questions:

★ What factors contributed to the economic prosperity of the 1920s?
★ What were the causes and effects of the Great Depression?
★ What has been the impact of the New Deal?

LOOKING AT ECONOMIC POLICY

reviously, you learned about our economy in *Looking at Economic Growth*. This section focuses on the role of government in the operation of our economy.

THE GOALS OF NATIONAL ECONOMIC POLICY

Since the late 19th century, the government's role in our economic life has changed. Earlier, the federal government rarely interfered in the economy, except to ensure fair competition. After the Great Depression, the federal government took on a greater role in the economy. Since the New Deal, the federal government has had these three goals:

promote maximum employment	promote maximum production	fight inflation (rising prices)

To keep the nation informed of what is happening in the economy, the President presents Congress each year with the *Economic Report of the President.*

MEASURING THE NATION'S ECONOMIC HEALTH

To measure the health of our national economy and to compare it to the economies of other nations, economists often look at several statistical indicators:

ECONOMIC INDICATORS

Gross Domestic Product (G.D.P.). This is the value in dollars of all the goods and services produced in the United States in a single year.

Per Capita Income. This is the G.D.P. divided by the population. It provides an indication of the average income of a single person.

Unemployment Rate. This measures the number of unemployed people who would like to work and are actively looking, divided by the total working population.

National Debt. This is the total amount of money owed by our national government to those who have lent it money.

Inflation Rate. This measures how quickly money loses its value because people are paying more for the same goods. When things cost more than before, this is a sign of inflation.

(continued)

ECONOMIC POWERS
OF THE NATIONAL GOVERNMENT

To achieve its economic goals, the federal government has several instruments at its disposal.

THE POWER TO PROVIDE PUBLIC GOODS

Public goods are goods paid for by tax money and used to serve the whole community, such as public parks, schools, and hospitals.

THE POWER TO REGULATE ECONOMIC ACTIVITIES

The government acts as a referee to ensure a free market by:

Encouraging Fair Competition. The federal government ensures that the marketplace will remain competitive. Unfair monopolies were outlawed by the Sherman Antitrust Act in 1890. The government also created commissions to act as watchdogs over certain industries.	**Protecting Workers and Consumers.** The federal government has passed laws to protect workers and consumers. For example, the Pure Food and Drug Act requires manufacturers to list product ingredients on their labels.	**Regulating International Trade.** The federal government regulates trade through its power to tax imports. Tariffs are used to protect American industries and jobs against unfair foreign competition. The government also imposes labeling requirements.

THE POWER TO REGULATE THE ECONOMY

Ensuring Equal Opportunity. The federal government has enacted legislation to promote equality in the workplace. In 1972, the federal government passed the Equal Employment Opportunity Act, requiring employers to pay equal wages for the same work regardless of race or sex.	**Protecting the Environment.** In 1972, the federal government created the Environmental Protection Agency, which sets strict standards for protecting the environment.

FISCAL POLICY

During the Great Depression, the economist **John Maynard Keynes** showed that a government can influence the rates of unemployment and inflation by its spending, taxing and borrowing policies. Keynesian theory states that:

If a country is in a depression, the government should spend more than it receives in taxes. By hiring more workers and buying more products, the government creates new jobs. Workers and businesses then spend more, increasing demand and stimulating production.

If there is a high rate of inflation, the government should collect more in taxes than it spends. People and businesses will become more cautious about spending or borrowing money. With less spending, producers will have to lower their prices.

Government should spend more than it receives in taxes

Government hires more workers, buys more goods

More people are employed; they buy more goods

Consumer demand creates more production jobs

IN AN ECONOMIC DEPRESSION

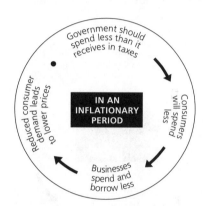

Government should spend less than it receives in taxes

Consumers will spend less

Businesses spend and borrow less

Reduced consumer demand leads to lower prices

IN AN INFLATIONARY PERIOD

Keynes thus urged governments to take an active role in maintaining high levels of employment and stable growth. One difficulty with Keynesian policy has been that Congress has often refused to cut spending or raise taxes to fight inflation because of the opposition of special interest groups. Although an excellent economic tool, fiscal policy can be affected by political considerations.

MONETARY POLICY

Monetary policy relies on the government's ability to control the nation's money supply to promote economic growth and stability. The money supply affects the overall level of business activity. **The Federal Reserve Act** (1913) established the Federal Reserve System. The Federal Reserve's role is to reduce swings in the economy by controlling the ability of banks to lend money.

The Federal Reserve controls the money supply in the economy

Bureau of Engraving and Printing

When there is an economic downturn, the Federal Reserve increases the money supply. As money is pumped into the economy, interest rates fall. Businesses and individuals borrow more because borrowing costs are less. This leads to increased spending, stimulating production and employment.

When there is a upswing in the economy and inflation is rising, the Federal Reserve reduces the money supply. By limiting the amount of money available, fewer loans are made to businesses or individuals. People borrow and spend less, and the pace of growth is slowed.

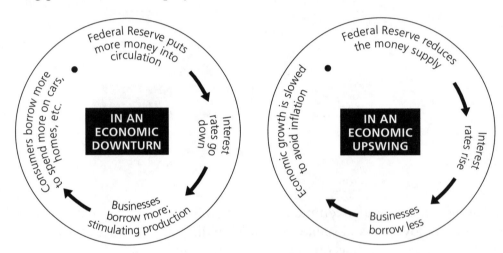

The chief limitations to the use of monetary policy are:

★   Monetary policy is controlled by the **Federal Reserve Board,** an independent agency. Congress and the President have no direct control over its policies other than through the appointment of its members.

★   The Federal Reserve assumes that businesses and consumers will respond to lower and higher interest rates. Sometimes they do not.

★   Monetary policy at home has effects overseas. Interest rates affect the strength of the dollar compared to foreign currencies. Federal Reserve policies influence the ability of American companies to compete overseas or to attract foreign investment.

BOOM TIMES: THE 1920s

THE ROARING TWENTIES, 1919–1929

The "**Roaring Twenties**" were good times for many Americans. Beneath an appearance of calm and prosperity, America was experiencing fundamental economic and social change.

ADJUSTING TO PEACE, 1919–1920

The decade of the 1920s opened with the difficult task of adjusting to peace. Disillusioned by the outcome of World War I, Americans returned to a policy of **isolationism** in foreign affairs — refusing to become involved in other nations' disputes or problems. On the domestic front, the government stopped its wartime spending and soldiers returned home looking for jobs. This led to a temporary economic recession, lasting from 1919 until 1921.

THREATS TO CIVIL LIBERTIES

The 1920s also witnessed attacks on American civil liberties.

★ **The Red Scare.** Communists seized power in Russia in 1917 and threatened to spread their revolution to other countries. When a wave of strikes hit the United States in 1919, some Americans feared this was the start of a Communist revolution. In 1919, anti-Communist hysteria led Attorney General Palmer to

Sacco and Vanzetti surrounded by marshals

Library of Congress

conduct raids against radicals accused of plotting to overthrow the government. Thousands were arrested, and several hundred immigrant radicals were deported. The hysteria affected immigrants in other ways as well. Two Italian immigrants, **Nicola Sacco** and **Bartolomeo Vanzetti,** were accused of committing murder during a robbery to obtain funds for an anarchist revolution. Despite insufficient evidence, they were convicted and later executed in 1927.

★ **Rise of Nativism and Racism.** The "Red Scare" and the Sacco and Vanzetti trial contributed to the rise of **nativism** — a dislike of foreigners which led to new restrictions on immigration in the early 1920s. The migration of African Americans from the South to Northern cities during World War I led to increased racial tensions after the war. The **Ku Klux Klan,** dead for decades, revived in the 1920s. The Klan was hostile to immigrants, Catholics, Jews, and African Americans.

THE REPUBLICAN PRESIDENCIES: HARDING, COOLIDGE, AND HOOVER

In 1920, Republicans triumphantly returned to the White House. They were to remain there for the next twelve years, overseeing the prosperity of the twenties and the arrival of the depression that ended it.

POLICIES FAVORING BUSINESS

In general, Presidents Harding, Coolidge, and Hoover followed policies favorable to American business. They supported laissez-faire policies, with minimal interference in business activities.

High Protective Tariffs. Congress passed tariffs that protected U.S. manufacturers by keeping out foreign-made goods. The **Hawley-Smoot Tariff Act** (1930) raised tariffs to their highest levels in history.

REPUBLICAN POLICIES FAVORING BUSINESS

Lower Taxes on the Wealthy and Corporations. Congress slashed taxes on the rich and corporate profits. As a result, a larger tax burden was shifted to the average wage earner.

Lax Enforcement of Antitrust Laws and Regulations. These Presidents were lax in regulating business. Business was given a much freer hand and a large number of business mergers took place in the 1920s.

THE HARDING ADMINISTRATION, 1921–1923

Warren Harding, elected President in 1920, captured the national spirit when he called for a "return to normalcy" — a less ambitious foreign policy and greater prosperity at home. Under Harding, the United States refused to join the League of Nations, enacted high tariffs, and restricted immigration. In the **Teapot Dome Scandal,** it was revealed that one high-ranking Harding Administration official had leased oil-rich government lands at Teapot Dome, Wyoming, to businessmen in exchange for personal bribes.

THE COOLIDGE ADMINISTRATION, 1923–1929

Vice-President **Calvin Coolidge** assumed the Presidency on Harding's death in 1923, and was elected in his own right in 1924. Coolidge symbolized old-fashioned values, like honesty and thrift. Continuing Harding's pro-business policies, Coolidge's motto was "the business of America is business." President Coolidge received much of the credit for the business expansion of the 1920s.

THE HOOVER ADMINISTRATION, 1929–1933

In his 1928 campaign for the Presidency, Herbert Hoover predicted an end to poverty in America. He was impressed by the achievements of business in raising American living standards. Hoover believed this was the result of a system in which individuals were given equal opportunities, a free education, and a will to succeed. This **"rugged individualism,"** as Hoover called it, spurred progress. He felt strongly that government interference in business could undermine the nation's prosperity.

President Hoover relaxes while fishing

FACTORS UNDERLYING PROSPERITY

For many Americans, the 1920s were prosperous times. Wages and employment opportunities increased, while business profits and production soared. Government policies favoring business were one factor behind this prosperity. However, there were several other factors that also explain this affluence:

THE RISE OF THE AUTOMOBILE

Probably the single greatest factor behind the prosperity of the 1920s was the expanded use of the automobile. The growth in automobile ownership, from 8 to 24 million, greatly affected American life. Automobile production required vast amounts of steel, glass, and rubber — stimulating those industries. By 1929, one out of every nine workers was employed in an auto-related industry. Cars gave people greater mobility, as families were now able to drive away on vacation. The growth of suburbs was made possible by the car. School buses allowed students in remote and rural areas to attend school regularly for the first time. Goods could be delivered by truck. Farmers could use tractors to grow and harvest crops.

FAMOUS AMERICANS: HENRY FORD (1863–1947)

Ford's goal was to build cars that everyone could afford. His Model T, introduced in 1905, was the first car that middle-class Americans could afford. He introduced the assembly line in 1914, increasing the efficiency of production by moving cars along a conveyor belt while workers completed their assigned task. By 1924,

Ford poses with his 10th millionth Model T

Ford Motor Corporation

Ford was producing 1.6 million cars a year at a price of under $300 per car. By 1925, one car was rolling off Ford's assembly line every ten seconds.

THE DEVELOPMENT OF OTHER NEW INDUSTRIES

Besides automobiles, other new industries emerged, largely based on new uses of electricity. Household appliances, like the vacuum cleaner, refrigerator, and toaster, were introduced. Radio and motion pictures became widespread. These new industries created new jobs and changed the ways Americans lived.

MORE EFFICIENT PRODUCTION TECHNIQUES

The **assembly line,** the use of standardized parts, and other labor-saving devices made American industry more efficient and productive. Some of these improved production techniques were developed for wartime production during World War I.

THE AGE OF MASS CONSUMPTION

The 1920s witnessed new patterns of consumption, creating larger mass markets for goods. Advertising stimulated demand, while workers with higher wages and more leisure time had greater purchasing power. Retailers developed programs for installment purchases and buying on credit.

SPECULATION BOOM

The emergence of new industries, improved production techniques, and mass markets helped fuel a speculative boom on the stock market, where millions of people invested in the hope of striking it rich.

CULTURAL VALUES OF THE 1920s

The 1920s also saw the emergence of new values. Greater mobility and material comfort had a key impact on social patterns and beliefs. Many groups, especially women, the young, and African Americans, felt a new sense of power and freedom. Others felt threatened and sought to preserve traditional values.

ATTEMPTS TO PRESERVE TRADITIONAL VALUES

At the start of the 1920s, rural America continued to regard the rise of urban society with suspicion. The best examples of the effort to defend traditional values were Prohibition and the Scopes Trial.

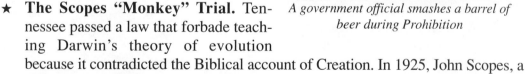

* **Prohibition.** Protestant reformers often saw liquor as the cause of poverty and crime. In 1919, the states ratified the **Eighteenth Amendment,** banning the sale of alcoholic drinks. By 1933, most saw this "experiment" as a failure because many people had refused to accept the ban on alcohol. The demand for illegal liquor stimulated the growth of organized crime in the 1920s. Prohibition was repealed by the **Twenty-first Amendment,** demonstrating that unpopular laws are sometimes unenforceable.

A government official smashes a barrel of beer during Prohibition

* **The Scopes "Monkey" Trial.** Tennessee passed a law that forbade teaching Darwin's theory of evolution because it contradicted the Biblical account of Creation. In 1925, John Scopes, a biology teacher, was tried and convicted for teaching evolution. The trial illustrated the clash between new scientific theories and some older religious beliefs.

* **New Restrictions on Immigration.** After World War I, nativist feeling against immigrants led Congress to restrict immigration from Southern and Eastern Europe. The Immigration Acts of 1921, 1924, and 1929 established quotas for each nationality based on America's existing ethnic composition. Under this system, Great Britain, Ireland, and Germany were allowed the greatest number of immigrants, while the number of "New Immigrants" was severely limited. Asian immigration was barred altogether.

THE EMERGENCE OF NEW VALUES

In opposition to traditional values stood the new values of the period, which encouraged greater openness and self-expression.

★ **Women.** New household appliances reduced housework, and greater numbers of women went to college. As more women worked, they demonstrated a new economic independence and became more assertive. This brought about changes in manners and morals. Women began to smoke and drink in public. They rejected restrictive fashions for shorter hair and skirts above the knees. Sexual behavior became more open, and young women went out unchaperoned. Flappers wore short dresses and danced the Charleston. Men and women both began reading **Sigmund Freud** and treating sexuality more openly.

★ **Youth and the Lost Generation.** Young adults were responsible for zany fads like flagpole sitting and marathon dancing. A new group of writers, known as the Lost Generation, rejected the desire for material wealth. Writers such as **Sinclair Lewis** in *Main Street* and *Babbitt,* ridiculed the narrowness and hypocrisy of American life. **F. Scott Fitzgerald** in *The Great Gatsby* hinted that the search for purely material success often led to tragedy.

★ **The Harlem Renaissance.** The 1920s are often referred to as the **Jazz Age,** reflecting the greater importance of African-American music. African Americans, who had begun migrating to Northern cities during World War I, continued to do so in the 1920s. The center of African-American life in the 1920s was Harlem in New York City. Here, jazz music flourished. An awakening of African-American culture in these years became known as the "**Harlem Renaissance.**" Poets and writers like **Langston Hughes** and **Alain Locke** expressed a new pride in their heritage, while attacking racism. **Marcus Garvey,** stressing racial unity through self-help, encouraged African Americans to set up their own shops and businesses.

Marcus Garvey planned a Back-to-Africa Movement, in which African Americans would return to Africa.

Schomburg Center for Black Culture

FAMOUS AMERICANS: LANGSTON HUGHES (1902–1967)

Langston Hughes is recognized as one of America's best poets. Born in Missouri, Hughes like other African American artists, writers, and painters, was drawn to Harlem. He drew on his personal experiences in writing about what it was like to be an African American growing up in America. His poems, novels, plays, and newspaper columns made him one of the most popular writers of the Harlem Renaissance. His writings expressed the new mood of rugged determination to overcome racial prejudice.

National Portrait Gallery

★ **Popular New Heroes.** More leisure time gave people greater opportunity for entertainment. They turned to spectator sports, the radio, movies, and magazines. The rise of new popular heroes resulted from the need to preserve a sense of personal identity in an increasingly impersonal age of machines. Popular sports heroes like Babe Ruth and Jack Dempsey served as new role models. **Charles Lindbergh** became the first person to fly solo across the Atlantic Ocean in 1927. Lindbergh made his historic flight in a single-engine plane. His daring trip made him an instant national hero and a worldwide celebrity.

Lindbergh after just landing in Paris

Library of Congress

THE GREAT DEPRESSION, 1929–1940

Economies historically pass through good and bad periods that regularly repeat themselves. These up-and-down periods of business activity are referred to as the **business cycle.** The bad times are called **depressions** — characterized by business failures and high unemployment. The **Great Depression** was the worst depression in our nation's history.

CAUSES OF THE GREAT DEPRESSION

A variety of factors caused the economy to move from the prosperity of the 1920s to the severe depression of the 1930s.

OVERPRODUCTION

The 1920s witnessed a rapid economic expansion, as manufacturers made and sold new products like cars, radios, and refrigerators. Many consumers, however, lacked the money to buy these goods. Manufacturers were soon producing more goods than they could sell.

UNEVEN DISTRIBUTION OF INCOME

Even in the 1920s, not all groups shared in the national prosperity. Many African Americans, Hispanics, Native Americans, and industrial workers already faced hard times. Railroad, coal, and textile workers in particular suffered from low wages or unemployment. Farmers suffered when crop prices dropped sharply, and many went bankrupt. Minority members had limited employment opportunities.

SPECULATION

In the 1920s, as stocks soared in value, many people bought stocks hoping to "get rich quick." This drove stock prices even higher. By 1929, stock prices had tripled since 1920. To make matters worse, people were buying stocks on margin — paying only a small percentage of a stock's value and promising to pay the rest later, when they sold the stock. However, if the stock's price fell, then buyers often did not have enough of their own money to cover the losses. People also invested in real estate with similar hopes of getting rich quickly. The frenzy of stock market and real estate speculation created an atmosphere of easy money but was subject to collapse.

SHAKY BANKING

The government failed to effectively regulate either the banking system or the stock market. Bankers invested their depositors' money in unsound investments. Many consumers were buying more than they could afford. This vast over-extension of credit made the entire economy extremely vulnerable.

RESTRICTED INTERNATIONAL TRADE

High U.S. tariffs protected American markets but made it hard for producers to sell abroad, since other countries retaliated by setting up high tariffs of their own.

THE GREAT DEPRESSION BEGINS

When the New York Stock Market crashed in 1929, it set off a chain reaction that toppled the American economy and quickly spread to the rest of the world.

THE STOCK MARKET CRASH

In 1929, the market turned sharply downward. People started to sell. On October 29th, the market crashed, with prices reaching all-time lows. Corporations could no longer raise funds. People who lost their money in the stock market could not repay their loans or rents, leading to bank failures. Thousands of people lost their life savings. In this new economic climate, the demand for goods decreased. As prices fell, factories closed, and workers lost their jobs. Demand was reduced still further, causing prices to fall more. Other factories closed, and the country became caught in the grip of a vicious downward spiral.

THE HUMAN IMPACT OF THE DEPRESSION

The Great Depression was a national nightmare. Businesses failed, farmers lost their farms, banks failed, and millions of people were out of work. There was no "safety net" — no unemployment insurance or bank deposit insurance. Private charities were overwhelmed. People lost their homes and went hungry. Millions depended on soup kitchens for their food. Writers like **John Steinbeck** and photographers like **Dorothea Lange** recorded the misery of the Great Depression.

THE IMPACT OF GEOGRAPHY ON AMERICAN HISTORY

The Dust Bowl. During the 1930s, in addition to financial disaster, the farmers of the Great Plains faced natural disaster. Since the 1870s, farmers had been plowing the Great Plains, exposing the topsoil, and tapping underground water supplies. A series of droughts (*long periods without rain*) in the early 1930s dried up crops and topsoil, turning the soil into dust. Heavy winds buried homes in dust,

Farm machinery buried under a sea of dust

National Archives

destroyed harvests, and carried topsoil across hundreds of miles. Unable to grow enough to pay their bills, farmers were forced to abandon their farms. Many farmers moved west to California. Over one million farmers were driven from their lands by the "dust bowl." Their troubles were described by the writer John Steinbeck in *The Grapes of Wrath* (1939).

PRESIDENT HOOVER
FAILS TO HALT THE DEPRESSION

Despite the spiraling economic catastrophe, President Hoover remained true to his belief in laissez-faire capitalism.

HOOVER'S PHILOSOPHY

Hoover rejected demands for the federal government to provide direct payments to the unemployed and needy. He believed that this would reduce the incentive to work, undermining American "rugged individualism." Instead, Hoover believed that voluntary and private organizations should provide emergency relief. Hoover was convinced that when prices got low enough, people would resume buying, production would pick up, and employment would increase again. Unfortunately, his predictions turned out to be incorrect.

HOOVER FINALLY RESPONDS

Hoover cut taxes, increased federal spending on public projects, and directed a federal agency to buy surplus farm crops. In 1932, Hoover established the **Reconstruction Finance Corporation** to give emergency loans to banks and businesses, believing that cheap loans would spur business. He thought this expansion would eventually "trickle down" to the average American. However, Hoover's policies were too little, too late. Americans found his lack of leadership frustrating. Shanty towns of the homeless and unemployed, sarcastically called **"Hoovervilles,"** sprang up on the outskirts of cities.

FRANKLIN D. ROOSEVELT AND THE NEW DEAL

During the Great Depression of the 1930s, the greatest challenge facing Americans was widespread unemployment. The Governor of New York, **Franklin D. Roosevelt,** was nominated as the Democratic candidate in the Presidential election of 1932. Roosevelt promised Americans a **"New Deal"** to put them back to work. Roosevelt easily defeated Hoover in a landslide election.

ROOSEVELT INTRODUCES THE NEW DEAL

The New Deal was a major turning point in American history. It established that the federal government bears the chief responsibility for ensuring the smooth running of the American economy.

ROOSEVELT'S NEW DEAL PHILOSOPHY

President Roosevelt saw the depression as a national emergency. He believed the President's task was to find a way back to prosperity. The New Deal marked an end to the view that government and the economy should be separated. Under Roosevelt, the New Deal permanently increased the size and power of the federal government, making it primarily responsible for managing the national economy.

ROOSEVELT'S STYLE

Roosevelt brought a new style to the Presidency. He assembled a group of very talented people, known as the **"Brain Trust,"** to serve under him. Roosevelt was an excellent communicator. In radio addresses to millions of listeners, known as **"fireside chats,"** he explained his policies in simple conversational terms. His cheerful optimism helped to restore public confidence.

Roosevelt (at right) meets with his "Brain Trust"

Franklin D. Roosevelt Presidential Library

FAMOUS AMERICANS: ELEANOR ROOSEVELT (1884–1962)

In mid-life, Roosevelt was struck by polio. He became unable to walk except with crutches for short distances. President Roosevelt's wife, Eleanor, served as her husband's eyes and ears by traveling throughout the country and later the world. A political activist, she strongly advocated women's rights and peace causes. She was also known as a champion of social causes to help the poor. Her greatest contribution was in helping to create the United Nations and to help write its Declaration of Human Rights.

Eleanor Roosevelt and Mayor La Guardia

Library of Congress

NEW DEAL LEGISLATION:
RELIEF, RECOVERY, AND REFORM

.....n as President Roosevelt took office, he called Congress into special session. Roosevelt then pushed through legislation that would have been difficult to pass in less critical times. Roosevelt explained the New Deal measures in terms of three R's — **Relief, Recovery,** and **Reform.**

RELIEF

Relief measures were short-term actions designed to tide people over until the economy recovered.

★ **The Banking Crisis.** Ten thousand banks had failed during the Great Depression. One of Roosevelt's first measures after his inauguration was to declare a **Bank Holiday** and close all the nation's banks. Each bank was permitted to reopen only after government inspectors found the bank financially sound.

★ **Relief to Homeowners and Farmers.** Many homeowners and farmers were unable to pay their mortgages. Banks were seizing their property and throwing them out of their homes and farms. The government passed legislation making emergency loans available.

★ **Relief for the Unemployed.** Over one-quarter of the nation's workforce was unemployed. There was no unemployment insurance, and many of the unemployed were without food or shelter. Roosevelt favored "**work-relief,**" giving people emergency public jobs.

Federal Emergency Relief Act (1933) funded state and local governments to provide emergency relief, and enabled millions of people to be hired on "make-work" projects.

Civilian Conservation Corps (1933) gave jobs to young men, such as planting trees and cleaning up forests. Members of the C.C.C. lived in camps and received free food. Most of their pay was sent to their parents.

"RELIEF" LEGISLATION DURING THE NEW DEAL

Public Works Administration (1933) created federal jobs by building public projects, such as schools, roads, courts, post offices, and bridges.

Works Progress Administration (1935) (W.P.A.) created jobs by hiring artists, writers, and musicians to paint murals and produce plays and other artworks.

RECOVERY

Roosevelt realized that the key to recovery was to stimulate production. His recovery measures were designed to restore the economy by increasing incentives to produce and by rebuilding people's purchasing power.

Priming The Pump. Roosevelt believed in pouring money into the economy to get it working again. By putting government money into consumers' hands, they would spend more, increasing the demand for products. This would lead to more workers being hired, further increasing purchasing power and consumer demand.

"RECOVERY" MEASURES DURING THE NEW DEAL

National Recovery Administration (1933) asked businesses to voluntarily follow codes which set standard prices, production limits, and minimum wages. In 1935, the Supreme Court found the N.R.A. unconstitutional because the federal government had no power to interfere with business activities conducted within a state.

Agricultural Adjustment Acts. In the first "A.A.A.," the government paid farmers to plant less in the hope of increasing crop prices. In 1936, the Supreme Court declared the A.A.A. unconstitutional. The second A.A.A. (1938) succeeded in raising farm prices. Under this act, the government bought farm surpluses and stored them in warehouses until prices went up.

REFORM

Reform measures were aimed at remedying defects in the structure of the American economy in order to ensure that another depression would never strike again. These reforms created new federal agencies and institutions, many of which still survive today. Many reform measures were based on the belief that government should protect individuals against risks they could not handle on their own.

F.D.R. arrives at the Tennessee Valley Dam dedication

Franklin D. Roosevelt Library

Federal Deposit Insurance Corporation (1933) insured bank deposits so that people would have confidence in their bank and would not lose their savings in the event of a bank failure.

"REFORM" LEGISLATION DURING THE NEW DEAL

Tennessee Valley Authority (1933) built 21 government-owned dams along the Tennessee River, controlling floods and producing electricity. Some feared the "T.V.A." as a form of socialism.

Securities and Exchange Commission (1934) was created to watch over the stock market, prevent fraud and guard against another stock market collapse.

National Labor Relations Act (1935), often called the **Wagner Act**, gave workers the right to form unions, to bargain collectively, and to submit grievances to a National Labor Relations Board.

Social Security Act (1935) was probably the most important measure of the New Deal. It provided workers with unemployment insurance, old age pensions, and insurance if they died early. Workers and their employers each paid new taxes to fund these benefits.

IMPACT OF THE NEW DEAL ON LABOR

The greatest growth in union membership in American history took place in the 1930s as a result of the New Deal. Roosevelt sought to raise wages to fight the depression.

Norris-LaGuardia Act (1932) prohibited the use of injunctions against peaceful strikes.

NEW DEAL LEGISLATION FAVORABLE TO LABOR

National Industrial Recovery Act (1933) guaranteed workers the right to form unions. Employers could not refuse to hire union members. This act was declared unconstitutional in 1935, but was replaced by the Wagner Act.

Wagner Act (1935) greatly stimulated the unionization of American workers by protecting the right of unions to bargain collectively with their employers. Union membership grew rapidly with this new law.

POST-NEW DEAL LEGISLATION: THE TAFT-HARTLEY ACT

Concern over the growth of union power led Congress to pass the **Taft-Hartley Act** in 1947. Union officials were required to file financial reports. Unions had to notify their employers of any strike and had to agree to a "cooling-off" period during which the government encouraged the union and employer to submit their dispute to an arbitrator.

REACTIONS TO THE NEW DEAL

Roosevelt's efforts to combat the depression gave him a landslide victory in the 1936 Presidential election. By the next election in 1940, Europe was in the middle of World War II. Roosevelt broke with tradition by running for a third term, and was again re-elected. In 1944, Roosevelt successfully ran for a fourth term. One year later, Roosevelt died. The 22nd Amendment was ratified in 1951, limiting Presidents to two elected terms.

THE SUPREME COURT AND THE NEW DEAL

The greatest threat to the New Deal came from the Supreme Court. In 1935–36, the Court ruled that both the N.R.A. and A.A.A. were unconstitutional.

A KEY COURT CASE: SCHECHTER POULTRY v. U.S. (1935)

The National Industrial Recovery Act gave the President the power to set up "codes of fair practices" for businesses involved in intrastate (*within a state*) commerce. The Schechter Poultry Company was convicted of failing to obey the act. It appealed the conviction, claiming the N.I.R.A. was unconstitutional. The Supreme Court agreed, holding that even during a national crisis, Congress could not give the President more powers than those granted in the Constitution.

ROOSEVELT'S COURT-PACKING PLAN (1937)

Roosevelt feared that the Court might declare other New Deal legislation unconstitutional. In 1937, he proposed to add six new justices to the Supreme Court, to give him control over the Court. The plan was viewed as an attempt to upset the traditional balance of power. Roosevelt's plan was condemned by the public and rejected by Congress. However, subsequent Supreme Court decisions upheld later New Deal legislation.

LEGACY OF THE NEW DEAL

The New Deal helped decrease unemployment, although full employment was only reached with the outbreak of World War II. The New Deal introduced new agencies and programs, to ensure that a Great Depression would not occur again.

SUMMARIZING YOUR UNDERSTANDING

KEY TERMS, CONCEPTS, AND PEOPLE

Make a vocabulary card for each of the following terms, concepts, and people.

Red Scare

Sacco and Vanzetti Trial

Teapot Dome Scandal

Herbert Hoover

Harlem Renaissance

Dust Bowl

Stock Market Crash

Franklin D. Roosevelt

New Deal

Social Security Act

Schechter Poultry v. U.S.

Court-Packing Plan

COMPLETING A TABLE

Briefly describe the following legislation associated with the New Deal.

Legislation	Major Provisions	Intent of this Legislation
Civilian Conservation Corps (1933)		
National Recovery Administration (1933)		
Federal Deposit Insurance Corp. (1933)		
Social Security Act (1935)		
National Labor Relations Act (1935)		

COMPLETING A GRAPHIC ORGANIZER

Briefly describe each of the following terms discussed in this chapter.

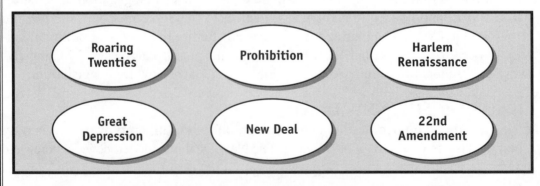

Roaring Twenties

Prohibition

Harlem Renaissance

Great Depression

New Deal

22nd Amendment

TESTING YOUR UNDERSTANDING

MULTIPLE-CHOICE QUESTIONS

1   What would someone be called who supported immigration quotas, the execution of Sacco and Vanzetti, and the rebirth of the Ku Klux Klan?
    1   a rugged individualist   3   a nativist
    2   an imperialist   4   a mercantilist

2   The boom years of the 1920s were characterized by
    1   decreases in both agricultural surpluses and farm foreclosures
    2   limited investment capital and declining jobs
    3   widespread use of the automobile and an increase in consumer purchases
    4   increased regulation of the economy by the federal and state governments

3   The "Harlem Renaissance" refers to the
    1   artistic style of the first Dutch settlers in New York
    2   regiment of African American soldiers in World War I
    3   flourishing of African-American literature and music during the 1920s
    4   blossoming of Hispanic culture in New York during the 1960s

4   Which generalization most accurately describes the literary works of Langston Hughes, Sinclair Lewis, and John Steinbeck?
    1   Politics and art seldom mix well.
    2   The best literature concerns the lives of the wealthy.
    3   Literature often reflects the times in which it is created.
    4   Traditional American themes are the most popular.

5   Which was an immediate effect of the use of new production techniques during the period 1900 to 1929?
    1   a loss of commitment to the work ethic
    2   a flood of new consumer products on the market
    3   an increase in the rate of unemployment
    4   decline in business profits

6   What was an important effect of the growth of the automobile industry after World War I?
    1   It stimulated other new industries.
    2   There were decreased employment opportunities.
    3   There was an increased number of railroad passengers.
    4   It encouraged the government operation of major industries.

7   Which lesson is best supported by a study of Prohibition?
1   Social attitudes can make some laws difficult to enforce.
2   Increased taxes can affect consumer spending.
3   Morality can be legislated successfully.
4   People will sacrifice willingly for the common good.

8   Which was an important cause of the Great Depression?
1   speculation on the stock market
2   shortages of consumer goods
3   the collapse of the international gold standard
4   higher oil and farm prices

9   Before the New Deal, the basic approach of the federal government toward handling depressions was to
1   allow the economy to adjust itself   3   enact public spending programs
2   ask other nations for economic aid   4   issue more silver coinage

10   Which statement best describes Franklin Roosevelt's New Deal programs?
1   They reduced the number of government employees.
2   They expanded the economic role of the federal government.
3   They relied mainly on local government leadership.
4   They emphasized the importance of the gold standard.

Base your answer to question 11 on the graph and your knowledge of social studies.

11   Which factor best explains the decline in the number of bank failures by 1937?

1   New banking laws restored public confidence in banks.
2   Most people were too poor to have any bank savings.
3   The government was now operating all the nation's banks.
4   Most Americans transferred their savings to foreign banks.

BANK FAILURES IN THE UNITED STATES, 1926-1937

1926

1931

1933

1937

KEY: One = 250 banks

12 Which groups were most helped by the Wagner Act and the Social Security Act?

1 farmers and homeowners
3 large businesses and corporations
2 stockbrokers and investors
4 labor unions and workers

13 The primary purpose of the Social Security Act of 1935 was to

1 achieve integrated public schools
2 provide old age and unemployment insurance
3 regulate international trade
4 guarantee collective bargaining

14 Many opponents of the New Deal claimed that its programs violated the American tradition of

1 welfare capitalism
3 government regulation of business
2 collective bargaining
4 individual responsibility

Base your answer to question 15 on the cartoon and your knowledge of social studies.

15 What is the main idea of the cartoon?

1 President Roosevelt used a system of trial and error to improve the economy.
2 Congress and the President were unable to cope with the Great Depression.
3 President Roosevelt always followed the recommendations of the Congress.
4 The President and Congress constantly fought over Depression era programs.

"Of course we may have to change remedies if we don't get results."

16 Which branch of the national government declared early New Deal legislation unconstitutional?

1 the Senate
3 the President
2 the Supreme Court
4 the House of Representatives

17 Roosevelt's election to a *fourth* Presidential term can be attributed to the

1 blame placed on Republicans for the country's economic problems
2 need to continue efforts to cope with rising farm prices
3 unwillingness of voters to change leadership during a major crisis
4 decreasing popularity of the New Deal

INTERPRETING DOCUMENTS

1. How many Americans were unemployed in 1937?

_____

2. What event led to increased unemployment in 1929–1931?

_____

3. What factors helped to lower unemployment in the mid-1930s?

_____

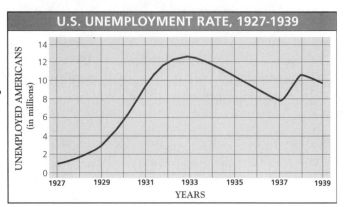

THEMATIC ESSAY QUESTION

Directions: Write a well-organized essay that includes an introduction, several paragraphs addressing the task below, and a conclusion.

Theme: Economic Systems

> Economic problems have been a major concern of Americans since the Civil War.

Task:

> Choose **two** economic problems from your study of American history.
>
> For _each_ economic problem:
> * Describe the economic problem
> * Show how that economic problem was dealt with by the federal government

You may use any example from your study of United States history. Some suggestions you might wish to consider include: the rise of monopolies, problems of farmers, unemployment, inflation, and the abuse of workers.

You are _not_ limited to these suggestions.

CHAPTER 11

THE AGE OF GLOBAL CRISIS

National Archives

The U.S.S. Shaw exploding during the surprise attack on Pearl Harbor

TIMELINE OF IMPORTANT EVENTS

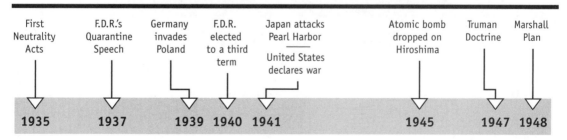

First Neutrality Acts	F.D.R.'s Quarantine Speech	Germany invades Poland	F.D.R. elected to a third term	Japan attacks Pearl Harbor ——— United States declares war	Atomic bomb dropped on Hiroshima	Truman Doctrine	Marshall Plan
1935	1937	1939	1940	1941	1945	1947	1948

WHAT YOU SHOULD FOCUS ON

In the 1920s and 1930s, dictatorships came to power in Italy, Germany, Spain, and other countries. When war broke out in Europe and Asia, Americans were reluctant to become involved. However, Japan's attack on Pearl Harbor ended U.S. neutrality. American participation helped achieve an Allied victory in World War II, the most destructive war in history. U.S. leaders later regretted not having stamped out Nazi aggression in its infancy. In the post-war years, they resolved not to make the same mistake in their struggle against Communism. In this chapter you will learn about the following:

National Archives

Smoke rises 60,000 feet as an atom bomb is dropped on Nagasaki (August 1945)

★ **American Isolationism.** After World War I, America became isolationist in foreign affairs. Despite the outbreak of war in Europe in 1939, the United States maintained a cautious neutrality.

★ **The United States in World War II.** On December 7, 1941, Japanese planes bombed Pearl Harbor, bringing the United States into the war against Germany, Japan, and Italy. After a long struggle, the allies achieved victory in 1945. Germany was divided, and Japan was occupied by U.S. forces.

★ **The Cold War.** Immediately after World War II ended, the United States and the Soviet Union became rivals in the "Cold War," which quickly spread from Europe to Asia. American leaders took steps to contain Communism.

In studying this period, you should focus on the following questions:

★ Why was the United States isolationist in the years 1920–1941?

★ What factors led to the outbreak of World War II?

★ What were the causes of the Cold War?

★ How did U.S. leaders attempt to contain Communism in Europe and Asia?

LOOKING AT FOREIGN POLICY

 any questions on the Regents Examination will concern foreign policy. This section will give you a brief overview of the nature of foreign policy in general.

WHAT IS FOREIGN POLICY?

Foreign policy is the conduct of one nation towards other nations. An example of foreign policy was the decision of President Clinton to bomb military targets in Yugoslavia. **Domestic policy**, in contrast, refers to a government's actions within its borders, such as passing a new income tax law. The main objective of U.S. foreign policy is to promote national interests. Many factors determine what those interests are.

National Security. The foremost goal of American foreign policy is to protect our way of life. The United States achieves this through military preparedness, by responding to acts of aggression, by developing its economy, by allying with friendly nations, and by participating in international organizations.

GOALS OF U.S. FOREIGN POLICY

Protection of U.S. Citizens and Investments. The United States acts to protect its citizens and investments overseas.

Promotion of American Trade. The federal government follows policies abroad that will help to promote the American economy.

Promotion of Democracy. The United States actively pursues spreading its political system of democracy.

Promotion of Human Rights and International Peace. The United States supports morality in both national and international affairs.

WHO MAKES FOREIGN POLICY?

The Constitution gave control of U.S. foreign policy to the federal government. To prevent any one branch of the federal government from becoming too strong, the Constitution divided control of foreign policy between the President and Congress.

(continued)

PRESIDENTIAL FOREIGN POLICY POWERS

The President has the day-to-day control of foreign policy. The President is assisted in making foreign policy by the Secretary of State and the State Department. Others assisting the President include the Central Intelligence Agency, the National Security Council, and the Joint Chiefs of Staff.

Serves as Commander-in-Chief of the armed forces	Negotiates treaties with foreign countries

FOREIGN POLICY POWERS OF THE PRESIDENT

Appoints and receives foreign ambassadors and ministers. This power gives the President the authority to extend or deny diplomatic recognition to new foreign governments.

CONGRESSIONAL FOREIGN POLICY POWERS

Congress was given partial power in formulating foreign policy. Primarily, this was done to act as a check on the President's powers over foreign policy.

Declare war	Approve treaties and Presidential appointments. A 2/3 vote of the Senate is required to ratify a treaty

FOREIGN POLICY POWERS OF CONGRESS

Regulate commerce with foreign nations	Decide how much money the President may spend on foreign affairs or national defense

The many crises of the twentieth century and the ability of the Presidency to respond quickly to these crises has made the executive branch dominant in conducting U.S. foreign policy, overshadowing the role of Congress. However, in times when the nation is not faced with military crisis, Congress has frequently attempted to re-assert greater control over foreign policy.

OTHER INFLUENCES ON FOREIGN POLICY

Although the President and Congress have the constitutional power to make foreign policy, they are often influenced in their decisions by others.

Special Interest Groups. Businesspeople, political action groups, environmental groups, and others often lobby Congress or contact the President's staff to express their views.

OTHER INFLUENCES ON FOREIGN POLICY DECISIONS

News Media. Newspapers, magazines, television, and radio are very influential, since they decide what news gets reported and how it is reported.

Public Opinion. Since the United States is a democracy, Congress and the President are very sensitive to public opinion.

HOW TO EVALUATE FOREIGN POLICY

To evaluate or discuss a particular foreign policy, you must decide whether the best means were chosen to achieve a particular goal. To illustrate how this is done, let us examine the **Cuban Missile Crisis,** which threatened Americans in the early 1960s.

STEP 1: WHAT IS THE GOAL?

The first step is to determine the immediate objective or goal of the policy or action. Usually the objective will be related to one of the foreign policy goals discussed on page 211.

Background: The Cuban Missile Crisis, October 1962

An American spy plane observed Soviet technicians building missile launch sites in Cuba. President Kennedy was told that missiles being shipped to Cuba could be activated in a few days . Kennedy sought to have the missiles removed before they could be used to threaten the United States.

Goal: National security by protecting the nation against a nuclear attack.

STEP 2: WHAT ARE THE ALTERNATIVES?

The second step is to examine the various choices that are open in order to achieve a goal or objective. In examining alternatives in foreign policy, there are always two extremes: fight to obtain your objective, or simply do nothing. Between these two extremes there are usually many other options.

Alternatives: The Cuban Missile Crisis, October 1962

Kennedy and his advisors had a number of options:

❑ *The United States could use nuclear weapons against Cuba.*
❑ *U.S. armed forces could invade Cuba.*
❑ *U.S. jet bombers could destroy the missile sites.*
❑ *The United States could impose a naval blockade.*
❑ *The United States could appeal to the United Nations for help.*
❑ *The United States could do nothing.*

❑ *Any Other Alternatives?_____*

STEP 3: WAS THE BEST CHOICE ACTUALLY MADE?

In the final step, you should evaluate the choice actually selected by the decision-makers. Was this the best option among the various alternatives? Did it succeed in obtaining the goal? Did the policy assume any unnecessary risks or dangers?

Evaluation: The Cuban Missile Crisis, October 1962

Kennedy decided on a naval blockade of Cuba, preventing further Soviet shipments of missiles. He also threatened Cuba with a full-scale invasion if the missiles were not removed. In return, the United States offered to withdraw some of its missiles aimed at the Soviet Union and promised never to invade Cuba. Kennedy's naval blockade and threatened invasion, combined with the offer of concessions, convinced Soviet leaders to withdraw the missiles from Cuba. Although the objective was achieved, some critics claim the risk of nuclear war assumed by Kennedy was too great.

ANSWERING A FOREIGN POLICY QUESTION

Throughout American history, our national government has followed a variety of foreign policies in its relations with other nations. On the Regents Examination, you may be asked about one or more of these policies on a multiple-choice, thematic essay, or document-based essay question. To help you answer such questions, you will find references to foreign policy throughout this book and a comprehensive chart at the back of the book summarizing U.S. foreign policy milestones.

PEACE IN PERIL, 1920–1941

Americans became disillusioned with involvement in foreign affairs following World War I. This disillusionment had a profound impact on U.S. relations with other nations in the 1920s and 1930s.

A RETURN TO ISOLATIONISM

In the 1920s, Americans returned to their traditional policy of isolation from European affairs. Americans became more concerned with events at home than abroad. They felt safe behind the oceans separating them from Europe and Asia. This isolationism revealed itself in several ways:

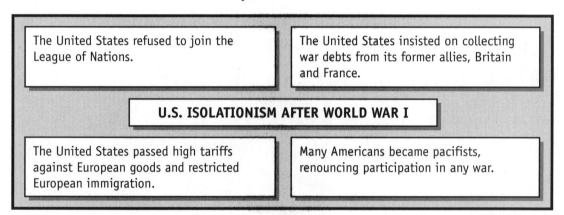

The United States refused to join the League of Nations.

The United States insisted on collecting war debts from its former allies, Britain and France.

U.S. ISOLATIONISM AFTER WORLD WAR I

The United States passed high tariffs against European goods and restricted European immigration.

Many Americans became pacifists, renouncing participation in any war.

THE UNITED STATES AND INTERNATIONAL AGREEMENTS

There were some exceptions to the trend towards isolationism. In 1921, the United States hosted the **Washington Naval Conference,** in which leading world powers agreed to limit the size of their navies. In 1928, the United States also promoted the **Kellogg-Briand Peace Pact,** signed by 62 nations, renouncing the use of war. In addition, between 1923 and 1930, American bankers lent funds to Germany to help it cover its reparation payments to Britain and France. In 1930, this help was withdrawn because of the Great Depression.

THE UNITED STATES AND LATIN AMERICA

Presidents Herbert Hoover and Franklin D. Roosevelt rejected Theodore Roosevelt's "Big Stick" policy and tried to improve relations with Latin America. Under the **"Good Neighbor Policy,"** the United States agreed not to interfere in the internal affairs of Latin America, and relations between the U.S. and Latin America began to improve.

THE ORIGINS OF WORLD WAR II IN EUROPE

Meanwhile, new political parties like the Italian Fascists and German National Socialists (*Nazis*) took advantage of feelings of intense nationalism and racism in Europe. The spread of the Great Depression in the early 1930s brought the Nazi leader **Adolf Hitler** to power in Germany. Hitler was determined to achieve German domination of Europe. Nazi aggression was the underlying cause behind the outbreak of World War II.

THE FAILURE OF THE LEAGUE OF NATIONS

The League of Nations, charged with the responsibility of preventing another war, proved powerless against the Fascist dictators. The idea of **collective security** — that peaceful nations would band together to stop aggressors — failed when major countries like the United States and the Soviet Union failed to become members of the League. Germany and Japan left the League in the 1930s.

APPEASEMENT FAILS: THE MUNICH CONFERENCE, 1938

German soldiers march into Austria in 1938

In 1938, Hitler annexed Austria. Next, he demanded the **Sudetenland** — a part of Czechoslovakia. At first, France and Britain promised to protect Czechoslovakia, but when Hitler threatened war, they backed down. At the **Munich Conference,** British and French leaders agreed to give Hitler a part of Czechoslovakia in order to avoid war. This policy of giving in to satisfy the demands of a potential enemy is known as **appeasement.** The appeasement policy failed, since it only encouraged Hitler to make further demands.

WORLD WAR II BEGINS: GERMANY INVADES POLAND

In 1939, Hitler made new territorial demands in Poland. Fearing that Hitler intended to dominate Europe, Britain and France refused to give in. Hitler responded by signing a treaty with the Soviet dictator Joseph Stalin, in which the two agreed to divide Poland. When Germany invaded Poland in 1939, Britain and France declared war on Germany, beginning World War II.

A Good Time for Reflection

WORLD WAR REMINDERS
AMERICAN CASUALTIES
·
UNPAID WAR DEBTS
·
ECONOMIC COLLAPSE

EUROPE

As this 1938 cartoon illustrates, as the threat of another European war loomed, Americans became increasingly critical of any future involvement.

AMERICA PRESERVES A CAUTIOUS NEUTRALITY

In the early 1930s, Americans were too absorbed with the Great Depression to become very involved in world affairs. A Senate investigation, the **Nye Commission,** revealed that a few individuals had profited greatly from American involvement in World War I. This helped to harden public opinion against new involvement in Europe.

THE NEUTRALITY ACTS, 1935–1937

As tensions rose in Europe, Congress passed a series of acts to keep the country out of war. America had been drawn into World War I when German submarines attacked American ships. To avoid similar events, the **Neutrality Acts** prohibited Americans from traveling on the ships of nations at war or from selling arms to countries at war. Americans could sell non-military goods, but only on a **"cash-and-carry"** basis. Congress later allowed Americans to sell arms to Britain and France, but only for cash payments and if the goods were carried on Allied ships.

AMERICA PREPARES FOR WAR

When Japan invaded China in 1937, President Roosevelt gave his **Quarantine Speech.** He said that peaceful nations had to act together to quarantine aggressive nations or aggression would spread. Most Americans remained opposed to any U.S. military action. When Germany invaded Poland, most Americans were willing to help the Allies, but only with measures short of war. Americans hoped to avoid war, but began preparing just in case. Congress increased spending on the army and navy. In 1940, Congress enacted the first peacetime draft. All men between the ages of 21 and 35 had to register and be eligible for one year of military service.

THE LEND-LEASE ACT, 1941

By the end of 1940, Britain stood alone against Nazi aggression. Roosevelt proposed the **Lend-Lease Act** to sell, lease, or lend war materials to "any country whose defense the President deems vital to the defense of the United States." Congress approved funds for ships, tanks, planes and other weapons. Under this act, the United States gave more than $50 million to Britain. American battleships began protecting British ships crossing the Atlantic. Critics feared the program might drag the country into the war. Most Americans, however, supported helping the British.

THE ATLANTIC CHARTER

In 1941, Roosevelt told Americans he hoped to establish a world based on **"Four Freedoms":** freedom of speech, freedom of religion, freedom from want, and freedom from fear. Later that year, Roosevelt met with British Prime Minister **Winston Churchill** aboard a warship in the Atlantic to discuss their common objectives for a postwar world. Roosevelt and Churchill announced that their

The Atlantic Charter Conference

Franklin D. Roosevelt Presidential Library

countries sought no territorial gains, and stood for freedom of the seas, and an end to war. They signed the **Atlantic Charter,** laying the foundation for the United Nations.

THE UNITED STATES ENTERS WORLD WAR II

President Roosevelt believed U.S. entry in the war was inevitable. In 1941, armed American merchant ships were authorized to carry supplies directly to Britain. It seemed that U.S. involvement in the war was just a matter of time.

INCREASING U.S. – JAPANESE TENSIONS

Surprisingly, events in East Asia, not Europe, finally brought the United States into the war. In 1937, Japan had gone to war with China. When Japan occupied Southern Indochina in 1941, Roosevelt reacted by freezing Japanese assets in the United States and cutting off all trade with Japan. Roosevelt offered to resume trade only if Japan withdrew from China and Indochina. Japan refused.

JAPAN PREPARES A SURPRISE ATTACK

Japanese military leaders decided to attack Indonesia to obtain oil for their war effort. Realizing such a move would bring America into the war, they decided to attack first. Japanese leaders believed a surprise attack would catch the Americans unprepared, eliminating U.S. naval power in the Pacific, and allowing Japan to fortify its position. Japanese leaders believed that Americans

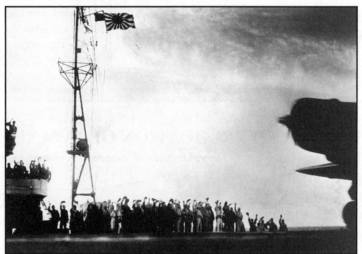

Japanese pilots receive encouragement as they take off to attack Pearl Harbor

National Archives

would soon tire of the war and negotiate a compromise peace — leaving Japan in control of East Asia. On the morning of December 7, 1941, Japanese airplanes attacked the U.S. Pacific fleet stationed in **Pearl Harbor,** Hawaii.

THE UNITED STATES AT WAR, 1941–1945

The day after the attack on Pearl Harbor, President Roosevelt asked Congress to declare war on Japan. Four days later, Germany and Italy, allies of Japan, declared war on America. Americans were now engaged in a war on two fronts — the Atlantic and Pacific.

THE HOME FRONT

The U.S. government now faced the giant task of mobilizing American manpower and production to meet its enormous wartime needs.

The Draft. All men between 18 and 45 were liable for military service. For the first time, women could also enlist. One million African Americans served, although forced to serve in segregated units. One out of ten Americans served at some point in the war.

Wartime Production. Special advisory boards managed the war economy. They instituted rationing to control the use of raw materials and provide for the conversion of factories to wartime production. Essential goods like gasoline were rationed.

THE WAR EFFORT AT HOME

The Labor Force. The draft and the expansion of production finally ended the Great Depression. Women, African Americans, and other minorities filled the gap as other workers went to war.

Paying For the War. The war cost $350 billion—ten times the cost of World War I. Americans bought war bonds to finance the war. The United States changed from a creditor to a debtor nation.

THE FORCED RELOCATION OF JAPANESE AMERICANS

The attack on Pearl Harbor created fear among many Americans, especially along the West coast, that Japanese Americans might commit acts of sabotage. These fears seemed racially motivated, since there was no evidence that Japanese Americans were disloyal. Nonethe-

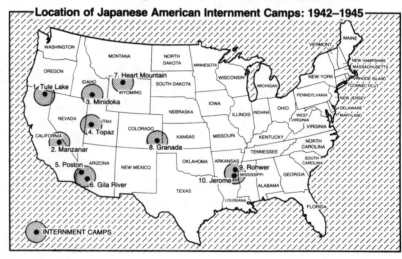

Location of Japanese American Internment Camps: 1942–1945

less, Roosevelt issued an Executive Order forcing Japanese Americans to relocate to internment camps. In the camps, they lived in primitive and crowded conditions. Roosevelt justified these measures as a military necessity. The Supreme Court upheld these relocations in *Korematsu v. U.S.*

KEY COURT CASES: KOREMATSU v. UNITED STATES (1944)

Korematsu was a Japanese American convicted of continuing to remain in a restricted area. He believed his constitutional rights had been violated. The Supreme Court upheld Roosevelt's order on the grounds that constitutional liberties may be limited in wartime.

THE WAR AGAINST GERMANY

Roosevelt decided to focus American energies on defeating Germany first. By the time the United States entered the war, Hitler controlled most of Europe and North Africa.

THE WAR IN EUROPE

Hitler made his greatest mistake when he both invaded the Soviet Union and declared war on the United States before defeating Britain. By late 1941, the German advance into the Soviet Union was stopped just short of Moscow. Roosevelt and Churchill promised Stalin they would open a second front against Germany in the West, to relieve pressure on the Soviet army. Late in 1942, Allied troops landed in North Africa. After defeating German forces there, the Allies advanced to Sicily

and Italy in 1943-1944. Meanwhile, Soviet forces defeated the German army at Stalingrad and advanced toward Germany.

THE COLLAPSE OF NAZI GERMANY

On June 6, 1944 — "**D-Day**" — Allied troops landed in France. They moved eastward, liberating Paris and reaching the German border. American, British, and Free French forces then invaded Germany from the west, while Soviet forces invaded from the east. In May 1945, Germany surrendered.

THE WAR AGAINST JAPAN

In these same years, Americans also remained at war with Japan. At first, the Japanese made significant gains in Asia and the Pacific while Americans rebuilt their navy and fought Nazi Germany. Japan invaded and occupied the Philippines, Hong Kong, Borneo, the Solomon Islands, Java, and Singapore. In 1943, the tide began to turn. The United States regained naval superiority in the Pacific, and American forces began "island-hopping," liberating Pacific islands from Japanese control one at a time.

THE INFLUENCE OF GEOGRAPHY ON AMERICAN HISTORY

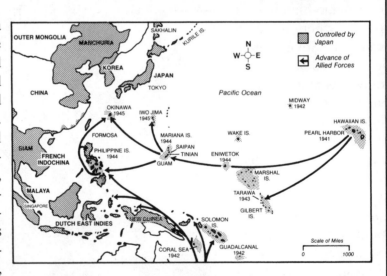

Geography played a critical role in the Pacific during World War II. The U.S. and Japan were separated by the Pacific Ocean. After attacking Pearl Harbor, Japan over-ran Malaya, Burma, Indonesia, the Philippines, and the Western Pacific Islands thus threatening Australia, India, Midway, and Hawaii. The Japanese attempted to use their control of the western Pacific as a cover to fortify their vast new empire. The Americans, who could decipher the Japanese codes, knew to attack the Japanese navy at Midway. The Americans then halted the Japanese advance, draining Japanese resources through a series of assaults on Pacific islands. This campaign nevertheless delayed the Allied assault on Germany. It was not until June 1944 that U.S. forces captured islands close enough to Japan to use as bases to attack the Japanese home islands.

THE DECISION TO USE THE ATOMIC BOMB

Albert Einstein, a famous German Jewish scientist who had emigrated to America, sent a letter persuading Roosevelt to develop an atomic bomb before the Nazis did. American scientists were sent to New Mexico, where they developed and exploded the world's first atomic bomb in 1945. By then, Germany was defeated, and America was preparing to invade Japan. President Roosevelt died of a stroke just before the end of the war. His successor, **President Harry Truman,** feared that an invasion might lead to a million American casualties. Truman preferred to use the atomic bomb against Japan rather than to sustain such high losses. Truman selected targets that were centers of Japanese military production. On August 6, an atomic bomb was exploded over **Hiroshima.** Three days later, a second bomb was exploded over **Nagasaki.** About 100,000 people were killed in each explosion. Japan surrendered shortly after the second explosion, when American leaders agreed to allow the Japanese emperor to remain on his throne.

THE LEGACY OF WORLD WAR II

World War II was a global disaster of unprecedented dimensions. Over 50 million people lost their lives. Much of Europe, Africa, and Asia lay in ruins.

THE NUREMBERG TRIALS, 1945–1946

During the war, Hitler had murdered millions of European Jews and other targets of Nazi hate in the **Holocaust.** The liberation of concentration camps in Europe revealed the full extent of Nazi brutality. The Allies put surviving Nazi leaders on trial for "crimes against humanity" in Nuremberg, Germany. Those on trial defended themselves by claiming they had only been following orders.

Nazi leaders stand trial at Nuremberg

Many were found guilty of committing **atrocities** and were hanged or imprisoned. The **Nuremberg Trials** demonstrated that individuals are responsible for their actions, even in times of war.

"DENAZIFICATION" AND THE DIVISION OF GERMANY

After the war, Germany was divided into four zones by the United States, Britain, France, and the Soviet Union. Each power occupied one zone. The occupying powers introduced programs explaining the evils of Nazi beliefs to the German people.

THE OCCUPATION OF JAPAN

General **Douglas Mac-Arthur,** Supreme Commander of Allied forces in the Pacific, was assigned the task of rebuilding and reforming post-war Japan. Under his leadership, important changes were introduced to make Japan less aggressive. Japan's overseas empire was taken away, and her military leaders were put on trial and punished. Japan renounced the use of nuclear weapons and the waging of war. Japan was

General MacArthur (at microphone) accepts Japan's surrender aboard the U.S.S. Missouri

Library of Congress

prohibited from having a large army or navy. A new constitution went into effect in 1947, turning Japan into a democracy.

THE RISE OF NEW SUPERPOWERS

The end of World War II left the United States and the Soviet Union as two **superpowers** in command of the world. The United States had tremendous economic power and control of the atomic bomb; the Soviet Union had the world's large army, which occupied most of Eastern Europe.

THE START OF THE COLD WAR, 1945–1960

Although allies during the war, these two superpowers soon became rivals in a **"Cold War."** The war was "cold" only in the sense that, because of nuclear weapons, the two superpowers never confronted one another directly in open warfare. However, their global competition led to frequent conflicts on every continent.

THE ROOTS OF THE COLD WAR

The roots of the Cold War lay in the competing ideological systems of the United States and the Soviet Union. The United States wanted to spread its democratic capitalist system, while the Soviet Union wanted to spread its system of **Communism.** It was inevitable that these two Superpowers would clash.

The Communist system was based on the ideas of **Karl Marx.** The Soviet Union became the world's first Communist state in 1917. Some of Communism's most important ideas were the following:

STAGES OF DEVELOPMENT IN COMMUNIST THEORY

Class Struggle. In non-Communist societies, landowners and businessmen (*capitalists*) use their wealth to take advantage of workers by taking most of what the workers produce. This conflict of interest leads to a class struggle.

Violent Revolution. The conditions of workers grow increasingly worse. In an attempt to correct these injustices, workers are driven to overthrow their capitalist rulers in a violent revolution.

Dictatorship of the Workers. After the revolution, Communist leaders establish a dictatorship to educate people in Communist ideas. This dictatorship is run for the workers' benefit.

The New Communist Society. Gradually, a new Communist society is created in which private property is eliminated and everyone works for the good of society. Each contributes according to his or her abilities and receives from society according to his or her needs.

THE YALTA AND POTSDAM CONFERENCES

In February 1945, Roosevelt, Churchill, and Stalin met at Yalta to plan for the reorganization of Europe at the end of the war. At the **Yalta Conference** they agreed on the formation of the United Nations, and that Germany would be divided into separate occupation zones. Finally, the three leaders agreed to create democratic governments and to allow free elections in the countries they had liberated from German rule. In particular, Stalin pledged to allow free elections in Poland after the war. However, when Truman met with Stalin at the **Potsdam Conference** in Germany in the summer of 1945, serious differences emerged over the future of Eastern Europe.

THE COLD WAR BEGINS

When Stalin refused to allow elections in Poland and the United States refused to share the secrets behind the atomic bomb, the "Cold War" began in earnest. The Soviet army continued to occupy Eastern Europe. The Soviets placed Communists in power in all the governments of Eastern Europe. Trade and contact between Eastern and Western Europe was cut off. An **Iron Curtain** fell over Eastern Europe, closing it off from the West. Over the next forty years, travel and contact between the East and West was limited, and Eastern European governments became "satellites" of the Soviet Union.

THE POLICY OF CONTAINMENT IN EUROPE

American leaders responded to the Soviet domination of Eastern Europe by developing the policy of **containment.** They attempted to avoid the mistakes of the appeasement of Hitler in the 1930s by reacting firmly against every attempt to spread Communist influence. Under this policy, American leaders would not attempt to overturn Communism where it already existed, but resolved to prevent it from spreading to new areas.

THE TRUMAN DOCTRINE

In 1947, when Communist rebels threatened the governments of Greece and Turkey, President Truman gave these countries military aid. To win public support, Truman turned this into a moral crusade. In his speech to Congress, Truman promised American support to any country fighting Communism. This declaration, known as the **Truman Doctrine,** marked the beginning of America's containment policy.

President Harry Truman

THE MARSHALL PLAN, 1948

Truman believed people were attracted to Communism when they were desperate and miserable. Secretary of State **George Marshall** proposed that massive aid be given to wartorn Europe to rebuild their economies and limit the spread of Communism. Marshall believed this aid would create strong European allies and trading partners for the United States, and avoid the chaos that followed World War I. The **Marshall Plan** succeeded in speeding the economic recovery of Western Europe and creating good will towards the United States.

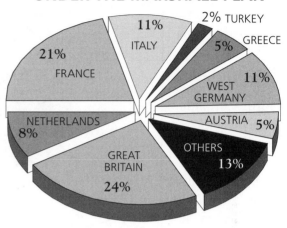

DISTRIBUTION OF AID UNDER THE MARSHALL PLAN

THE DIVISION OF GERMANY AND THE BERLIN AIRLIFT, 1948

In 1948, the French, British, and Americans decided to merge their zones into a single West German state. Berlin, the old capital of Germany, was in the Soviet zone. It had also been divided into four sectors, each occupied by a different power. The Soviets reacted to the merging of the Western zones by closing all highway and railroad links to West Berlin. The Western Allies refused to abandon Berlin, and began a massive airlift to feed and supply the city. Within a

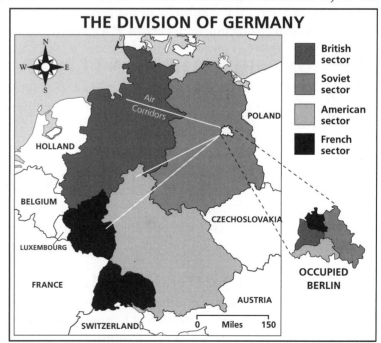

THE DIVISION OF GERMANY

year, Stalin lifted the blockade. However, over the next 15 years, the Soviets placed renewed pressure on Berlin whenever a crisis flared up.

THE FORMATION OF NATO AND THE WARSAW PACT

In response to Cold War tensions, the U.S., Canada, and ten Western European countries formed the North Atlantic Treaty Organization (**NATO**) in 1949 to protect against Communism. NATO was based on the concept of **collective security**

— each member pledged to defend every other member if attacked. Through NATO, the United States extended its umbrella of nuclear protection to Western Europe. The Soviet Union responded by creating the **Warsaw Pact** with its Eastern European satellites in 1955.

FRICTION BEHIND THE IRON CURTAIN

Although the U.S. condemned Soviet force, it never intervened behind the Iron Curtain. Soviet leaders successfully suppressed an anti-Communist revolution in Hungary in 1956, erected the Berlin Wall in 1961 to prevent East Germans from escaping to the West, and invaded Czechoslovakia in 1968 to overthrow a reform government.

CONTAINMENT IN ASIA

Just when the U.S. believed it had checked the spread of Communism in Europe, China, turned Communist in Asia. This raised the question: could American leaders check the spread of Communism, not only in Europe, but everywhere on the globe?

CHINA FALLS TO COMMUNISM, 1949

Since the 1920s, Chinese Communists had sought to overthrow the Nationalist government in China. The two groups had temporarily united during World War II against the Japanese invaders. In 1949, the Communists, led by **Mao Zedong,** defeated the Nationalist government. Nationalist leaders fled to the island of Taiwan. Now fully in control of China, Mao proceeded to create the world's largest Communist state.

President Truman denied diplomatic recognition to the Communist government in China. Using its veto power in the United Nations, the United States prevented admission of Mao's China to the United Nations. Truman also pledged to protect the Nationalist government on Taiwan from Communist attack.

THE KOREAN WAR, 1950–1953

Many Americans complained that the United States had not done enough to prevent the fall of China to Communism. This criticism of U.S. foreign policy affected America's actions at the time of the outbreak of the Korean War.

★ **The War Begins.** After World War II, Korea had been divided into two zones: in North Korea, the Soviet zone, a Communist government was established; South Korea elected a non-Communist government. In 1950, North Korea invaded South Korea to unify the country under Communist rule. Truman saw this as parallel to Nazi aggression and ordered U.S. forces into South Korea to resist the invasion. Since the Soviet Union was boycotting the United Nations at the time, the United States was also able to pass a resolution sending U.N. troops to South Korea. This action marked the first time an international peacekeeping organization used military force to oppose aggression.

MAP 1

A: North Koreans attack, June 25, 1950
B: North Koreans advance, Sept. 1950
C: U.N. landing at Inchon, Sept. 15, 1950
D: U.N. advance, October 27, 1950

MAP 2

E: Chinese advance, Nov. 1950
F: Chinese advance, Jan. 1951
G: Armistice line, July 27, 1953

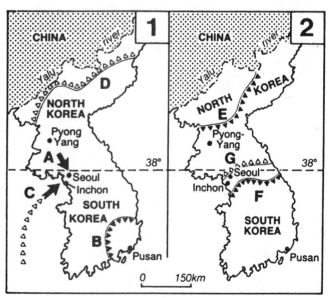

★ **The Truman-MacArthur Controversy.** Truman sent General Douglas MacArthur to Korea to command U.N. forces. MacArthur landed his forces at Inchon and then attacked North Korea, advancing to the border between North Korea and China. This brought a large Chinese army into the war, forcing MacArthur to retreat. MacArthur wanted to recapture China from the Communists, by using atomic weapons if necessary. When Truman failed to agree, MacArthur publicly criticized Truman. Truman dismissed MacArthur from his command, successfully asserting civilian control over the military.

★ **The War Ends.** In 1952, **Dwight Eisenhower,** former Allied commander on D-Day, was elected President after pledging that he would end the war in Korea. An armistice was signed in 1953, ending the war. It left Korea divided exactly as it had been before the North Korean invasion.

THE NUCLEAR ARMS RACE BEGINS

In 1945, America was the sole atomic power. However, by 1949 the Soviet Union had developed its own atomic bomb, initiating a nuclear arms race. In 1952, the United States developed the hydrogen bomb, vastly more powerful than the atomic bomb. The Soviet Union exploded its first hydrogen bomb a year later, showing that the technology gap between the two superpowers was narrowing.

MASSIVE RETALIATION

American leaders in the 1950s decided to rely more on nuclear weapons for defense than on a large military force. These nuclear weapons acted as a **deterrent** — the Soviets would be *deterred* from attacking because if they did, the United States would destroy them with its nuclear weapons. The threat of massive retaliation was cheaper than a large military force, but was also less flexible. American leaders soon realized that in most situations nuclear weapons could not be used. Mass destruction could only be justified if the nation's survival was at stake.

MAJOR U.S. AND SOVIET MISSILE SITES

SOVIET UNION

NORTH + POLE

CANADA

EUROPE

UNITED STATES

AFRICA

Intercontinental Ballistic Missile sites

THE SOVIETS LAUNCH SPUTNIK, 1957

In 1957, the Soviet Union launched **Sputnik,** the first man-made satellite, into space. This not only marked the start of the "**Space Race,**" but also had tremendous military significance. With space missiles, the Soviet Union had the ability to send nuclear weapons to the United States. This prompted the United States to launch its own first man-made satellite into space in 1958 and to increase missile production.

EFFECTS OF THE COLD WAR ON U.S. SECURITY

As the Cold War grew more intense, Americans became ever more concerned with their internal security.

THE HOUSE UN-AMERICAN ACTIVITIES COMMITTEE

Following World War II, Americans were concerned about a possible Communist threat within the United States. President Truman ordered the establishment of **Loyalty Review Boards** to investigate individual "un-American" acts, such as participation in extremist organizations like the American Communist Party. On very little evidence, many people were accused of "un-American" acts. These unfortunate targets were prevented from defending themselves or even from knowing who accused them — serious violations of their constitutional rights. Congress conducted its own loyalty checks through the **House Un-American Activities Committee.** The Committee questioned actors, directors and writers, among others, about possible Communist sympathies.

THE ROSENBERG TRIALS

In 1950, **Julius and Ethel Rosenberg** were charged with selling secret information to the Soviet Union about the atomic bomb. The Rosenbergs were tried, found guilty, and executed for spying. Like the Sacco and Vanzetti case in the 1920s, many Americans had serious doubts about the Rosenbergs' guilt.

THE McCARTHY HEARINGS

In 1950, Senator **Joseph McCarthy** shocked the nation by claiming that he knew the names of hundreds of Communists who had infiltrated the U.S. State Department. Although McCarthy never proved any of his claims, his charges frightened most Americans. McCarthy was finally discredited when he had no evidence. The term **"McCarthyism"** has become identified with making wild accusations without evidence. Like the Red Scare of the 1920s, McCarthy's allegations created fears of a domestic Communist conspiracy.

National Archives

SUMMARIZING YOUR UNDERSTANDING

KEY TERMS, CONCEPTS, AND PEOPLE

Make a vocabulary card for each of the following terms, concepts, and people.

Good Neighbor Policy	D-Day	Iron Curtain
Appeasement	*Korematsu v. U.S.*	Cold War
Neutrality Acts	Nuremberg Trials	NATO
Lend-Lease Acts	United Nations	Korean War
Atlantic Charter	Truman Doctrine	Douglas MacArthur
Pearl Harbor	Marshall Plan	McCarthyism

COMPLETING A TABLE

Briefly describe each of the following conflicts involving the United States.

War	Causes	Major Results
World War II		
Cold War		
Korean War		

COMPLETING A GRAPHIC ORGANIZER

Briefly describe each of the following foreign policies discussed in this chapter.

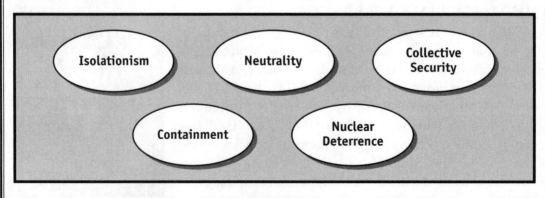

TESTING YOUR UNDERSTANDING

MULTIPLE-CHOICE QUESTIONS

1   Throughout our nation's history, the main aim of American foreign policy has been
 1   participation in international organizations
 2   advancement of the national interest
 3   containment of Communism
 4   participation in military alliances

2   Which was an example of appeasement?
 1   the Neutrality Acts of 1935 and 1937
 2   the conquest of Poland in 1939
 3   the agreement to give Germany the Sudetenland in 1938
 4   American entry into World War II

Base your answer to question 3 on the map below and your knowledge of social studies.

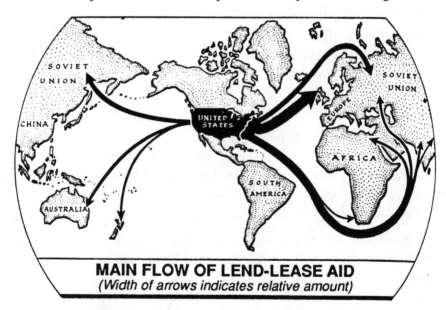

MAIN FLOW OF LEND-LEASE AID
(Width of arrows indicates relative amount)

3   The aid shown on the map was provided as part of the U.S. effort to
 1   help the Allies fight the Axis powers
 2   persuade other nations to join the United Nations
 3   provide technical assistance to developing nations
 4   force other nations to pay their debts to the United States

4 Between World War I and World War II, the United States followed a policy of
1   isolation from European military conflicts
2   containment of Communism
3   active membership in the League of Nations
4   military alliances with France and Great Britain

5 Which description best characterizes world politics in the periods immediately before the outbreaks of both World Wars I and II?
1   a division into armed alliances
2   increasing Communist influence
3   increased acts of aggression by Western democracies
4   a decline in the extent of European imperialism

6 Which group of American citizens was subject to the greatest loss of constitutional rights during a period of U.S. military involvement?
1   Hispanic Americans during the Spanish-American War
2   German Americans during World War I
3   Japanese Americans during World War II
4   Chinese Americans during the Korean conflict

7 The bombing of Hiroshima and Nagasaki resulted in
1   the outbreak of World War II
2   U.S. entry into the war against Japan
3   the surrender of Japan
4   a decrease in the spread of Communism

8 Which was a major result of World War II?
1   Great Britain and France helped rebuild the Soviet Union.
2   A Cold War began between the United States and Soviet Union.
3   Germany gained control of Eastern Europe.
4   Italy was divided into two countries.

9 The decisions of *Dred Scott v. Sandford*, *Plessy v. Ferguson*, and *Korematsu v. United States* all demonstrate that the Supreme Court has
1   continued to extend voting rights to minorities
2   frequently protected itself from internal dissent
3   sometimes failed to protect the rights of minorities
4   often imposed restrictions on free speech during wartime

10 Which was a fundamental principle expressed by the war crimes tribunal at Nuremberg following World War II?

   1   National leaders are responsible for their wartime actions.

   2   National policies during wartime cannot be criticized after a war.

   3   Persons acting in the national interest cannot be prosecuted.

   4   The use of nuclear weapons can never be justified.

11 How did the personal diplomacy conducted by President Roosevelt during World War II affect the Presidency?

   1   Subsequent Presidents refused to use this method.

   2   The President's role in shaping U.S. foreign policy was strengthened.

   3   The President's war powers as Commander in Chief were reduced.

   4   Congress was able to increase its power over the executive branch.

12 After World War II, the United States was better able than its allies to adjust its economy from wartime to peacetime because the United States

   1   possessed nuclear weapons

   2   raised tariffs on imports

   3   had collected all its war debts immediately after the war

   4   had suffered less wartime destruction

13 The term "Cold War" refers to

   1   U.S. neutrality in the early years of World War II

   2   Prime Minister Chamberlain's attempts to appease Hitler

   3   the border dispute between the Soviet Union and Communist China

   4   a period of hostility between the United States and Soviet Union

14 Which is a governmental action consistent with the "Cold War" mentality?

   1   establishing Loyalty Review Boards   3   eliminating the C.I.A.

   2   reducing military spending   4   adopting the G.I. Bill of Rights

15 U.S. economic aid to Western Europe after World War II was mainly intended to

   1   create a tariff-free Common Market

   2   provide the United States with badly needed raw materials

   3   unify Europe under U.S. leadership

   4   make European nations more resistant to Communism

16 A study of the Red Scare (1920s) and McCarthyism (1950s) best shows that

   1   many Communists have infiltrated the federal government

   2   fears of subversion can lead to the erosion of constitutional rights

   3   Communism gains influence in times of economic recession

   4   loyalty oaths by government employees prevent espionage

17 General Douglas MacArthur was relieved of his command during the Korean War because he
1   threatened the principle of civilian control over the military
2   ordered the use of nuclear weapons against China
3   refused to follow a Presidential order to invade China
4   failed to unify North and South Korea into one nation

18 In the late 1940s, an American statesman made the following observation:

> "There is nothing [the Soviets] admire so much as strength, and there is nothing for which they have less respect than for weakness, especially military weakness."

This perception of the Soviet Union by U.S. leaders contributed most to the creation of the
1   Lend-Lease Program
2   United Nations
3   North Atlantic Treaty Organization
4   War Mobilization Board

INTERPRETING DOCUMENTS

"Korematsu was not excluded because of hostility to him or his race. [Our] military authorities feared an invasion of our West Coast and felt it necessary to take proper security measures. There was evidence of disloyalty on the part of some, the military authorities considered that the need for action was great, and time was short. We cannot now say that these actions were unjustified."

— Justice Hugo Black delivering the majority opinion in *Korematsu v. U.S.*

"Racial discrimination in any form has no part in our democratic way of life. All residents of this nation are kin in some way by blood or culture to a foreign land. Yet they are primarily a part of the United States [and are] entitled to all rights and freedoms guaranteed by the Constitution."

— Justice Frank Murphy delivering the minority opinion in *Korematsu v. U.S.*

Briefly state the main point expressed by each opinion:

• Justice Black: _____

• Justice Murphy: _____

THEMATIC ESSAY QUESTION

Directions: Write a well-organized essay that includes an introduction, several paragraphs addressing the task below, and a conclusion.

Theme: Political Systems

The U.S. has pursued a variety of foreign policies to advance its interests.

Task:

Choose **two** foreign policies from your study of American History.

For *each* foreign policy:
- Describe the foreign policy identified.
- Describe an action taken by the United States in pursuit of that foreign policy goal.

You may use any example from your study of U.S. history and government. Some suggestions you might wish to consider include: purchase of the Louisiana Territory (1803), declaring war on Spain (1898), acquisition of colonies during the Progressive Era, the building of the Panama Canal (1903), entry into World War I (1917), and entry into World War II (1941).

You are *not* limited to these suggestions.

DOCUMENT-BASED ESSAY QUESTION

Directions: Read the documents in Part A and answer the questions after each document. Then read the directions for Part B and write your essay.

Historical Context:

The federal government's power over American society expanded tremendously in the first half of the twentieth century. While some have applauded this development, others have viewed the growth of federal power suspiciously.

Task:

Evaluate the expansion of federal power in the early twentieth century by comparing its advantages and disadvantages.

PART A
Short Answer

Directions: Analyze the documents and answer the questions that follow each document.

DOCUMENT 1

Act	Description
Pure Food and Drug Act (1906)	Banned the manufacture and sale of impure foods and drugs, and required medicines to be truthfully labeled.
Federal Reserve Act (1914)	Established the Federal Reserve System to regulate the nation's currency supply.
Income Tax of 1913	First direct federal tax on citizen's incomes, permitted by the Sixteenth Amendment.
Federal Trade Act (1914)	Established the Federal Trade Commission to investigate unfair business practices.
Securities and Exchange Commission (1934)	Established the Securities Exchange Commission to regulate the stock market.
National Labor Relations Board (1935)	Established the National Labor Relations Board to enforce the right of workers to organize into unions.
Social Security Act (1935)	Provided workers with federal unemployment insurance and old age pensions paid for by a tax on payrolls.

1a. How did the Pure Food and Drug Act affect the power of the federal government?

_____

b. What trend about the role of government is revealed by this table? _____

_____

_____

DOCUMENT 2

> *"I insisted upon the theory that the executive power was limited only by specific restrictions and prohibitions in the Constitution or imposed by Congress. My view was that every executive officer in high position was a steward of the people. I refused to adopt the view that what was necessary for the nation could not be done by the President unless he could find some specific authorization to do it."*
>
> — Theodore Roosevelt, on Presidential power, 1913

2. What did Theodore Roosevelt see as the main limits on the expansion of Presidential power? _____

_____

DOCUMENT 3

"My view of the executive function is that the President can exercise no power which cannot be reasonably traced to some specific grant of power or implied and included as proper and necessary to its exercise. Such a specific grant must be either in the federal Constitution or an act of Congress. There is no undefined power which he can exercise simply because it seems to him to be in the public interest."

— Former President William Howard Taft, 1916

3. In what way did Taft view Presidential power as limited?_____

_____

DOCUMENT 4

"If somebody puts a derrick improperly on top of a building, then the government has the right to see that derrick is so secure that you can walk under it and not be afraid that it is going to fall. Likewise, it is the privilege of the government to see that human life is protected, that human lungs have something to breathe .... The first duty of law is to keep sound the society it serves."

— President Woodrow Wilson, 1916

4. Why did Wilson reject the idea of a laissez-faire role for government?_____

_____

DOCUMENT 5

"There are ... an additional 3.5 million people who are on relief. This group was the victim of a nationwide depression caused by conditions which were not local but national. The federal government is the only government with sufficient power and credit to meet this situation. We have assumed this task, and we shall not shrink from it. It is the duty of national policy to give employment to these 3.5 million people now on relief, pending their absorption by private employment."

— President Franklin D. Roosevelt, 1935

5. What did Franklin D. Roosevelt argue was the responsibility of the federal government in the face of widespread national unemployment? _____

_____

DOCUMENT 6

6. What is the cartoonist's view of Roosevelt's New Deal?

_____

_____

_____

_____

_____

Library of Congress

DOCUMENT 7

> "We have seen these gigantic expenditures and this torrent of waste pile up a national debt which two generations cannot repay. We have seen the increase of a horde of political officials. We have seen the pressures on the helpless and destitute to trade political support for relief. Both pollute foundations of liberty. There are some principles that cannot be compromised. Either we shall have a society based on liberty and the initiative of the individual, or we shall have a planned society that means dictation, no matter what you call it ."
>
> — President Herbert Hoover on the New Deal, 1936

7. Why did Hoover believe that the federal government was becoming dangerously powerful under the New Deal? _____

PART B - ESSAY

Directions: Write a well-organized essay that includes an introduction, several paragraphs and a conclusion. Use evidence from at least **four** documents in the body of the essay. Support your response with relevant facts, examples, and details. Include additional outside information.

> Using information from the documents and your knowledge of U.S. history and government, write an essay in which you:

- Describe the expansion of federal power in the early twentieth century.
- Evaluate this expansion of federal power by comparing its advantages and disadvantages.

CHAPTER 12

AMERICA IN UNCERTAIN TIMES

John F. Kennedy delivering his inaugural speech, January 20, 1961

J.F. Kennedy Presidential Library

TIMELINE OF IMPORTANT EVENTS

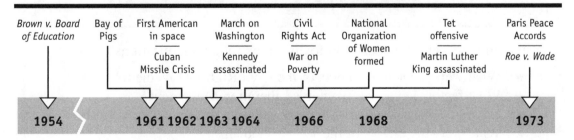

Brown v. Board of Education	Bay of Pigs	First American in space	March on Washington	Civil Rights Act	National Organization of Women formed	Tet offensive	Paris Peace Accords
		Cuban Missile Crisis	Kennedy assassinated	War on Poverty		Martin Luther King assassinated	*Roe v. Wade*

1954   1961 1962 1963 1964   1966   1968   1973

WHAT YOU SHOULD FOCUS ON

The 1950s and 1960s were times of prosperity and social reform. The Civil Rights Movement sought equality for African Americans; the Women's Liberation Movement helped achieve greater rights for women; Presidents Kennedy and Johnson introduced programs to help the poor; an activist Supreme Court enlarged individual rights. This reform period was brought to a close by the Vietnam War. In this chapter you will learn about:

Dr. Martin Luther King, Jr.

National Archives

★ **The Civil Rights Movement.** African Americans moved toward ending racial segregation in the public schools and other public places, and obtained equal civil rights. Their success helped inspire other minority groups and women.

★ **The Post-War Presidents.** President Kennedy introduced a new style to the Presidency, but was assassinated in 1963. President Johnson introduced Civil Rights legislation and "Great Society" programs to help the poor.

★ **The Sixties.** The 1960s saw a new rebelliousness among young people. Women demanded greater equality. There was a growing militancy among African Americans. The Supreme Court issued important rulings protecting individual rights.

★ **The War in Vietnam.** The United States became involved in defending the government of South Vietnam from Communist attack. Despite sending massive aid and half a million troops, the United States was unable to win the war. The Vietnam War was one of the most divisive conflicts in U.S. history.

In studying this period, you should focus on the following questions:

    ★ What were the achievements of the Civil Rights Movement?
    ★ What factors led to the Women's Liberation Movement?
    ★ How did Johnson's "Great Society" attempt to achieve social reform?
    ★ What were the effects of the war in Vietnam?

LOOKING AT OUR LEGAL SYSTEM

 mericans justly rejoice that they live under the rule of law — a system that protects each individual from impulsive acts by government or from unfair treatment by neighbors. This section reviews how our system of laws works.

WHAT IS LAW?

A **law** is a rule that tells people *to do* or *not to do* something. Usually there is a penalty for breaking the law. In the United States, there are several law-making bodies. The most familiar are legislatures — such as the U.S. Congress or the New York State Legislature. Executives can also issue orders which have the force of law. A Presidential order, for example, has legal authority. In addition, agencies sometimes make rules that have the binding power of law. For example, the Internal Revenue Service has the power to make rules with the force of law.

WHAT DO THE COURTS DO?

You have often heard that courts "apply" or "interpret" the law, but what does this mean? No rule can ever be so precise that it can foresee all the situations that might arise. For this reason, we need courts to apply the laws to specific situations to see whether or not particular circumstances fall within the rule.

> A sign reads, **"NO VEHICLES IN THE PARK."** We are certain this means no cars or trucks in the park, but what about bicycles? What about baby strollers and wheelchairs? Are they vehicles in the same sense intended by the sign?

As you can see, courts must interpret the words of a law to decide just what the law means. Sometimes they might want to consider the purpose of the rule to determine whether it applies to a particular situation or not. A court might say the purpose of the rule, **"NO VEHICLES IN THE PARK,"** is to avoid danger to pedestrians. Since wheelchairs and baby strollers pose no danger to pedestrians, they are not "vehicles" in the sense intended by the rule.

Because we live under the rule of law, we want all persons to be treated similarly. Courts look to the decisions of other courts to see how to treat particular cases. The opinions of judges therefore provide another source of law — known as the **common law.** Rules made by judges still control many areas of the law.

(continued)

In a court proceeding, each party has certain rights — the right to an attorney, the right to hear opposing evidence, the right to present its case, and the right to appeal the decision. A defendant also often has the right to have a case tried by a jury. The judge decides what evidence can be considered, and instructs the jury on the legal issues. These guarantees — known as "due process" rights — ensure that each side gets a fair opportunity to persuade the judge and jury.

OUR FEDERAL SYSTEM OF JUSTICE

In our federal system we have two levels of government: the state governments and the federal government. We also have two levels of courts: the state courts and the federal courts.

Trial courts at the state level can hear almost any kind of case. The federal courts, in contrast, are more limited. They can only try cases which involve federal law or which involve citizens from different states. When a trial court gives its verdict, the parties have the right to appeal the decision. An **appellate court** cannot overturn a trial court's decision on the basis of the facts, since it can only review the issues of law presented by the case. If the appellate court decides the trial court misapplied the law, it can overturn the decision.

THE ROLE OF THE SUPREME COURT

The U.S. Supreme Court operates as our highest "Court of Appeals." It hears appeals from both the federal and state courts. Because so many decisions are appealed to the Supreme Court, it is left up to the Supreme Court which appeals it will review.

The members of the Constitutional Convention debated whether the Supreme Court should review federal laws before they are passed to decide their constitutionality. They rejected this approach, believing it was better if the Court waited to hear real cases. Thus, the Court never decides the constitutionality of a law until an actual dispute arises and is appealed to the Supreme Court.

The Supreme Court plays two roles. First, it determines how an ordinary law should be applied to a case. Secondly, the Supreme Court also decides if that law is constitutional. The Supreme Court can reject a law passed by Congress if it feels the law violates the Constitution. The only way to override such a decision by the Court is to amend the Constitution.

AREAS OF GREATEST SUPREME COURT ACTIVITY

The Supreme Court has had its main impact in the following areas:

THE GROWTH OF FEDERAL POWER

Case	Importance of Decision
Judicial Review (Decisions establishing the power of the Court)	
Marbury v. Madison (1803)	The Supreme Court has the power to declare laws unconstitutional.
Commerce Power (Decisions regulating interstate commerce)	
Schechter Poultry v. U.S. (1935)	Early New Deal legislation interfering with intrastate business was unconstitutional.
The "Necessary and Proper" Clause	
McCulloch v. Maryland (1819)	Congress can exercise expanded powers on the basis of the "necessary and proper" clause.

INDIVIDUAL RIGHTS

Case	Importance of Decision
Free Speech (First Amendment)	
Schenck v. U.S. (1919)	An individual cannot exercise the right to free speech where it presents a "clear and present danger" to the public.
Rights of Criminal Defendants (4th, 5th, 6th, and 8th Amendments)	
Mapp v. Ohio (1961)	Evidence unlawfully seized in an unreasonable search by the police cannot be used in a court of law.
Gideon v. Wainwright (1963)	A state must provide a free lawyer to a defendant if he or she is too poor to afford one.
Miranda v. Arizona (1966)	A person in custody must be informed of his or her constitutional rights *before* being questioned.
Rights of Privacy (5th and 14th Amendments)	
Roe v. Wade (1973)	A woman has the right to an abortion in the first three months of her pregnancy.
Equal Protection of the Laws (5th and 14th Amendments)	
Plessy v. Ferguson (1896)	As long as a state government provided "separate but equal" facilities, it could practice racial segregation.
Korematsu v. U.S. (1944)	The President was justified in detaining Japanese-Americans in wartime.
Brown v. Board of Education (1954)	This decision overturned *Plessy* by holding that segregated public schools were "inherently unequal".

THE CIVIL RIGHTS MOVEMENT

One of the most important developments of the 1950s and 1960s was the struggle for equal rights by African Americans. The **Civil Rights Movement** was a major turning point in the history of American society. Women, other ethnic minorities, the disabled, and youths all followed the trail-blazing efforts of the Civil Rights Movement in making America a more open and pluralistic society.

ORIGINS OF THE CIVIL RIGHTS MOVEMENT

The United States had held out the promise of equality to African Americans at the end of the Civil War, but this promise was cut short in the aftermath of Reconstruction. Many Americans felt that the treatment received by African Americans was inconsistent with the ideals expressed in the Declaration of Independence and the Constitution. Indeed, it seemed ironic for America to pose as the defender of freedom throughout the world, while denying equality at home.

THE TRUMAN YEARS, 1945–1953

In 1947, **Jackie Robinson** became the first African-American baseball player to cross the "color line" and join the major leagues. Some states, like New York, passed laws outlawing discrimination in housing, employment, and the use of public services. In 1948, President Truman ordered the desegregation of the armed forces and an end to discriminatory hiring practices in the federal government.

BROWN v. BOARD OF EDUCATION, 1954

The Supreme Court's decision in *Brown* was central to the emergence of the Civil Rights Movement.

Jackie Robinson

Schomberg Center for Black Culture

★ **Background.** In *Plessy v. Ferguson* (1896), the Supreme Court had upheld the constitutionality of state segregation laws. Starting in the 1930s, NAACP lawyers began challenging this "separate-but-equal" doctrine. In 1953, they appealed a Kansas court ruling to the Supreme Court. A young African-American student had been denied admission to an all-white public school near her home.

The NAACP alleged that segregated public schools denied African-American children the "equal protection" of the law due to them under the Fourteenth Amendment. In addition, the NAACP argued that the education received by African-American students was inherently (*by its very nature*) inferior since it gave them the message that they were not good enough to be educated with others.

★ **The *Brown* Decision. (1954) Chief Justice Earl Warren** wrote the unanimous decision, ruling that segregation in public schools was unconstitutional: "Separate-but-equal has no place in the field of public education. Separate educational facilities are *inherently* unequal." The Court ruled that desegregation should be done "with all due deliberate speed." Enforcement of this decision was left to the lower federal courts, which were to see that local school districts complied with the order. Nevertheless, it took many years before the *Brown* decision was carried out.

Thurgood Marshall, attorney for the NAACP, later became the first African American on the Supreme Court

Collection of the U.S. Supreme Court

★ **Significance.** The *Brown* decision marked the end of legal segregation in public schools, and was a key turning point in the Civil Rights Movement. The decision also demonstrated that the Supreme Court was willing to become involved in controversial social issues.

THE MARCH TO EQUALITY

Dr. Martin Luther King Jr., a Baptist minister, emerged in the late 1950s as the main leader of the Civil Rights Movement. Like Thoreau and Gandhi before him, King believed in **non-violence** — that passive resistance to unjust laws could change the attitudes of oppressors. King carried out this resistance through **civil disobedience** — if the government passed an unjust law, people should oppose it with non-violent tactics such as boycotts, picketing, sit-ins, and demonstrations.

THE MONTGOMERY BUS BOYCOTT, 1955–1956

In the 1950s, old "Jim Crow" laws in Southern states still prevented African Americans from sharing restaurants, water fountains, or public buses with whites. When **Rosa Parks,** a seamstress, was arrested in Montgomery, Alabama, for refusing to give up her seat on a bus to a white passenger, local black leaders began a 13-month boycott of the city's public buses. Dr. Martin Luther King emerged as the leader of the boycott. Eventually the buses were desegregated. The boycott showed that African Americans could unite successfully to oppose segregation.

LITTLE ROCK, ARKANSAS, 1957

Most Southern states delayed putting the *Brown* decision into effect. In Arkansas, the governor refused to provide special protection to nine black students attending an all-white high school in Little Rock who were being threatened by angry mobs. President Eisenhower ordered federal troops to Little Rock to ensure that the students could attend the school. The following year, the governor closed down the school and asked for a postponement of the integration plan. The Supreme Court ruled against any delay and forced the reopening of the school.

THE CIVIL RIGHTS ACTS OF 1957 AND 1960

These laws created the Civil Rights Division of the U.S. Justice Department and gave federal courts the power to register African-American voters in the South. Registration procedures were so complex, however, that these acts proved ineffective.

SIT-INS AND FREEDOM RIDES IN THE SOUTH, 1960–1961

In 1960, African-American students held a "**sit-in**" at a "Whites Only" lunch counter in North Carolina. The tactic was soon copied by students who supported the Civil Rights Movement throughout the South. In 1961, interracial groups rode buses in **Freedom Rides** throughout the South. The Freedom Riders sought to create confrontations in the hope that the federal government would intervene. Freedom Riders often faced violence and death from those opposed to integration.

DR. KING'S LETTER FROM A BIRMINGHAM JAIL, 1963

When Dr. Martin Luther King led a march in Birmingham, Alabama, in opposition to segregation, he was arrested. He wrote a "Letter from a Birmingham Jail" explaining why African Americans could no longer patiently wait for their constitutional rights. Television revealed to the entire nation the brutal tactics used by the Birmingham police to break up marches and peaceful demonstrations. As a result of protests and boycotts, downtown stores finally agreed to desegregate lunch counters and to hire African Americans.

THE MARCH ON WASHINGTON, 1963

In 1963, Dr. King and other Civil Rights leaders called for a **March on Washington** in support of a new Civil Rights bill pending in Congress. A quarter of a million people attended the march. King gave his famous **"I Have a Dream" Speech,** in which he looked forward to the day when all Americans would live together peacefully.

Dr. King leads the March on Washington

National Archives

THE CIVIL RIGHTS ACT OF 1964

As a result of the March on Washington and the assassination of President Kennedy, President Johnson pushed this bill through Congress. The act prohibited discrimination based on race, color, religion, or ethnic origin in hotels, restaurants, and in places of employment doing business with the federal government or engaged in interstate commerce. The act cut off federal aid to districts with segregated schools. Finally, the federal government was given power to register voters and to establish the **Equal Employment Opportunity Commission** to enforce the act's provisions.

THE STRUGGLE TO ACHIEVE VOTING RIGHTS

After passage of the Civil Rights Act of 1964, Civil Rights leaders next turned their energies to registering black voters and encouraging them to vote.

Twenty-Fourth Amendment (1964) eliminated poll taxes in federal elections.

THE ROAD TO EQUAL VOTING RIGHTS

Selma Marches. In 1965, Dr. King went to Selma, Alabama, to organize a march demanding the vote for African Americans. When demonstrators were attacked, President Johnson reacted by introducing a voting rights bill.

Voting Rights Act of 1965. This act ended poll taxes, suspended literacy tests where they were used to prevent African Americans from voting, and led to a substantial increase in the number of African-American voters.

AFFIRMATIVE ACTION, 1965

In 1965, President Johnson signed an executive order requiring employers with federal contracts to take steps to raise the number of their minority and female employees to correct past imbalances. **Affirmative action** programs also increased minority representation in colleges and the professions. Some critics have challenged these programs as a form of reverse discrimination.

KEY COURT CASES: UNIVERSITY OF CALIFORNIA v. BAKKE

In 1987, Alan Bakke, a white male, was denied admission to a medical school which had accepted minority candidates with lower test scores. The medical school contended that special admissions were being used to correct past racial discrimination. Bakke argued this was reverse racial discrimination. The Supreme Court held that schools could not have specific quotas for different racial groups, but that they could take race into account as a factor in admissions. The decision upheld the principle of affirmative action.

Although affirmative action was upheld by the Supreme Court in the *Bakke* decision, many affirmative action programs have been phased out over time as the United States has moved closer to becoming a more pluralistic society.

THE POST-WAR PRESIDENTS:
EISENHOWER, KENNEDY, AND JOHNSON

THE EISENHOWER YEARS, 1953–1960

In addition to witnessing the beginnings of the Civil Rights Movement, the 1950s were a period of recovery and economic growth. People whose lives had been disrupted by the Great Depression and World War II settled down to work and having families.

U.S. SOCIETY UNDER EISENHOWER

Dwight D. Eisenhower, the popular hero of World War II, won the Presidential election of 1952. Although a Republican, Eisenhower continued to preserve New Deal programs. His years in office were marked by several important developments.

Bureau of Engraving and Printing

Housing Boom. This was a time of high birth rates, known as the "baby boom." This boom and the **G.I. Bill** helping veterans led developers to build cheaper, mass-produced housing. Home ownership increased by 50%. The movement of middle-income families to suburbs led to a declining urban tax base and decaying inner cities.

DOMESTIC DEVELOPMENTS DURING THE EISENHOWER PRESIDENCY

Economic Prosperity. The demand for consumer goods reached all-time highs. Millions of autos and TV sets were sold. The use of refrigerators and other appliances became widespread. The gross domestic product doubled between 1945 and 1960. America dominated world trade.

Conformity. In the 1950s, there was a greater emphasis on conformity. Unusual ideas were regarded with suspicion. Fear of Communism strengthened the dislike of non-conformist attitudes.

THE IMPACT OF GEOGRAPHY ON HISTORY

For much of the 19th century, rural Americans had migrated into cities. In the middle of the 20th century, this pattern shifted. The building of highways and the construction of new homes after World War II allowed millions of city-dwelling Americans to move to the suburbs — areas where homeowners enjoyed grassy backyards and fresh air, but were close enough to the city to work and shop there. As suburban populations grew, freeways became more congested. Suburbanites began to shop in local malls, and some suburbs grew so much that they became cities themselves.

State Archives of Michigan

FOREIGN POLICY UNDER EISENHOWER

Eisenhower ended the Korean War, just as he had promised in his election campaign. He gave control of foreign policy to his Secretary of State, **John Foster Dulles.** Dulles sought to contain the spread of Communism by preventing Communists from gaining any additional territory. In 1957, Eisenhower announced he would send U.S. forces to any Middle Eastern nation that requested help, to defend against Communism. This extension of containment policy became known as the **Eisenhower Doctrine.**

THE KENNEDY PRESIDENCY, 1961–1963

In 1960, Democratic candidate **John F. Kennedy** became the youngest man ever elected to the Presidency. In his inaugural address, he challenged Americans to "ask not what your country can do for you, but what you can do for your country." His speech sought to ignite the spirit of American idealism.

THE NEW FRONTIER

Kennedy's **New Frontier** symbolized the vigor of youth. The President and his wife, Jackie, brought an elegant style to the White House. Kennedy sought to use the powers of the federal government to solve the nation's problems. He proposed a tax cut to stimulate the economy, the creation of Medicare, civil rights legislation, and increased aid to education. None of these proposals passed during Kennedy's Presidency.

FOREIGN POLICY

One of the greatest challenges Kennedy faced was the establishment of a Communist government by **Fidel Castro** in Cuba, only 90 miles from Florida.

Fidel Castro

★ **Bay of Pigs Invasion.** In 1961, Cuban exiles, trained in the United States, invaded Cuba in an attempt to overthrow Castro. Kennedy refused to give them air support during their invasion, and they were defeated by Castro's army. This was a major foreign policy failure for Kennedy.

★ **Alliance For Progress (1961).** To meet the Cuban challenge, Kennedy created this program to offer grants and loans to Latin American nations to promote economic progress, land reform, and trade.

★ **Cuban Missile Crisis.** In 1962, the United States discovered that Cuba was secretly building bases for Soviet nuclear missiles. Kennedy imposed a naval blockade on Cuba and threatened to invade if the missiles were not withdrawn. For a brief moment, the world stood on the brink of nuclear war. Soviet leader Khrushchev agreed to withdraw the missiles for a pledge that the United States would not invade Cuba.

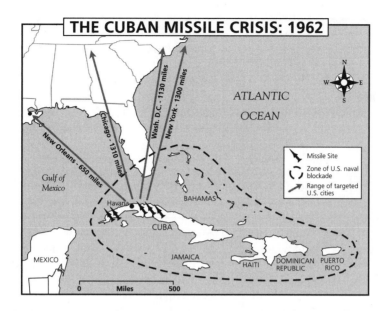

★ **Peace Corps.** Kennedy created the Peace Corps, a program in which American volunteers went to live in developing countries in Africa, Asia, and Latin America in order to help local people. The program continues today.

★ **The Space Race.** To counter the Soviet space program, Kennedy announced that America would place a man on the moon. In 1962, **John Glenn** became the first American to orbit the earth.

THE JOHNSON PRESIDENCY, 1963–1968

The nation was shocked when Kennedy was assassinated on November 22, 1963, in Dallas, Texas. Vice-President **Lyndon Johnson** became the next President.

THE GREAT SOCIETY

Soon after taking over the Presidency, Johnson proposed the most far-ranging program of social legislation since the New Deal. Johnson's aim was to turn the United States into a **"Great Society"** by opening up opportunities and improving the quality of life for all Americans. When Johnson was elected President in his own right in 1964, he sponsored additional legislation extending his Great Society programs.

Lyndon Johnson takes the oath of office following the assassination of President Kennedy

L.B.J. Presidential Library

Civil Rights. Johnson pushed through a broad program of Civil Rights legislation, including the **Civil Rights Act** (1964) and the **Voting Rights Act** (1965).

War on Poverty. Johnson called for a "war on poverty." The **Economic Opportunity Act** (1964) created a new government office to administer programs established by the act. These included the **Job Corps**, to train underprivileged youths, and a domestic "Peace Corps" to help in depressed areas.

JOHNSON'S GREAT SOCIETY PROGRAMS

Medicare Act of 1965. Social Security was expanded to provide medical care, hospital insurance, and post-hospital nursing for people over age 65.

Aid to Cities. A new cabinet post was created to help the nation's cities. Money was provided for urban planning, slum clearance, rental assistance for the poor, and the reconstruction of buildings.

CHANGES IN THE NATION'S IMMIGRATION POLICY

Enacted shortly after World War II, the **McCarren-Walter Act** (1952) kept immigration quotas at 1920 levels, favoring Western Europe. Asian countries received only token immigration. The **Immigration Act of 1965,** enacted during the Johnson Presidency, aimed to be less biased, reflecting changes in national values. Each country was allowed up to 20,000 immigrants, with a cap on total immigration. Preference was given to those with relatives already in the United States or to those with valuable skills. The act restricted immigration from Latin America for the first time.

THE GREAT SOCIETY FALLS VICTIM TO THE VIETNAM WAR

Despite these Great Society programs, many Americans remained in poverty. Involvement in the Vietnam War eventually forced Johnson to withdraw much of the funding from domestic programs. Because of his failure to achieve victory in Vietnam, Johnson did not seek another term as President in 1968.

THE SIXTIES: A DECADE OF CHANGE

The 1960s and early 1970s were a watershed in American history. Many groups — the young, women, African Americans — became more militant in their demands for a more equal and diverse American society.

THE YOUTH CULTURE OF THE SIXTIES

A large number of "baby boomers" reached their twenties in the 1960s and 1970s. This generation was influenced by the post-war prosperity, new permissive methods of child care, and exposure to television. By the mid-1960s, some baby boomers adopted a spirit of rebelliousness. They challenged the materialism of those in charge of American society — whom they called the "Establishment." These youths were shocked at the Establishment's indifference to poverty and other social problems.

NEW LIFE-STYLES

The new **"youth culture"** was especially affected by rock music. The **Beatles** introduced new fashions and long hair for males, which became a symbol of the new culture. The new youth culture experimented openly with drugs and sex. They adopted new fashions to set them apart from traditional styles. Some **hippies** left mainstream society and went to live on self-sufficient communes.

THE ANTI-WAR MOVEMENT

In the late 1960s, many youths focused on American involvement in Vietnam. By 1968, millions of young people were actively protesting the war. Protests continued until the United States withdrew from the war in 1973. The Vietnam War also brought about an amendment lowering the voting age, since eighteen-year olds were being drafted to fight but could not even vote.

Protesters burn their draft cards to show their opposition to the war

THE WOMEN'S LIBERATION MOVEMENT

One of the most important events of the 1960s was the **Women's Liberation,** or **Feminist Movement.** In the 1950s and early 1960s, most women accepted traditional roles as wives and mothers. Movies and television reinforced this image. Married women who did not conform to the image of the ideal housewife were regarded as outcasts. Although they could vote, women still had not achieved full equality at work or in the home. Unlike the earlier Suffrage Movement, which focused on securing the vote, the Women's Liberation Movement sought to achieve economic and social equality.

REASONS FOR THE EMERGENCE OF THE WOMEN'S LIBERATION MOVEMENT

Dissatisfaction. Many women were dissatisfied with their roles as housewives and sought freedom to express themselves in careers and work.

Influence of Civil Rights Movement. Many women leaders had been active in the Civil Rights Movement. Its success inspired them to adopt the same techniques to promote women's rights—lobbying, sit-ins, demonstrations, boycotts, and strikes.

Impact of Social Science. Social scientists, especially women like anthropologist **Margaret Mead**, began to see women's low status in Western society as the creation of a male-dominated power structure rather than a biological necessity.

The "Sexual Revolution." Sex education courses began to be taught in the schools. Birth control pills protected women from pregnancy. The Women's Movement attacked the myth of female passivity. Women objected to being treated as "sex objects" instead of as full human beings.

Dynamic Leadership. Highly educated and talented women provided dynamic leadership. Feminist leaders included Betty Friedan and Gloria Steinem, who founded *Ms. Magazine*, devoted to women's concerns and viewpoints decidedly different from traditional woman's magazines.

FAMOUS AMERICANS: BETTY FRIEDAN

Friedan wrote *The Feminine Mystique* in 1963. The book denied that all women were content leading traditional lives as mothers and housewives. Friedan wrote that women were as capable as men and should be permitted to compete for the same jobs. In 1966, she helped form the **National Organization for Women** (NOW), which became the chief voice of the Women's Movement.

ACHIEVEMENTS OF THE WOMEN'S LIBERATION MOVEMENT

Feminist goals were far-reaching. Women sought greater freedom and a fuller social and economic life.

★ **Education.** As a result of affirmative action, universities receiving federal support could no longer discriminate on the basis of sex in their admissions policy. Most colleges became co-educational and hired women professors. Greater gender equality was also achieved in admissions to military academies, law schools, and medical schools.

★ **Employment.** Feminists sought to end discrimination in hiring, to establish equal job opportunities for women, and to place women in positions of greater responsibility. In 1963, Congress passed the "Equal Pay" Act requiring companies to pay women the same wages as men for the same work.

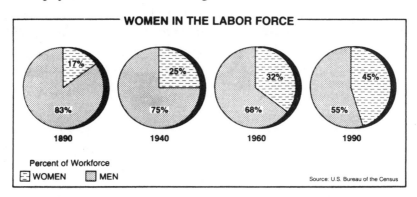

★ **New Attitudes.** Feminists objected to beauty contests and introduced the title Ms. to replace Miss and Mrs. They opposed sexist language ("policeman" and "fireman") and the use of women as sex objects in advertising. Feminist leaders opposed sexual discrimination in textbooks that ignored women's contributions. They lobbied for more funds to research women's diseases.

THE ABORTION ISSUE

Abortion is the deliberate termination of an unwanted pregnancy. Many states had laws banning abortion. Feminists believed that women should have the right to decide whether or not to have an abortion. "Pro-choice" rights became a rallying cry for the Women's Movement. The abortion issue became one of the most divisive issues in American history. The Supreme Court finally became involved in this highly controversial issue.

*Demonstrators outside the Supreme Court
on the 20th anniversary of Roe v. Wade*

KEY COURT CASES: ROE v. WADE (1973)

Jane Roe (*assumed name*) tried to terminate her pregnancy. She was arrested for violating a state law making abortion a crime unless the mother's life was endangered. The Court ruled that a woman's constitutional right to privacy guaranteed her the right to an abortion in the first three months of pregnancy. The decision overturned all state laws prohibiting abortions in the first three months.

INCREASING AFRICAN-AMERICAN MILITANCY

Despite the gains of the Civil Rights Movement, by the late 1960s many young African Americans disagreed with Martin Luther King's policy of cooperation with sympathetic whites and his program of non-violence.

THE GHETTOS ERUPT, 1965–1968

In the North, African Americans faced segregation based on residential living patterns. Many African Americans were confined to decaying inner cities. In 1968, Dr. Martin Luther King was assassinated in Memphis, Tennessee. African-American frustration erupted in a series of riots that shook Northern cities three summers in a row. Rioters in cities across the nation smashed windows, overturned cars, and started fires. The

Cities like Detroit erupted in riots following the assassination of Dr. King

State Archives of Michigan

Kerner Commission concluded that the lack of job opportunities for African Americans, urban poverty, and white racism were the chief factors behind the riots.

THE BLACK POWER MOVEMENT

The new militants believed in **Black Power** — that African Americans should use their votes to win concessions from government and that they should control their own communities, patronize their own businesses, and free themselves from the economic, cultural, and political domination of whites.

Search for a New Identity. In the late 1960s, many African Americans began to search for the roots of their cultural identity. They rejected imitating whites or being absorbed into American culture, believing that they should be proud of themselves and that "Black is Beautiful."

SPOTLIGHT ON THE BLACK POWER MOVEMENT

New Groups Emerge. New groups challenged the leadership of traditional, non-violent organizations like the NAACP. The militant Student Non-Violent Coordinating Committee (**SNCC**) barred white participation. **Black Muslims** believed Islam should be the religion of African Americans, who should form their own black state. **Black Panthers** demanded reparations to the black community for centuries of oppression.

Malcolm X, a leading black Muslim, questioned King's policy of non-violent resistance. Malcolm X believed that African Americans should meet violence with violence and should not depend on the goodness of white people. He urged African Americans to obtain control of their own businessses and communities. He was assassinated by rival black Muslims in 1965.

NATIVE AMERICAN INDIANS BECOME MILITANT

Even Native American Indians grew restless in the 1960s. Back in 1953, the federal government had transferred its responsibility for Native American Indians on reservations to state governments, and encouraged Native American Indians to blend into mainstream American life. Many states were unable to provide the same level of services previously provided by the federal government. The new policy turned out to be largely a failure.

FORMATION OF THE AMERICAN INDIAN MOVEMENT ("AIM")

In 1963, the federal government reversed its policy again, and swung back to encouraging tribal life on the reservations. The Civil Rights Act prohibited discrimination against Native American Indians. In 1970, President Nixon announced the federal government would honor its treaty obligations. Nevertheless, many Native American Indians felt they were still mistreated. Under the slogan **"Red Power,"** they formed the **American Indian Movement** to mobilize favorable public opinion. Native American Indians sought greater pride and respect for their heritage. They introduced the term "Native American" and protested the racial biases and stereotypes commonly found in textbooks, television, and movies. They even dramatized the plight of Native American Indians by temporarily occupying government monuments like Alcatraz Island and Wounded Knee, South Dakota.

THE WARREN COURT

Under Chief Justice **Earl Warren,** the Supreme Court also acted as a major instrument of social change in this era — starting with the *Brown* decision. Many of the Justices shared Warren's view that the Court should protect individual rights and minority groups from abuses by the majority. This even went so far as to require the protection of those accused of crime. Critics argued that the Warren Court went too far — increasing rights for the accused to the point where it became difficult for police to protect society.

Collection of the U.S. Supreme Court

Earl Warren

MAPP v. OHIO, 1961

Dollree Mapp was suspected of hiding gambling equipment in her home. When she tried to prevent police from entering her home, Ms. Mapp was arrested. A search of her home turned up obscene materials, prohibited under Ohio law. Mapp believed her Fourth Amendment rights had been violated by the search. The Supreme Court agreed with Mapp that her right to be protected against "unreasonable searches and seizures" had been violated by the police. The Supreme Court ruled that officials could not use evidence obtained in an unlawful search in court.

BAKER v. CARR, 1962

In the late 19th and early 20th centuries, large numbers of people had moved from rural areas to cities. Frequently, state legislatures failed to redraw their election districts. As a result, rural areas were over-represented in many states while more heavily populated cities were under-represented. The Supreme Court ruled that these legislative districts must be reapportioned on the principle of "one person, one vote."

GIDEON v. WAINWRIGHT, 1963

Clarence Gideon was arrested for petty larceny. His request for a lawyer was rejected because under Florida law a lawyer was only appointed for defendants in capital cases. The Supreme Court ruled that Gideon's Sixth Amendment right to a lawyer had been violated. The case required states to provide a free lawyer to any criminal defendant facing imprisonment who could not afford one.

MIRANDA v. ARIZONA, 1966

Ernesto Miranda was arrested for raping a young woman. Under interrogation, Miranda confessed to the crime. The police never told him that he had the right to remain silent and did not have to answer their questions. He was also never informed that he could have a lawyer present to advise him. The Supreme Court overturned Miranda's conviction. The ruling requires police to inform suspects of their "Miranda" rights: the constitutional right to remain silent, the right to have a lawyer present during questioning, and the right to know that their remarks could be used against them.

THE VIETNAM WAR, 1954–1973

The "decade of change" ended with Americans deeply divided over the Vietnam War. Vietnam was once a French colony in Indochina. In 1954, Vietnamese led by **Ho Chi Minh** defeated the French. At the **Geneva Conference** that followed, Laos and Cambodia were made into independent states. Vietnam was divided into two: Ho Chi Minh and the Vietnamese Communists controlled the north, while a pro-Western state was established in the south. The country was to be reunited after elections were held in 1956. After the Geneva Conference, the United States replaced France as South Vietnam's principal supporter. South Vietnamese leaders refused to hold elections for the unification of Vietnam, however, since they feared elections in the North would not be free. Soon afterwards, South Vietnamese Communists (**Vietcong**) with North Vietnamese support began a guerrilla war against the government of South Vietnam.

THE WAR UNDER PRESIDENT KENNEDY, 1961–1963

President Kennedy, responding to requests from the South Vietnamese government for help, sent aid and military advisers to assist in fighting the Vietcong. American leaders believed in the **domino theory:** they feared if South Vietnam fell to Communism, other Southeast Asian countries would also fall, like a row of dominos. This would allow Communism to spread to other areas until it posed a direct threat to the United States. Resisting Communism in Vietnam therefore became crucial to the "free world." Kennedy and his advisers also felt that a successful democracy in South Vietnam might serve as a model for other developing countries in Asia, Africa, and Latin America.

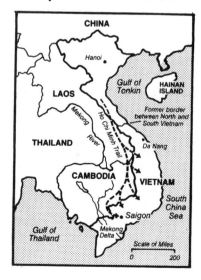

THE WAR UNDER PRESIDENT JOHNSON, 1963–1968

Under President Johnson, the United States became even more actively involved in the defense of South Vietnam.

★ **Gulf of Tonkin Resolution.** In 1964, Johnson announced that the North Vietnamese had attacked U.S. ships in international waters in the Gulf of Tonkin. Congress voted to give Johnson full military powers to act to stop North Vietnamese aggression. Years later it was revealed that the U.S. ships had been in North Vietnamese waters acting in cooperation with South Vietnamese warships, which were shelling North Vietnam.

★ **Johnson Escalates the War.** Although Congress had not officially declared war, President Johnson used the Gulf of Tonkin Resolution to escalate the war. Johnson ordered massive bombing raids over North Vietnam. He also sent in more combat troops to South Vietnam. By 1968, half a million U.S. soldiers were stationed in South Vietnam. New weapons like **napalm,** a type of fire bomb, inflicted great damage on the Vietnamese, while herbicides like **Agent Orange** destroyed the jungle cover used by the Vietcong to hide.

★ **The Tet Offensive.** In 1968, the Vietcong launched a massive offensive throughout South Vietnam, seizing many major cities. Once in control, the Vietcong committed brutal acts of terror against South Vietnamese officials. Although American forces finally drove the Vietcong from these strongholds, the offensive marked a major turning point in the war, demonstrating to the American public that, even with half a million troops in Vietnam, victory was far away.

INCREASING DIFFICULTIES IN VIETNAM

By the end of 1968, the United States had dropped more bombs on Vietnam than it had in all of World War II. The war was costing $25 billion a year. Despite these efforts, the United States was proving unable to win the war for a number of reasons:

POPULARITY OF THE NATIONALIST CAUSE

The North Vietnamese and many South Vietnamese saw Ho Chi Minh as the father of their country. They felt they were fighting for their independence and were willing to suffer large losses to unify their nation. On the other hand, the disruptions of the war had weakened the government of South Vietnam. Corruption became widespread. Successive South Vietnamese governments failed to gain popular support.

THE DIFFICULTIES OF GUERRILLA WARFARE

Most American soldiers were unfamiliar with the Vietnamese language, people, or physical environment. American forces were unable to tell who was friendly and who was the enemy. The jungles of Vietnam provided an ideal cover for guerrilla warfare and secret enemy movements. Vietnam's location next to Communist China made it easy for Communists to send a steady flow of supplies.

DISCONTENT AND DIVISION ON THE HOME FRONT

The Vietnam War grew increasingly unpopular in the United States. President Johnson told Americans they were winning the war, but journalists reported otherwise. This **"credibility gap"** led many Americans to lose faith in the government's reliability. Opponents of the war joined in marches, demonstrations, and rallies. Young men burned their draft cards, and youthful demonstrators protested at national political conventions. American "doves" wanted the United States to withdraw, since they saw the contest as a civil war between North and South Vietnamese. They believed American leaders were acting immorally by bombing civilians and burning villages. The "hawks" supported the war, which they saw as an attempt to defend free Vietnamese from Communist repression.

THE WAR UNDER PRESIDENT NIXON, 1969–1973

Divisions among Democrats over the war and the assassination of Robert F. Kennedy, younger brother of the late President, led to the election of Republican **Richard Nixon** as President in 1968. During the campaign, Nixon promised Americans "peace with honor." However, during Nixon's Presidency the war dragged on for five more years. During these years:

Vietnamization. Under Nixon's "Vietnamization" policy, the army of South Vietnam gradually took over the brunt of the fighting, allowing the withdrawal of U.S. forces. At the same time, Nixon increased American bombing of North Vietnam and provided military aid to South Vietnam.

NIXON'S VIETNAM POLICY

Invasion of Cambodia. Nixon believed the war would be shortened if supply routes through Cambodia from North to South Vietnam could be cut. In 1970, American troops invaded Cambodia.

Diplomatic Overtures. Nixon negotiated with Vietnam's Communist allies, China and the Soviet Union, to put pressure on North Vietnam.

THE LEGACY OF THE VIETNAM WAR

In 1973. Nixon's negotiators, led by Henry Kissinger, worked out a cease-fire agreement with the North Vietnamese known as the **Paris Peace Accords.** Nixon agreed to pull out all U.S. troops from Vietnam, and the North Vietnamese agreed to release American prisoners of war. After the U.S. withdrawal, fighting continued. South Vietnam and Cambodia finally fell to Communist forces in 1975, when Vietnam was reunited under Communist rule.

DEATH AND DESTRUCTION

Over 58,000 American soldiers died in the war, and thousands of others suffered physical and psychological injuries. Over a million Vietnamese were killed, while almost half the population of South Vietnam was left homeless.

IMPACT OF PUBLIC OPINION

Public division over the Vietnam War demonstrated that the success or failure of government actions can be greatly affected by public opinion.

LIMITS ON PRESIDENTIAL WARTIME POWERS

As in earlier wars, Presidential power greatly expanded during the Vietnam War. After the war, Congress attempted to reclaim greater authority in determining policy by passing the **War Powers Act (1973).** The act set limits on the power of the President to involve the nation in conflict without a formal declaration of war by Congress. The act requires the President to inform Congress within 48 hours of sending troops to fight overseas. If Congress does not approve the use of these forces within 60 days, the President must withdraw the troops.

LOSS OF U.S. CONFIDENCE ABROAD

The Vietnam War led to a crisis of confidence. Many Americans grew concerned about our foreign commitments. As a result, Americans became more aware of the limits of U.S. power and cautious about where they should act abroad.

ECONOMIC AND SOCIAL IMPACTS

Wartime expenses led to the end of some Great Society programs. The war brought rising inflation and a new distrust of government leaders.

THE BOAT PEOPLE AND INCREASED U.S. IMMIGRATION

When Communists finally seized control of South Vietnam in 1975, thousands of South Vietnamese fled on small boats to neighboring non-Communist countries. Many of these refugees later emigrated to the United States.

SUMMARIZING YOUR UNDERSTANDING

KEY TERMS, CONCEPTS, AND PEOPLE

Make a vocabulary card for each of the following terms, concepts, and people.

March on Washington
Affirmative Action
Bay of Pigs Invasion

Cuban Missile Crisis
Great Society
War on Poverty

Black Power
Domino Theory
War Powers Act

COMPLETING A TABLE

Briefly describe each of the following Supreme Court cases.

Case	Issue in the Case	Supreme Court Decision
Brown v. *Bd. of Education*		
Mapp v. *Ohio*		
Baker v. *Carr*		
Gideon v. *Wainwright*		
Miranda v. *Arizona*		
Roe v. *Wade*		

COMPLETING A GRAPHIC ORGANIZER

Identify the following people and describe their importance.

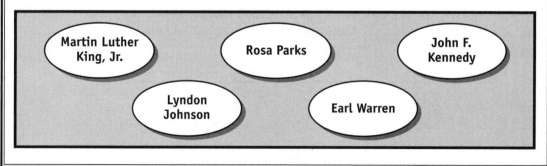

TESTING YOUR UNDERSTANDING

MULTIPLE-CHOICE QUESTIONS

1 In *Brown v. Board of Education,* the Supreme Court ruled that
1 busing children to overcome segregation is constitutional
2 laws requiring racially segregated public schools are unconstitutional
3 the use of civil disobedience to achieve legal rights is constitutional
4 delaying integration to avoid violence is constitutional

2 Which statement is best illustrated by the Supreme Court's decision in *Brown v. Board of Education*?
1 The Constitution ensures federal control of state academic requirements.
2 Racial prejudice no longer exists in the United States.
3 Non-whites have gained economic and political equality with whites.
4 The Court's interpretation of the Constitution may change over time.

Base your answers to questions 3 and 4 on the following quotation from a Supreme Court decision and your knowledge of social studies.

"We conclude that in the field of public education the doctrine of 'separate but equal' has no place. Separate educational facilities are inherently unequal. Therefore, ... the plaintiffs ... are, by reason of the segregation ..., deprived of the equal protection of the laws guaranteed by the Fourteenth Amendment."

3 This quotation marked the reversal of principles earlier stated in
1 *Plessy v. Ferguson*   3 *Roe v. Wade*
2 *Gideon v. Wainwright*   4 *Miranda v. Arizona*

4 This court decision was based on the idea that public school segregation
1 creates unnecessary administrative problems
2 places excessive burdens on school transportation systems
3 results in unfair tax increases to support dual school systems
4 denies individuals their equal rights

5 Which development was a result of the other three?
1 African Americans were barred from voting in several states.
2 State laws supported racial segregation in schools and housing.
3 Federal Civil Rights and Voting Rights Acts were passed.
4 Civil Rights advocates held boycotts, demonstrations and sit-ins.

6   With which statement would a follower of Martin Luther King, Jr. most likely agree?
    1   All properly enacted laws must be obeyed.
    2   Demonstrations against unfair laws are morally justified.
    3   Civil disobedience is damaging to society.
    4   Violence is acceptable if the cause is just.

7   The movements led by Mohandas Gandhi in India and Martin Luther King, Jr. in the United States were similar in that both
    1   supported attempts to overthrow the established government
    2   used civil disobedience to bring about social change
    3   boycotted British goods
    4   elected their leaders to national political office

8   Roosevelt's New Deal and Johnson's Great Society both shared the idea that
    1   foreign imports should be cut to a minimum
    2   the federal government should help the less fortunate
    3   taxes should be raised to stimulate consumer spending
    4   key industries should be nationalized

9   Lyndon Johnson's Great Society programs illustrated
    1   the increased power of the states to deal with economic problems
    2   direct federal action to address poverty
    3   laissez-faire capitalism
    4   decreased support for the concerns of minority groups

10 Which best illustrates affirmative action?
    1   A company actively recruits qualified women and minority members.
    2   A corporation hires people on a "first come, first serve" basis.
    3   A university's sole criterion for admission is its entrance examination.
    4   A graduate school accepts all students who apply.

11 What has been a major criticism of affirmative action programs in recent years?
    1   They have been too costly to the federal government.
    2   Such programs are no longer needed to obtain full equality.
    3   Very few minority persons have been hired under these programs.
    4   Most state governments have been unwilling to enforce affirmative action.

12 A member of NOW would most likely favor

  1   greater power for state governors   3   greater opportunities for women

  2   increasing military spending   4   African-American separatism

Following are quotations from several African-American authors. Base your answers to questions 13 and 14 on their statements and your knowledge of social studies.

Author A:	African Americans must have a country and a nation of their own. Don't encourage them to believe they will be social equals and leaders of whites in America, without first proving to the world they are capable of evolving an advanced civilization of their own.
Author B:	Our greatest danger is that, in the leap from slavery to freedom, we may overlook the fact that most of us will live by the production of our hands. We shall prosper in proportion as we learn to dignify and glorify common labor and put brains and skill into the common occupations of life.
Author C:	We went in for agitation. We pushed our way into the courts. We demanded the right to vote. We urged our children into college. We encouraged African-American art and literature. We studied African history. We declared that the colored races are destined to share in the heritage of the earth.

13 Twentieth-century black nationalist leaders would probably most agree with the statements of

  1   Authors A and B   3   Authors B and C

  2   Authors A and C   4   all three authors

14 The opinion of Author B is closest to the views of

  1   Booker T. Washington   3   Malcolm X

  2   W.E.B. DuBois   4   Martin Luther King, Jr.

15 Malcolm X and Martin Luther King, Jr. chiefly disagreed over the

  1   use of violence to achieve equality   3   issue of U.S. aid to Africa

  2   desirability of racial equality   4   degree of pride in being black

16 The terms "hippies," "youth culture," and "anti-establishment" would most likely be used in an essay dealing with which decade?

1   The 1940s   3   The 1960s
2   The 1950s   4   The 1980s

17 The decisions of the U.S. Supreme Court in *Miranda v. Arizona, Gideon v. Wainwright,* and *Mapp v. Ohio* all advanced

1   the voting rights of minorities   3   the rights of accused persons
2   free speech   4   women's rights

18 The Equal Protection Clause of the Fourteenth Amendment has been used by the federal government to justify its intervention in state matters concerning

1   civil rights   3   granting of corporation charters
2   appointment of judges   4   regulation of currency

19 In *Roe v. Wade,* the Supreme Court ruled that

1   racial segregation in public schools is unconstitutional
2   the Court has the power to declare federal laws unconstitutional
3   women deserve equal pay for equal work
4   the right to privacy allows women to have abortions in early pregnancy

20 Presidents Kennedy, Johnson, and Nixon sent American troops to Vietnam in an effort to

1   prevent violations of U.S. neutrality
2   support the policy of containment
3   protect freedom of the seas
4   create a new colonial empire

21 The primary purpose of the War Powers Act of 1973 was to

1   limit Presidential power to send troops into combat
2   encourage a quicker response to military attack
3   assure adequate defense of the Western Hemisphere
4   prevent the use of troops for non-military purposes

22 As a result of the experience of the Vietnam War, Congress attempted to

1   increase the number of men drafted into the military
2   take a larger role in shaping foreign policy
3   recall most U.S. troops stationed overseas
4   increase economic aid to Southeast Asia

INTERPRETING DOCUMENTS

> "His legislative leadership was remarkable. No President since Lincoln has done more for civil rights. Yet much of this has been forgotten as American society became increasingly divided over U.S. participation in a bloody, undeclared war."

1. Which President does this statement describe? _____

_____

2. Describe one piece of legislation proposed by this President in the field of civil rights. _____

_____

THEMATIC ESSAY QUESTION

Directions: Write a well-organized essay that includes an introduction, several paragraphs addressing the task below, and a conclusion.

Theme: Justice and Human Rights

> Many U.S. Supreme Court decisions have dealt with important issues and have had an important impact on American society.

Task:

> Choose **two** Supreme Court cases from your study of American history.
>
> For *each* Supreme Court case:
> • Explain how the case dealt with an important issue.
> • Discuss the impact of the decision on American society.

You may use any example from your study of U.S. history and government. Some suggestions you might wish to consider include: *Marbury* v. *Madison*, *McCulloch* v. *Maryland*, *Korematsu* v. *U.S.*, *Brown* v. *Board of Education*, *Miranda* v. *Arizona*, and *Roe* v. *Wade*.

You are *not* limited to these suggestions.

CHAPTER 13

CONTEMPORARY AMERICA

Presidents Ford, Nixon, Bush, Reagan, and Carter

The White House

TIMELINE OF IMPORTANT EVENTS

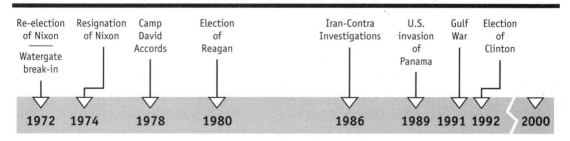

Re-election of Nixon	Resignation of Nixon	Camp David Accords	Election of Reagan		Iran-Contra Investigations	U.S. invasion of Panama	Gulf War	Election of Clinton	
Watergate break-in									
1972	1974	1978	1980		1986	1989	1991	1992	2000

WHAT YOU SHOULD FOCUS ON

In this chapter, you will learn about American society in the past 40 years. Under President Nixon, the United States withdrew from Vietnam and opened diplomatic relations with Communist China. In the 1970s, the nation sank into a recession. U.S. prestige suffered when American hostages were taken in Iran. Under Presidents Reagan and Bush, America moved toward conservatism and witnessed the end of the Cold War. Under President Clinton, Americans enjoyed unparalleled prosperity. Under President George W. Bush, Americans fought a "War on Terrorism" after the 9/11 attacks. Under President Obama, Americans faced a major financial crisis. In this chapter you will learn about:

President Bush meets with Russian President Yeltsin

★ **The Presidency in Crisis.** Under Nixon, failure in Vietnam and the Watergate scandal weakened the prestige of the Presidency. Presidents Ford and Carter had to deal with rising oil prices, economic recession, new acts of aggression by the Soviet Union, and the Iranian Revolution of Ayatollah Khomeini.

★ **The New Conservatism.** President Reagan cut taxes and domestic spending, while increasing military spending. His policies restored prosperity but greatly increased the national debt. In foreign policy, he aided anti-Communist rebels and held talks with Soviet leader Gorbachev. Bush followed similar policies and witnessed the successful end of the Cold War.

★ **The United States in Recent Times.** Under President Clinton, Americans enjoyed unparalleled economic prosperity at home while they searched for a new role in promoting international stability and justice. Under President G.W. Bush, Americans responded to terrorist attacks by sending troops to Afghanistan and Iraq.

In studying this period, you should focus on the following questions:

★ How was the U.S. Presidency weakened in the post-Vietnam years?
★ How have recent Presidents coped with domestic problems?
★ How well have recent Presidents protected U.S. interests in foreign affairs?
★ What changes can Americans expect in the future?

LOOKING AT DIVERSITY

uch of your study of American history has focused on our nation's leaders. They have frequently been wealthy, white, Protestant males. To truly understand our nation's history, it is also necessary to study the experiences of other groups. We sometimes refer to these other groups as **minorities.** Let's look at the patterns of prejudice many minorities have faced.

THE ROOTS OF PREJUDICE

Prejudice refers to attitudes and beliefs about people from other racial, ethnic, or gender groups. What causes people to be prejudiced? Social scientists have identified several mechanisms that explain how prejudices develop:

Psychological Factors. People often feel more familiar with those from the same racial, ethnic, class, or gender group. Lack of familiarity leads people to look at other groups as outsiders. Such **ethnocentrism** increases their own self-esteem, since they believe their group is superior to others.

Influence of Tradition. We are not born with prejudices: we learn them from family and friends. Dominant groups often look upon other groups as inferior. For example, many men once thought women incapable of rational decision-making. Such thinking led women to limit their expectations.

HOW PREJUDICES DEVELOP

Economic Competition. Prejudice is increased by fears of competition. Badly paid workers fear competition from poor immigrants who work for even lower wages.

THE MANY FACES OF DISCRIMINATION

While prejudice refers to attitudes about members of a group, **discrimination** refers to actual acts against someone from a different group. It can take many forms.

★ **Private Acts of Discrimination.** Private discrimination can make it difficult for members of disadvantaged groups to get the best education or jobs, blocking their economic and social advancement. For example, residents of some neighborhoods once signed agreements promising not to sell their homes to members of certain ethnic or racial groups.

(continued)

★ **Legal Discrimination and Segregation.** In more extreme cases, minorities have faced discrimination supported by law. "Jim Crow" laws in the South once excluded African Americans from white public schools or from the use of "whites-only" public facilities.

A segregated fountain in Mississippi, 1940

★ **Enslavement, Expulsion and Genocide.** Earlier in our history, African Americans were brought to the U.S. by force and enslaved. Native Americans were forcibly resettled on reservations. World history has witnessed attempts to eliminate minorities through extermination, known as **genocide.**

THE CHALLENGE OF A PLURALISTIC SOCIETY

In the 19th century, many disadvantaged groups organized reform movements. Abolitionists helped end slavery. More recently, the Civil Rights Movement marked an important milestone on the road to a more equal society. The Supreme Court read new meaning into the Equal Protection Clause, and Congress passed laws against discrimination. Other groups followed African Americans in fighting for equality. As a result, our nation today is making efforts to foster a society in which all groups participate equally. This goal has presented two major challenges.

THE NEED FOR AGREEMENT

Americans still need to agree on what should be done to overcome past prejudice to achieve equality. Should we establish a "color-blind" society in which race is never a factor in any decision, or should we compensate the members of disadvantaged groups for past discrimination?

THE NEED TO PRESERVE DIVERSITY

Americans must find new ways to preserve their identities as members of diverse cultural and social groups while also cooperating with members from different groups in maintaining a common American identity. Will Americans be able to strike a balance between loyalty to their particular group and loyalty to their society as a whole? This is the challenge for the future.

THE PRESIDENCY IN CRISIS

Presidential power greatly increased when the New Deal gave the federal government increased authority over the economy. The two World Wars and the Cold War also made the President's role in foreign affairs more important. Some historians have referred to this growth of Presidential power as the **"Imperial Presidency."** The increasing power of the Presidency seemed ready to threaten the fragile balance among our separate branches of government. Under Presidents Nixon, Ford, and Carter, many wondered whether the Presidency had become overwhelming — with more responsibilities than any one person could handle effectively.

THE NIXON PRESIDENCY, 1969–1974

The expansion of Presidential power reached its height during the Nixon Presidency. Nixon made major decisions without consulting Congress. He failed to consult Congress about the bombing and invasion of Cambodia and Laos, the mining of North Vietnam's harbor, and the decision to open relations with Communist China. Nixon also used public funds to remodel his private homes in California and Florida, while he used the CIA and FBI to collect information about his political opponents.

DOMESTIC POLICY UNDER NIXON

Nixon, a Republican, moved the nation in a more conservative direction. He believed that federal social programs were often inefficient, and that most social problems were best dealt with at the local level. Under his policy of **New Federalism,** Nixon reversed the trend of increasing federal control by turning some federal revenues over to state governments.

Nixon delivers his inaugural address

The 1970s saw rising prices, a new trade deficit, and rising unemployment. To combat inflation, Nixon cut spending on social programs but also imposed wage and price controls. These attempts to control inflation proved unsuccessful.

FOREIGN POLICY UNDER NIXON

Nixon's foreign policy successes included U.S. withdrawal from Vietnam, a resumption of contact with mainland China, and beginning a détente with the Soviet Union.

★ **The Vietnam War, 1969–1973.** As we have seen, Nixon pursued a policy of "Vietnamization," shifting the fighting from American troops to the South Vietnamese army. In 1973, Nixon and the North Vietnamese agreed to the **Paris Peace Accords,** and U.S. troops were withdrawn.

★ **Re-Opening Relations with China, 1972.** Ever since the Communist Revolution in China in 1949, U.S. leaders had refused to establish diplomatic relations with their government. Instead, they had treated the Nationalist Chinese government on Taiwan as the government of China. Nixon made a breakthrough in relations when he visited Communist China and took steps toward the normaliztion of diplomatic relations with the Communists.

★ **Détente with the Soviet Union, 1972.** Nixon also introduced a policy of **détente** — a relaxing of strained relations — with the Soviet Union. In 1972, Nixon visited Moscow and signed the **SALT I Accord,** limiting the development of certain missile systems. Nixon also agreed to sell grain to the Soviet Union, to help them cope with a severe food shortage. In 1973, when war broke out in the Middle East, the U.S. and the Soviet Union cooperated in pressuring Israel and the Arab states to conclude a cease-fire.

THE WATERGATE CRISIS

In his election campaign, Nixon had promised Americans a return to "law and order," but Americans soon learned that the government itself was corrupt.

★ **The Vice President Resigns.** In 1973, **Spiro Agnew** resigned as Vice President when it was discovered he had taken bribes as Governor of Maryland. Under the **Twenty-fifth Amendment,** Nixon appointed U.S. Congressman **Gerald Ford** as his new Vice President.

★ **The Watergate Scandal.** In 1972, a group of former CIA agents, working for Nixon's re-election, were caught breaking into Democratic Party headquarters at the Watergate complex in Washington, D.C.

★ **The Cover-up.** Nixon tried to cover up an investigation of the break-in on the grounds of national security. A group of investigative reporters were the first to report possible links between the Watergate break-in and the White House. The Senate appointed a committee to investigate the scandal. The Attorney General also appointed a Special Prosecutor to examine the break-in.

★ **The Watergate Tapes.** In the Senate hearings, it was revealed that Nixon had secretly recorded all his White House conversations in the oval office. When the Senate Committee asked to hear the tapes, Nixon refused, claiming **executive privilege** — that Congress could not question members of the executive branch without Presidential approval. In ***United States v. Nixon*** (1974), Nixon contended that to obey a lower court order would lead to judicial control of the Presidency, violating the separation-of-powers provisions of the Constitution. The Supreme Court ruled that Nixon must turn over the tapes, reaffirming the principle that no one, not even the President, is above the law.

★ **Nixon Resigns.** The tapes revealed that Nixon had lied when he said he was not involved in the cover-up. The House of Representatives moved to impeach Nixon. Fearing impeachment, Nixon became the first President to resign.

THE FORD PRESIDENCY, 1974–1977

Gerald Ford became the next President. Ford had never even been elected as Vice President; instead he was a Nixon appointee, and Nixon had now resigned in disgrace. One of Ford's first acts as President was to pardon Nixon for any crimes he had committed. The pardon came under heavy public criticism.

CONTINUING STAGFLATION

In office, Ford's main worries were over the economy. The nation suffered from **stagflation** — high unemployment combined with high inflation. Part of the problem was the reduction in government spending after the Vietnam War. Stagflation was also caused by drastic increases in oil prices. During the Arab-Israeli War of 1973, Arab nations had learned to cooperate in using oil as a political weapon. After the war, the Organization of Petroleum Exporting Countries (**OPEC**), containing both Arab and non-Arab members, realized that this cooperation could also be used to raise world oil prices.

INDOCHINA FALLS

In 1975, during Ford's Presidency, South Vietnam finally fell to North Vietnamese' forces. When Ford asked Congress for funds to save the South Vietnamese government, Congress refused. Ford was forced to watch passively as both South Vietnam and Cambodia were taken over by Communist governments.

THE HELSINKI ACCORDS

Ford continued Nixon's policy of détente with the Soviet Union. In 1975, the United States, the Soviet Union, and other countries signed the **Helsinki Accords,** recognizing post-World War II borders and promising to respect human rights.

THE CARTER PRESIDENCY, 1977–1981

President Ford lost the 1976 Presidential election to the Democratic candidate, **Jimmy Carter,** in part because many Americans identified Republicans with the Watergate scandal. Carter, a former Georgia governor, was elected as an "outsider" who promised to clean up Washington. Although free of the corruption that had plagued the Nixon Administration, Carter was unable to solve some of the nation's major problems.

DOMESTIC POLICY

Like Ford, Carter's chief problems at home were economic. The United States was heavily dependent on imported oil. As oil prices skyrocketed, inflation went over 10%, interest rates rose to 20%, and unemployment remained high.

The Energy Crisis. To deal with the crisis, Carter created the Department of Energy. He also increased the nation's fuel reserves. Carter sought a special tax on large automobiles, and the power to ration gas, but Congress denied him those powers.

Stagflation. Inflation and interest rates soared in 1979, partly due to the oil crisis. Carter cut federal spending, but inflation did not come down until two years into the Reagan Presidency.

CARTER'S DOMESTIC PROGRAM

The Environment. Carter provided funds to clean up toxic dumpsites. Following an accident at the **Three Mile Island** nuclear reactor in 1979, Carter created the Nuclear Regulatory Commission to develop stricter standards for nuclear

Diversity. Carter appointed women and minority members to government posts. He also sponsored a bill requiring public schools to provide instruction to students in their native language while trying to learn English.

FOREIGN POLICY

Carter wanted the United States to assert its world leadership by setting a moral example for other nations. Carter made human rights a very high priority: he condemned apartheid in South Africa, pressured the Soviet Union to allow Soviet Jews to emigrate, and cut aid to dictatorships that violated human rights.

★ **The Panama Canal Treaty, 1977.** Carter signed a treaty returning control of the Canal Zone to Panama, except for the canal itself. The United States further agreed to turn over the canal to Panama in 1999. In exchange, Panama gave the United States the right to defend the canal from attack.

★ **Camp David Accords.** Egypt and Israel had fought one another since 1948. In 1978, Carter invited Egypt's President **Anwar Sadat** and Israel's Prime Minister **Menachem Begin** to Camp David, where an agreement was reached. Under the agreement, Israel agreed to return the Sinai Peninsula to Egypt in exchange for a peace treaty and the establishment of normal diplomatic relations. Many Arab leaders denounced the agreement because it failed to provide a homeland for the Palestinians. Sadat was later assassinated.

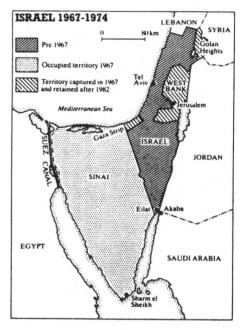

★ **China.** Carter restored full diplomatic relations with Communist China in 1979.

★ **U.S.-Soviet Relations.** At first, Carter continued the policy of détente with the Soviet Union. However, in 1979, the Soviet Union invaded Afghanistan, bringing a temporary end to détente. Carter halted grain sales to the Soviets, boycotted the 1980 Olympics in Moscow, and advised the Senate to postpone ratification of a new arms control agreement, **SALT II.**

★ **The Iranian Revolution and the Hostage Crisis (1978–1979).** The Shah (*ruler*) of Iran was an ally of the United States. However, **Shah Pahlavi** was also a dictator who used brutal measures against his opponents. In 1978, widespread demonstrations broke out across Iran against the Shah. When the Shah fled the country, **Ayatollah Khomeini** and other religious leaders hostile to Western influences took control. The new rulers resented the United States for helping the Shah and backing Israel. In retaliation, Iranian students seized the staff of the U.S. embassy in Iran. The staff was held hostage for 444 days. America's image throughout the world suffered because of Carter's inability to free them. Negotiations finally led to their release, but only on the day that Carter left office and Ronald Reagan became President.

THE NEW CONSERVATISM: REAGAN AND BUSH

Under Ronald Reagan and George H.W. Bush, the federal government moved in an even more conservative direction than under Nixon — further cutting social spending and federal regulations, but also taking a more aggressive stance in foreign affairs.

THE REAGAN PRESIDENCY, 1981–1989

Carter was defeated by **Ronald Reagan** in the Presidential election of 1980. Once in office, Reagan introduced far-reaching changes that brought a return to prosperity for many, but not all citizens.

Bureau of Engraving and Printing

DOMESTIC POLICY

Reagan felt individuals and businesses were better able to solve economic problems than government. He believed businesses would be more successful if they could make decisions with less governmental interference. Reagan supported the policy of **New Federalism** begun under President Nixon a decade earlier.

★ **Reaganomics.** When Reagan took office the nation was still facing stagflation. Reagan tried to solve the problem by introducing "**supply-side economics.**" He believed a large supply of goods would bring down prices and stop inflation. Reagan gave tax breaks to businesses and the wealthy. Some called this new strategy "**Reaganomics.**" In 1983, the economy came out of recession. Under Reagan, the nation enjoyed prosperity based on a variety of factors:

Tax Cuts and Domestic Spending. Reagan cut taxes on businesses and the wealthy: he felt these groups would invest their tax savings to raise productivity and increase employment, resulting in benefits that would "trickle down" to other groups. To finance the tax cut, Reagan reduced spending in federal welfare programs.	**Deregulation.** Reagan eliminated many federal regulations on industry, making it easier for new companies to compete. He ordered many regulatory agencies to cut back their rule-making and to allow businesses greater freedom.

REAGANOMICS IN ACTION

Increased Military Spending. Reagan increased military spending, which he financed through borrowing. This increased spending stimulated the entire economy, creating a demand for many goods and services.	**Other Factors.** World oil prices stabilized. New employment patterns created new jobs, such as computer programming and health care. Reagan took steps against unions to allow more flexible work practices.

★ **The Federal Deficit and the National Debt.** The **federal deficit** is any amount the federal government spends each year beyond what it collects in taxes. Reagan promised a budget in which government spending would be limited to the amount of taxes raised. Nevertheless, because of military spending, the federal deficit increased greatly, and the national debt more than doubled.

★ **The Trade Imbalance.** Reagan's policies led to growing trade imbalances. Americans bought more goods and services from abroad than they sold overseas. This imbalance led to the loss of millions of jobs, the closing of steel and auto plants, and a drop in the disposal income of many Americans.

THE IMPACT OF GEOGRAPHY ON HISTORY

Until the 1970s, most Americans lived in the Northeast and Midwest. The Southeast was considered too hot in summers, while the West was too dry and remote. Certain technological developments

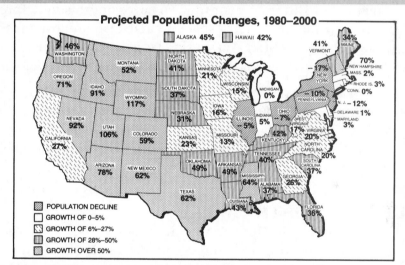

changed this situation. Government-built dams made more water available to Western cities. Air conditioning and hydroelectric power made homes and offices cooler in summer. The result was a shift of population to the West and South — known as the "**Sunbelt.**" With rising oil prices, Americans chose warm winters over snow and cold. California and Texas became the nation's most populous states, with Atlanta and Las Vegas as the nation's fastest growing urban areas.

★ **Immigration Policy.** The Reagan years saw changes in our immigration laws. To deal with problems posed by massive illegal immigration, the **Mazzoli-Simpson Act of 1986** "legalized" illegal aliens who had been in the U.S. since 1981.

FOREIGN POLICY

Reagan set out to rebuild American confidence. He believed that the United States had to continue to act as the world's defender of freedom and democracy.

★ **Military Intervention.** In 1983, Reagan sent U.S. Marines to **Grenada** in the Caribbean after Communists had taken control. The intervention showed Reagan's willingness to use force to protect Americans and to prevent Cuba and the Soviet Union from using the island to export Communism to other nearby republics.

★ **The Reagan Doctrine.** In 1986, President Reagan announced the **Reagan Doctrine** — the United States would no longer confine itself to containing Communism, but would attempt to roll back Communism by aiding anti-Communist "freedom fighters" in Afghanistan, Nicaragua, and Cambodia.

★ **Increased Military Spending.** To carry out this new foreign policy, Reagan sharply increased military spending. He also proposed research into a defense system, known as **Star Wars,** using lasers to prevent nuclear attack. This prospect disturbed Soviet leaders, who feared the expense of developing their own system.

★ **The War against Terrorism. Terrorism** refers to the use of bombing, assassination, kidnapping, and other acts of terror to ensure that a political group's voice will be heard and that governments will meet their demands. Reagan announced that he would not negotiate with terrorists and even bombed Libya when he thought its leader was implicated in terrorists' activities.

THE IRAN-CONTRA AFFAIR

In 1986, officials in the Reagan Administration secretly sold arms to Iran in exchange for the release of American hostages in Lebanon. Profits from the sale were diverted to support rebels fighting the Communist government of Nicaragua, even though Congress had passed a law denying U.S. aid to the rebels. An investigation cleared the President of wrongdoing. Several officials, however, were convicted of lying to Congress.

THE TRIUMPH OF DEMOCRACY

Reagan's second term witnessed the triumph of democracy in many parts of the world. In the Philippines and Latin America, dictatorships and military governments were replaced by democratically elected governments. The last years of Reagan's Presidency saw the coming of the end of the Cold War. The failure of the Soviet economic and political system forced Soviet leaders to introduce new reforms. Soviet leader **Mikhail Gorbachev** agreed to withdraw troops from Afghanistan and to allow peaceful changes in Eastern Europe. Reagan and Gorbachev signed an agreement dismantling thousands of nuclear missiles.

THE BUSH PRESIDENCY, 1989–1993

In 1988, Reagan's Vice President, **George H.W. Bush**, was elected to the Presidency on a promise to continue Reagan's policies, but with greater compassion in dealing with the homeless and poor, improving education, and fighting drug use.

DOMESTIC POLICY

Bush had served as the Director of the CIA and as Ambassador to the United Nations under Presidents Nixon and Ford. Bush's experience was mainly in foreign policy, and critics felt his approach to domestic policy sometimes lacked focus and direction.

★ **The Budget Deficit.** Bush's greatest domestic challenge was to reduce the growing budget deficit. Events in Eastern Europe and the Soviet Union allowed cuts in military spending. In late 1990, Bush agreed to increase income taxes for the very wealthy. Nevertheless, Bush was never able to significantly reduce the deficit.

★ **Supreme Court Appointments.** Bush made several appointments to the Supreme Court, which finally gave conservatives a majority on the Court by 1991. The new Supreme Court toughened its treatment of criminal defendants, reduced the scope of abortion rights, and introduced other important changes.

★ **The Recession.** The United States gradually moved into a recession by 1990. Economists blamed the economic downturn on reduced spending by consumers, corporations, and federal and state governments. In addition, lay-offs in key industries increased, due to greater foreign competition.

★ **Civil Rights and Civil Unrest.** African-American frustration led to riots in Los Angeles and other cities in 1992, when a jury found policemen not guilty of brutality in the **Rodney King** case. Buildings in Los Angeles and other cities were looted and burned, and seventy people were killed. The riots highlighted the plight of minorities and continuing racial tensions throughout the nation.

★ **Americans with Disabilities Act of 1990.** Bush signed this act prohibiting discrimination against people with disabilities in employment and public accommodations. The act guaranteed that those with disabilities be given equal treatment in their jobs and be given easy access to buildings, stores, trains and buses.

FOREIGN POLICY

Bush proved more successful in his foreign policy than in his domestic policy.

★ **The Invasion of Panama** (1989). Shortly after becoming President, Bush took steps against Panamanian dictator and drug-dealer **Manuel Noriega**. He sent U.S. forces to Panama, where they restored democratically elected leaders. Noriega was captured and taken back to the United States, where he faced drug charges.

★   **The End of the Cold War.** The most important event of the Bush Presidency was the end of the Cold War. From 1989 to 1991, Eastern Europe moved from Communism to democracy, the Berlin Wall was torn down, and Germany was reunited. Gorbachev's reforms set in motion a series of events that, by 1991, led to the dissolution of the Soviet Union and its replacement by the Commonwealth of Independent States led by Russia. Bush recognized the newly independent republics and offered them economic assistance.

President Bush

The White House

★   **The Persian Gulf War, 1991.** In the summer of 1990, Iraqi leader **Saddam Hussein** invaded Kuwait, capturing its vast oil wealth and extending Iraq's borders. Hussein refused requests by the United Nations to withdraw. In response, U.N. forces, under U.S. leadership, launched an attack against Iraq. The invasion succeeded in only a few days. In February 1991, Hussein agreed to remove all Iraqi troops from Kuwait and to pay Kuwait for damages. President Bush declared a cease-fire. Critics, however, argued that Bush should have removed Saddam Hussein when he had the chance. The crisis was significant as the first major challenge to world order after the end of the Cold War. American prestige was greatly enhanced by its success in the war. Bush used the upsurge in American prestige to bring about peace talks between Israel and its Arab neighbors in late 1991.

★   **Somalia.** In 1992, Bush began a humanitarian airlift of food to war-torn Somalia in Africa, where millions faced starvation. When local warlords threatened food shipments, Bush sent in U.S. troops in the final month of his Presidency.

THE UNITED STATES IN RECENT TIMES

THE CLINTON PRESIDENCY, 1993–2000

The Presidential election of 1992 saw **Bill Clinton** unite several groups in the Democratic Party, who sought to end twelve years of Republican rule. The public believed Bush was not doing enough to fight the recession. Criticisms from third-party candidate **Ross Perot** further weakened Bush's prestige. Clinton was elected with 43% of the vote.

DOMESTIC POLICY

Clinton promised Americans an ambitious agenda of reform. However, like many Presidents, he found difficulty in obtaining Congressional support for many of his proposals.

★ **The Budget.** Clinton's first budget limited federal spending, increased income taxes for wealthy Americans, and introduced a gasoline tax.

Clinton addresses Congress

★ **Health Care Reform.** In the election, Clinton promised to reform health care. He appointed his wife, **Hillary Clinton,** to head a task force. Clinton proposed to give every American guaranteed health insurance. No plan was able to be passed by Congress. The failure to reform health care was a major defeat for Clinton.

★ **Economic Recovery.** Clinton pushed **NAFTA,** first proposed in the Bush years, through Congress — creating a trade association between the U.S., Mexico, and Canada. This association is gradually phasing out tariffs between the three countries. The closing of many U.S. military bases gave the economy a boost. The growth of computer sales and the birth of the Internet also greatly stimulated the economy. By the end of Clinton's Presidency, unemployment was down, and business profits were at all-time highs. The federal budget was enjoying a surplus for the first time in years.

★ **Impeachment and Scandal.** Clinton became subject to a major scandal when an independent prosecutor, investigating Clinton's personal finances, uncovered a sexual affair between Clinton and a White House intern. After finding Clinton had lied about the affair under oath, the prosecutor recommended impeachment. Voting along party lines, the House of Representatives impeached the President. In the Senate, Republicans fell short of the two-thirds vote needed to remove Clinton.

FOREIGN POLICY

Unlike Bush, Clinton came to the White House with little experience in foreign affairs. Nevertheless, some of his greatest successes were in foreign policy.

★ **Russia.** Clinton followed President Bush's policy of maintaining friendly relations with Russian President **Boris Yeltsin.**

★ **Yugoslavia, Bosnia, and Kosovo.** After years of fighting among Bosnian Muslims, Croats, and Serbs, Clinton intervened to force a compromise peace. When Serb nationalists began persecuting Muslims in Kosovo, Clinton used NATO forces to bombard Serbia and force an end to the bloodshed in Kosovo.

★ **Israel.** The Clinton Administration followed Bush's lead by promoting peace between Israel and two of its traditional enemies, the P.L.O. and Jordan.

★ **Terrorism.** Terrorists, led by **Osama bin Laden,** orchestrated explosions in two U.S. embassies in Africa. Clinton retaliated with air strikes in Afghanistan and Sudan, but his attempts to capture bin Laden failed.

Osama bin Laden

★ **Iraq.** Clinton airlifted U.S. troops to the Middle East to persuade dictator Saddam Hussein to remove thousands of Iraqi troops along the Kuwait border. Later, Clinton forced Hussein to allow U.N. weapons inspectors into Iraq.

★ **China.** At first, President Clinton tried to link U.S. trade with China to the promotion of human rights. He soon abandoned this policy. In 1999, U.S. missiles accidentally hit the Chinese embassy in Yugoslavia. U.S.-Chinese relations suffered a setback, but there was no attempt to halt U.S.-Chinese trade. China became increasingly important as a U.S. trading partner.

★ **Mexico.** In 1995, President Clinton extended a $20 billion loan to Mexico. This was offered to help Mexico avert financial collapse, strengthening friendly ties between the two nations.

THE GEORGE W. BUSH PRESIDENCY, 2000–2008

George W. Bush, son of former President George H.W. Bush, enjoyed great popularity as Governor of Texas. In November 2000, Bush was elected President in the closest Presidential election contest in U.S. history.

THE 2000 ELECTION: BUSH vs. GORE

Bush's Democratic opponent was Clinton's Vice President, **Al Gore.** Despite Bill Clinton's successes, the Democrats were badly weakened by Clinton's impeachment scandal. Bush's campaign took an upswing when he performed better then expected in the Presidential debates. On election night, Gore won the popular vote, but in some states the margin was so narrow the winner of the electoral vote was unclear. After weeks of indecision, Florida election officials declared Bush the winner, giving Bush the electoral votes he needed for victory. Gore challenged these results and demanded a manual recount. When the U.S. Supreme Court ordered manual recounts stopped in several counties for their lack of uniform standards, Bush was finally declared the victor.

DOMESTIC POLICY

As President, Bush pushed through a tax cut in an attempt to revitalize a lagging economy. The Federal Reserve Board also dropped interest rates to their lowest levels in decades. The Bush tax cuts revived the economy, but brought a return to high deficits. Critics also argued his cuts favored the rich. As Governor of Texas, Bush had been active in educational reform. As President, he introduced the **No Child Left Behind Act,** requiring states to test all students in English and mathematics from third grade on.

TERRORIST ASSAULT ON AMERICA

On **September 11, 2001,** Islamic terrorists boarded four different U.S. airliners. Once airborne, the planes were hijacked and flown into the World Trade Center in New York City and the Pentagon building in Washington, D.C. As many as five thousand people were killed — making this the worst attack in U.S. history.

Corbis-Bettman Archives

THE WAR ON TERRORISM

President Bush vowed to launch a war against terrorism, including nations that harbored terrorists. The primary suspect emerged as **Osama bin Laden.** Bin Laden was a member of a wealthy Saudi family who had helped organize the radical al-Qaeda terrorist network. Osama was sheltered by a friendly government in Afghanistan. The **Taliban,** the Islamic Fundamentalist rulers of Afghanistan, refused to turn bin Laden over to the United States. In October 2001, Bush ordered air and ground assaults, which toppled the Taliban and destroyed bin Ladin's bases. Although many members of **al-Qaeda** were caught, bin Laden himself eluded capture.

Bush also took steps to curb terrorism at home. Federal agents took over security at U.S. airports, and all passengers and luggage were subjected to more thorough screening. Bush also created a new Cabinet post, the **Office of Homeland Security**, and sponsored the *Patriot Act*, greatly expanding law enforcement powers.

THE WAR IN IRAQ

After defeating the **Taliban** in Afghanistan, President Bush turned his attend to Iraq. He feared Iraqi dictator **Saddam Hussein** might provide biological, chemical, or even nuclear weapons to Islamic terrorists like Osama bin Laden.

Iraq repeatedly denied that it possessed any weapons of mass destruction (WMDs). In March, 2003, the U.S., Britain, and Spain warned Iraq to surrender its WMDs or face invasion. France, Germany, and Russia favored a more cautious approach, believing U.N. weapons inspectors should be given more time. American leaders feared Hussein would use such time to better hide his weapons. In March 2003, President Bush gave Hussein 48 hours to leave Iraq or face invasion. When Hussein rejected the ultimatum, the U.S. and coalition forces took military action.

As in the **First Gulf War of 1991,** the United States began its campaign with a series of air strikes to control Iraqi's army's movements. In early April, U.S. forces entered Baghdad, where they faced little resistance. Hussein's dictatorship quickly collapsed. On May 1, President Bush declared an end to U.S. combat operations. In December, Hussein himself was captured, tried by Iraqis and executed in 2006. Meanwhile, coalition forces established a provisional authority to govern Iraq. In early 2005, Iraqi voters elected representatives to draw up a constitution. Soon afterwards, a newly elected Iraqi national government took office, becoming the first Arab democracy in the Middle East.

★   **An Insurgency Emerges.** Nevertheless, coalition casualties continued to mount. An insurgency consisting of Hussein loyalists, Shiite radicals, and Iraqis angry at foreign intervention soon arose. Moreover, Iraq is generally divided among Kurds in the north, Shiite Muslims in the south, and both Shiite and Sunni Muslims in the center. Differences between these ethnic groups greatly added to the conflict. American forces also committed some key missteps. For example, Iraqi prisoners at **Abu Ghraib** prison were tortured and humiliated. This added to the unpopularity of the foreign troops on Iraqi soil.

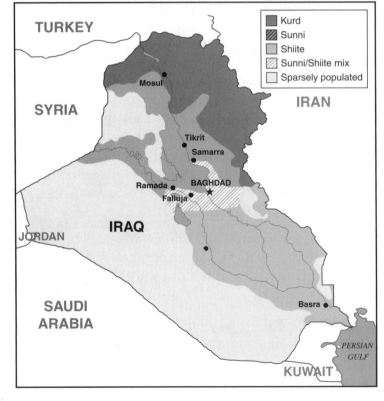

★ **The 2004 Presidential Election.** President Bush decided to run for a second term. His opponent was Senator **John Kerry,** an outspoken critic of Bush's handling of the war in Iraq. Bush defeated Kerry in another closely contested election.

★ **The "Surge."** By the end of 2006, as many as 1,000 people were being killed in Iraq each month. President Bush announced a new "surge" strategy early in 2007. Thousands of additional U.S. troops were added to secure local neighborhoods, guard Iraq's bordera, and strike at al-Qaeda forces. This led to a significant reduction in the violence in Iraq. Meanwhile, a petition of leading Iraqi legislators called for the with-

The "surge" of U.S. troops in Iraq helped stabilize the situation.

drawal of U.S. forces from Iraq. American withdrawal from Iraq became a central issue in the 2008 U.S. Presidential campaign.

★ **Hurricane Katrina.** The second term of the Bush Presidency also witnessed the arrival of Hurricane Katrina, which led to the evacuation and flooding of New Orleans and others parts of the Gulf Coast. When the levees failed to hold back the storm surge, more than 1,800 people lost their lives in subsequent floods, making it one of nation's the deadliest hurricanes. The storm was responsible for $81.2 billion in damages. Critics blamed the Bush Administration for its slow response to the crisis.

THE LEGACY OF PRESIDENT BUSH

At times during his Presidency, Bush achieved some of the highest approval ratings in U.S. history, but he managed to leave office as one of the nation's most unpopular Presidents. His Presidency was highlighted by keeping the nation safe from any further terrorist attacks, the nomination of U.S. Supreme Court Justice **John Roberts,** a push for Social Security and immigration reform, and the successful surge of U.S. troops in Iraq.

President Bush's critics point to the severe economic downturn that occurred at the end of his Presidency, including the banking system collapse and the mortgage crisis. These are described below. President Bush has also come under harsh criticism for the weak federal response to Hurricane Katrina, "warrantless" surveillances, and record federal budget deficits.

PRESIDENTIAL POWER IN THE AGE OF TERROR

How far should the government go, in an age of global communications, to protect Americans against future acts of terrorism? Following the September 11, 2001 attacks, Congress authorized the President to use "all necessary and appropriate force against nations, organizations or persons" he felt were behind the attacks. Congress also passed the **Patriot Act,** giving the President special powers to combat terrorism, and making it easier to wiretap potential terrorists. The Bush administration also authorized the National Security Agency (NSA) to wiretap suspect callers without first obtaining a warrant. The constitutionality of these "warrentless" wiretaps has been questioned.

To protect America from terrorism, the Bush administration also permitted the use of torture on some prisoners of war in Iraqi detention centers, especially at Abu Ghraib in Iraq. This practice violated the **Geneva Convention,** an international agreement prohibiting torture. Bush officials denied using torture, but admitted that the government had used "enhanced interrogation" techniques to uncover and prevent acts of terrorism.

Guantanamo Bay has long been a source of conflict over treatment of detainees.

On June 29, 2006, the Supreme Court ruled in ***Hamden v. Rumsfield,*** that the Bush administration, without the authorization of Congress, did not have the authority to set up a military commission to try detainees at Guantanamo Bay. Because Guantanamo Bay and Iraqi detention centers were not on American soil, officials had argued that detainees did not enjoy "due process" rights. Detainees were held for long periods without a trial, or were convicted by military courts based on evidence that they could not see, hearsay evidence, or even evidence gathered through coercion.

In June 2006, the U.S. Supreme Court ruled that the Bush administration lacked the authority to set up military commissions to try Guantanamo detainees. It held that detainees were protected by the Geneva Convention and could not be subject to "cruel treatment and torture" or "humiliating and degrading treatment."

In the 2008 Presidential campaign, both John McCain and Barack Obama announced their opposition to the use of torture. One of Obama's first Presidential acts was to announce the closure of the detention facility at Guantanamo Bay.

THE OBAMA PRESIDENCY, 2009–PRESENT

The 2008 Presidential campaign was one of the hardest-fought campaigns in U.S. history. Because neither the President nor the Vice President was in the running, a large number of candidates appeared on both sides. Democrats generally attacked the conduct of the war, while Republican candidates supported it. Former First-Lady **Hillary Clinton** was seen as the early Democratic frontrunner because her popularity with women and her reputation in American politics. However, a young senator from Illinois, **Barack Obama,** emerged as the Democratic nominee after a closely contested and historic primary contest. The Republican Party nominated Senator **John McCain,** a candidate with a distinguished war record.

Few believed Obama had a chance to be elected when he first announced his candidacy.

★   **Obama Becomes President.** Barack Obama, a strong critic of the war in Iraq, presented himself as the best candidate to bring about change. His appeal was strongest among young people, African-Americans, and opponents of the war. John McCain mainly emphasized his record as "maverick" Republican. He nominated a woman, Alaska Governor **Sarah Palin,** as his running mate. Obama identified McCain with President Bush, criticizing both the war in Iraq and the state of the American economy. A severe financial crisis, which broke out in the months just before the election, further helped Obama. In the historic election, Obama became the first African-American to be elected President — 135 years after the Emancipation Proclamation and 44 years after the Civil Rights Act.

Obama became the first African American elected President.

THE FINANCIAL CRISIS OF 2008–2009

President Obama's election coincided with the worst financial crisis since the Great Depression of 1932. For decades, the federal government and the Federal Reserve had been following policies to reduce swings in the U.S. economy. These efforts, combined with the growth of globalization, now contributed to an unexpected downturn.

★ **Roots of the Financial Crisis.** Back in 2000, many investors lost money buying stocks of overvalued Internet companies. When the stock market crashed in value, the Federal Reserve lowered interest rates to help stimulate the economy. Many took advantage of these lower interest rates to buy new homes. Changes in the system of government regulation also made it much easier to lend money. Some banks began lending money to borrowers who could not really afford homes. These loans were bundled with other investments and sold to other banks or investors, who did not know what they were buying. To further stimulate the economy, President Bush pushed through a series of tax cuts. To pay for the Iraq war and other expenses, the government sold bonds. Many of these bonds were bought by foreign governments, especially China and the Middle East. This further stimulated the American economy.

★ **The Financial Crisis Accelerates.** By 2007, overbuilding led housing prices to fall. Some people had specialized mortgages that adjusted to higher interest rates. When interest rates started to rise again, many homeowners could no longer afford to pay for their mortgages. A rising number of home foreclosures took place. A foreclosure occurs when a homeowner can no longer afford to pay the mortgage, and the bank takes

The housing crisis threatened the economy.

back the house to sell it. Many loans made to homeowners lost their value.

In September 2008, the federal government stepped in and took over **Fannie Mae** and **Freddie Mac,** the nation's largest mortgage lenders. Despite these actions, the crisis began to spin out of control. Firms that held these mortgage-backed securities mortgages started to fail. Banks stopped lending, even to one another. Credit dried up for individuals and businesses. In its final months in office, the Bush Administration sought to bail out several large companies and banks, such as AIG and Citibank. Congressional leaders approved a $700 billion bailout package.

★ **Obama Attempts to Stem the Crisis.** President Obama moved quickly to increase the size of the government bailout. He sought money to simulate the economy by creating jobs and rebuilding roads and schools, bridges and tunnels. He also proposed new funding for education and research. The Obama Administration also proposed important changes to a national health care system, phasing out earlier tax cuts for more affluent Americans, and reforming education.

FOREIGN PROBLEMS CLOUD THE HORIZON

President Obama also faced serious threats to American security from overseas:

★ **North Korea.** Both the Bush and Obama Administration expressed concerns about North Korea's attempts to develop nuclear weapons. North Korea has continued to test ballistic missiles that could reach Alaska. Despite its failing economy, North Korea has a conventional army of more than 100,000 special forces, and continues to remain a global security threat.

Kim Jong-il, North Korea's leader

★ **Iran.** Iran continues to refine its nuclear ores, claiming it is developing a new source of energy for peacetime domestic purposes. Critics fear Iran is developing its own nuclear weapons which will tip the regional balance of power in the Middle East. Iran also sponsors terrorist groups in the Middle East. Iran's leaders openly threaten Israel's existence and Iran's President has questioned the existence of the Holocaust. President Obama has been taking a "diplomatic" approach to Iran.

★ **Afghanistan and Pakistan.** President Obama has been refocusing American resources on the ongoing threat to U.S. security from the resurgence of al-Qaeda and the Taliban in Afghanistan and Pakistan. Obama increased U.S. troop levels in Afghanistan, and pressed NATO allies to do the same. Obama has also been spending greater resources to revitalize Afghanistan's economic development while pressing the Afghan government to reduce corruption and eradicate the opium trade. President Obama wants Pakistan to take a more aggressive role in securing its border with Afghanistan.

President Obama appointed two Special Envoys — Richard Holbrook (left) for Afganistan and Pakistan and George Mitchell (right) for the Middle East.

★ **Israeli-Palestinian Conflict.** Israel is America's strongest ally in the Middle East. President Obama has repeatedly affirmed Israel's right to defend itself from raid and rocket attacks. Obama seeks to work with both Israelis and Palestinians to achieve the goal of two states, a Jewish state in Israel and a neighboring Palestinian state, living side-by-side in peace and security.

TOWARD A POST-INDUSTRIAL WORLD: LIVING IN A GLOBAL AGE

Over the past thirty years, changes have gradually altered the American way of life.

TECHNOLOGY

Modern technology is based on the application of science to meet our needs.

THE SHIFT TO A SERVICE ECONOMY

After the Industrial Revolution, most Americans became involved in manufacturing. In the last fifty years, this nation has experienced a shift from manufacturing to a service economy. Americans are now more likely to find work in a store, office, or school than in a factory.

THE COMPUTER REVOLUTION

Much of the increased productivity in the 1990s is due to computers. The computer industry has added millions of jobs to the economy. The **Internet,** a world-wide linking of computers, is making it easier to communicate and find information.

MEDICINE AND HEALTH

Since World War II, the development of antibiotics, vaccines, and other medicines have increased life-spans and enabled Americans to cure many fatal diseases. Americans have also become more health conscious, limiting fat in their diets, drinking less alcohol and cutting down on tobacco use. Scientists are also studying each of the estimated 100,000 human genes, permitting **genetic engineering.** However, with the rising cost of medical care, millions of Americans are unable to obtain health insurance, posing a major challenge for future health care.

ENERGY

Population growth and rising living standards have led to a greater demand for energy. It was once thought that nuclear power plants would meet our energy needs without pollution. The **Three Mile Island** accident in 1979 showed that nuclear power might also be unsafe. New sources of oil in Alaska have helped meet our energy needs.

United Nations

A modern hydroelectric plant

GLOBALIZATION

In the 1950s, American manufacturers mainly sold to the American market. Today, our economy is more integrated into the world economy. Huge **multinational corporations** (*corporations with local companies in several countries*) sell their products in every corner of the world. By the 1990s, these multinationals controlled half of the industrial assets of the United States and employed millions of workers here and abroad.

American companies like Ford are now multinational corporations

Ford Motor Company

Competition among American and foreign multinational corporations is intensifying. The United States now produces only 15 percent of the world's steel, compared to 60 percent forty years ago. Likewise, American automobile manufacturers now face stiff competition from multinational corporations originating in Japan, Germany, Britain, and Korea.

GLOBAL INEQUALITIES

Vast differences separate the "have" and "have-not" nations of the world. Nearly one-fourth of the world's population live in industrialized nations like the United States, where people are relatively well-fed, healthy, consume more energy, are wealthier, and live longer lives. Three-fourths of the world's population still live in

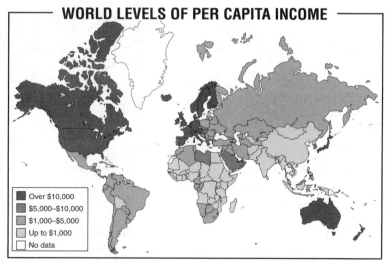

WORLD LEVELS OF PER CAPITA INCOME

Over $10,000
$5,000–$10,000
$1,000–$5,000
Up to $1,000
No data

the developing nations of the **Third World.**

The gap between the United States and poorer nations continues to widen, posing a challenge for the future. Although the United States is sensitive to the problems of developing nations, this gap has created tensions. To help poorer nations, the United States contributes aid to established international relief agencies that strive to improve education and to raise living standards in the Third World. The United States is the major contributor to the **World Bank,** which provides credit to developing nations seeking to build stronger economies.

THE ENVIRONMENT

In the past thirty years, Americans have become increasingly aware of growing dangers to our environment. As countries become more developed and the world's population grows, pollution of the earth's air, water, and other resources becomes an ever-increasing threat to the future survival of humankind.

★ **Global Warming.** Some pollutants in the atmosphere prevent heat from escaping into space. This **greenhouse effect** may eventually raise world temperatures enough to cause farmland to become desert, or polar ice to melt, raising seas to dangerous levels. The United States has been the leading offender, producing 25% of the gases that cause this effect. As more fuels are burned to supply electricity, the problem only worsens.

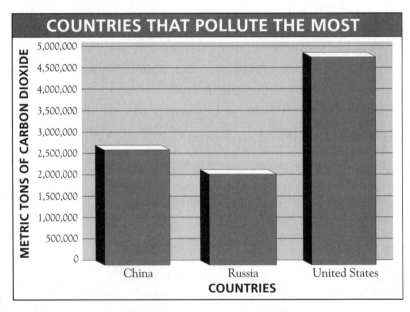

★ **Acid Rain.** When coal and oil are burned to create energy, they dump pollutants into the atmosphere. Many pollutants released by industry and automobile exhaust turn into acids. These acids get washed out of the air when it rains. When these pollutants return in the form of rain, they are highly toxic, killing fish, destroying forests, eroding soil and further endangering the environment.

★ **Erosion of the Ozone Layer.** The ozone layer absorbs ultraviolet radiation passing through the earth's atmosphere. Too much radiation can cause skin cancer. The ozone layer is rapidly being eroded by the use of certain types of fluorocarbons.

★ **Water Pollution.** As cities become more crowded, their ability to handle increased sewage and waste is strained.

★ **Solid Waste.** Modern societies generate millions of tons of garbage — bottles, cans, plastic, and other waste. Much of it is placed in landfills, but these sites are now filling up. Burning this waste or dumping it into oceans and rivers also creates pollution. The disposal of toxic chemical by-products or radioactive materials poses special dangers.

A tugboat tows a garbage barge out to sea for dumping

Stewart Milstein, Photographer

★ **New Efforts.** To deal with these problems, the **Environmental Protection Agency (E.P.A.)** and state agencies set standards for permissible pollution levels. New buildings pass through detailed environmental impact reviews before being approved and constructed. The United States is also cooperating with other countries for a global strategy to reduce pollution and conserve the environment.

TERRORISM

Terrorism uses violence against civilians as a weapon to draw attention to a group's grievances and to frighten governments into making concessions. Many radical groups in the world have used or still use terrorism. Afghanistan, Libya, Iran, Iraq, and Syria are alleged to have sheltered terrorists.

★ **The Irish Republican Army (I.R.A.)** once used terrorism against England to force British troops out of Ireland.

★ **The Palestine Liberation Organization (P.L.O.)** once used terrorism in what they considered as Israel's occupation of Palestinian lands.

★ **The Al-Qaeda Network.** Terrorism reached new levels of destruction when terrorists of Osama bin Laden's al-Qaeda network hijacked commercial airplanes and smashed them into the World Trade Center and Pentagon on September 11, 2001, killing over five thousand people.

Future terrorists may use biological, chemical, or even nuclear weapons — posing a serious threat for the twenty-first century.

SUMMARIZING YOUR UNDERSTANDING

KEY TERMS, CONCEPTS, AND PEOPLE

Make a vocabulary card for each of the following terms and concepts.

Imperial Presidency	Camp David Accords	Americans with Disabilities Act
Détente	Reaganomics	Gulf War of 1990
Watergate Scandal	New Federalism	NAFTA
Panama Canal Treaty	Iran-Contra Affair	Multinational Corporations

COMPLETING A TABLE

Briefly describe each of the following Presidential administrations of this period.

President	Major Domestic Policies	Major Foreign Policies
Nixon Administration		
Carter Administration		
Reagan Administration		
Bush Administration		
Clinton Administration		

COMPLETING A GRAPHIC ORGANIZER

Identify and describe some of the major post-war developments occurring in the United States during this period.

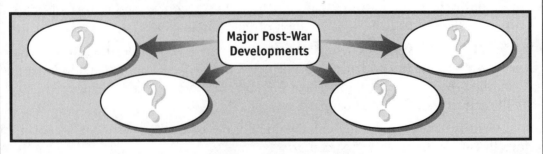

Major Post-War Developments

TESTING YOUR UNDERSTANDING

MULTIPLE-CHOICE QUESTIONS

1 The outcome of the Watergate scandal reinforced the idea that
1 our government is based on the rule of laws, not of individuals
2 our chief executive has unlimited powers
3 Congress is not effective in dealing with a constitutional crisis
4 the Supreme Court cannot make decisions affecting the Presidency

2 During the administration of President Nixon, U.S. policy toward China was characterized by
1 repeated attempts to introduce democracy into China
2 increasing hostility and isolation
3 the signing of a mutual defense pact
4 a resumption of communications

3 Which is the best explanation of why Presidential power increased during the Vietnam War?
1 Congress was afraid to exercise its constitutional powers.
2 The Constitution was suspended during wartime.
3 The President was in the best position to act quickly and decisively.
4 In wartime, the Bill of Rights puts all power into the President's hands.

4 Gerald Ford was the first President who
1 won the office by running on a third-party ticket
2 resigned from the Presidency
3 was impeached
4 was neither elected to the Presidency nor the Vice-Presidency

5 The Camp David Accords negotiated by President Carter were significant because they represented
1 the first peace agreement between Israel and an Arab nation
2 the establishment of a worldwide human rights policy
3 a lasting arms-reduction treaty
4 the end of the hostage crisis in Iran

6   During President Reagan's two terms in office, his federal budget proposals came under sharp criticism because they
1   lowered interest rates   3   raised income taxes
2   increased social welfare spending   4   included very large deficits

7   The Reagan Presidency faced its greatest difficulties in Central America in
1   Nicaragua   3   Guatemala
2   Honduras   4   Costa Rica

8   Which statement best reflects President Reagan's "New Federalism"?
1   The federal government should be given greater power.
2   Taxes should be raised to reduce the federal deficit.
3   The federal government should give power back to the states.
4   Military spending should be cut to provide funds for social programs.

9   According to the "supply-side" economics promoted by President Ronald Reagan, economic growth should occur when
1   corporate business taxes are reduced
2   business is regulated by antitrust legislation
3   unemployment benefits are increased
4   investment in capital goods is decreased

10   Which event took place during the administration of George Bush?
1   invasion of Panama   3   Cuban Missile Crisis
2   passage of the Civil Rights Act   4   the Watergate scandal

11   One direct result of the Persian Gulf War was that the United States
1   gained control of oil resources in the Middle East
2   liberated Kuwait from Iraqi control
3   promoted peaceful relations between Iran and its neighbors
4   seized colonies in the Middle East

12   "I believe that it must be the policy of the United States to support free peoples who resist attempted subjugation by armed minorities or by outside pressures. I believe that our help should be primarily through economic and financial aid...."
— Harry Truman

The ideas expressed in the quotation above were used by President Reagan to justify U.S. intervention in the affairs of
1   Central America   3   Vietnam
2   Western Europe   4   Canada

13 Which statement accurately describes U.S. immigration policy since 1965?
1   Any person wishing to immigrate has been welcome.
2   There are limits on the total number of immigrants allowed to enter.
3   Only immigrants with jobs or relatives in this country are admitted.
4   Immigrants have been required to speak English for admission.

14 **"Johnson Decides Not To Run"**
"Nixon Resigns Presidency"
"Bush Defeated by Clinton"
Based on these headlines, a valid conclusion about the contemporary Presidency is that
1   incumbent Presidents are guaranteed success in seeking re-election
2   Vice Presidents seldom become Presidents
3   Presidents are accountable for their performance
4   Presidential power has become nearly unlimited

15 NAFTA is based on the belief that
1   protective tariffs raise the standard of living
2   nations benefit from a greater flow of goods and services
3   foreign imports to the United States should be halted
4   the United States must be self-reliant in producing strategic products

16 One similarity between the "Open Door" Policy and NAFTA is that both were intended to
1   raise tariffs between nations
2   expand economic links between nations
3   improve relations in East Asia
4   relax restrictions on immigration

17 Some programs specifically designed to increase the number of minorities and women in the workforce have been attacked in recent years because
1   minorities and women are now satisfied with the gains they have made
2   laws guaranteeing equal opportunity have been found unconstitutional
3   affirmative action has sometimes been considered reverse discrimination
4   the economy has been too weak to absorb more workers

18 President Theodore Roosevelt's Russo-Japanese Treaty at Portsmouth, President Wilson's Fourteen Points, and President Carter's Camp David Accords are all examples of U.S. actions aimed at promoting
1   international trade   3   improved environmental standards
2   world peace   4   effective communication networks

INTERPRETING DOCUMENTS

"Government is not the solution to our problem. Government is the problem."

1. Place a check next to the President most likely to have made this statement.
    ❏ Franklin D. Roosevelt   ❏ Lyndon B. Johnson
    ❏ Ronald Reagan   ❏ Bill Clinton

2. Describe some of the programs or policies followed by this President to reflect

    his belief in the idea expressed in the quotation. ─────────────────────

    ──

THEMATIC ESSAY QUESTION

Directions: Write a well-organized essay that includes an introduction, several paragraphs addressing the task below, and a conclusion.

Theme: Justice and Human Rights

> Throughout American history, members of certain groups in society have faced prejudice or discrimination.

Task:

Choose **two** groups from your study of American history.

For *each* group:
- Discuss the discrimination or bigotry faced by members of that group.
- Describe how the group overcame that discrimination or bigotry.

You may use any examples from your study of American history. Some suggestions you might wish to consider include: Native Americans, African Americans, women, Irish Americans, new immigrants, Japanese Americans, Jewish Americans, Hispanic Americans, and Americans with Disabilities.

You are *not* limited to these suggestions.

CHAPTER 14

A FINAL REVIEW

Congratulations! You have just finished reviewing more than two hundred years of American history. At this point you might be thinking — how am I ever going to remember all of these dates, terms, concepts, events, and people?

This chapter will provide you with various ways of completing your final review of the information that appears most frequently on the United States History and Government Regents Examination. Let's look at what each section provides:

★ **Glossary of Major Concepts.** This section provides a short glossary identifying the major concepts of American history.

★ **Checklist of Important Terms.** This section provides a checklist of important terms used throughout this book.

★ **Notable Americans.** This section provides a checklist of the individuals most often asked about on the Regents Examination.

★ **Principles of the U.S. Constitution.** This section contains a chart summarizing the major principles of U.S. government.

★ **Milestones of American History.** This section is divided into three parts showing milestones in the fields of economic history, domestic history, and U.S. foreign policy.

GLOSSARY OF MAJOR CONCEPTS

Capitalism: The economic system of the United States. Under capitalism, resources and the means of production are privately owned rather than state controlled. Prices, production, and distribution are determined mainly by competition among sellers. Consumers are free to choose what they wish to buy.

Democracy: A system of government in which citizens participate in the decisions of government either by voting directly or by electing representatives to make decisions. The United States is an example of a representative democracy.

"Due Process of Law": The right to a fair and impartial trial or proceeding before being punished or deprived of property or other rights. Due process is guaranteed by the Constitution in the Fifth and Fourteenth Amendments.

Equal Protection: The right of each American to equal treatment before the law. State segregation laws were overruled on the basis of the Equal Protection Clause of the 19th Amendment.

Freedom of Expression (*also known as "free speech"*): The right of a person to speak or publish statements freely without fear of punishment. Free expression is vital to democratic government. However, even in the United States, free speech does not permit one to make statements that threaten the safety of others.

Imperialism: The political and economic rule of one country by another. For example, the United States followed an imperialist policy when it annexed the Philippines after the Spanish-American War.

Isolationism: The policy of any nation refusing to become involved in the affairs of other countries. Countries generally follow isolationist policies to avoid involvement that might lead to war. For example, the United States followed an isolationist policy in the 1920s and 1930s.

Laissez-faire: A policy followed by the American government in the 1800s which left businesses free to operate with minimal government interference or regulation, especially in their relations with consumers and workers. *Laissez-faire* comes from the French for "let do."

Nationalism: The belief that each ethnic group or "nation" should have its own government and country. Nationalism can be either a unifying or divisive force.

Neutrality: The policy of a country that refuses to take sides among warring nations. For example, the United States followed a policy of neutrality when war first broke out in Europe in 1914 and again in 1939.

Progressive Movement: A middle-class reform movement in the early 20th century, favoring the adoption of government regulations to prevent government corruption and the abuses of big business.

Social Mobility: The movement of individuals from one social class to another.

Union: An organization formed by workers for bargaining collectively with their employers to obtain more pay and better working conditions.

Urbanization: The movement of people from the countryside into cities.

CHECKLIST OF IMPORTANT TERMS

Following is a checklist of important terms, events, organizations, and Supreme Court cases that are frequently the focus of multiple-choice, thematic, and document-based essay questions.

- ❏ Affirmative Action
- ❏ Articles of Confederation
- ❏ Bill of Rights (1791)
- ❏ *Brown v. Board of Education* (1954)
- ❏ Civil War (1861–1865)
- ❏ Civil Rights Movement
- ❏ Cold War (1945–1991)
- ❏ Collective Bargaining
- ❏ Collective Security
- ❏ Compromise of 1850
- ❏ Concurrent Powers
- ❏ Containment
- ❏ Declaration of Independence (1776)
- ❏ Elastic Clause
- ❏ Electoral College
- ❏ Fourteen Points (1918)
- ❏ Fourteenth Amendment (1868)
- ❏ Frontier
- ❏ Good Neighbor Policy (1930–1945)
- ❏ Grange Movement
- ❏ Great Compromise (1787)
- ❏ Great Depression (1929–1940)
- ❏ Great Society (1964–1968)
- ❏ Harlem Renaissance (1920s)
- ❏ Impeachment
- ❏ Industrial Revolution
- ❏ Isolationism
- ❏ Jacksonian Democracy (1830s)
- ❏ Jim Crow Laws
- ❏ Judicial Review
- ❏ Korean War (1950–1953)
- ❏ Ku Klux Klan
- ❏ League of Nations
- ❏ Manifest Destiny
- ❏ *Marbury v. Madison* (1803)

- ❏ Marshall Plan (1948)
- ❏ Mexican-American War (1846–1848)
- ❏ Miranda v. Arizona (1966)
- ❏ Missouri Compromise (1820)
- ❏ Monroe Doctrine (1823)
- ❏ Muckrakers
- ❏ NATO
- ❏ New Deal
- ❏ New Immigrants
- ❏ Nineteenth Amendment
- ❏ Open Door Policy (1899)
- ❏ *Plessy v. Ferguson* (1896)
- ❏ Popular Sovereignty
- ❏ Populist Party (1891–1896)
- ❏ Progressive Income Tax
- ❏ Progressive Movement (1890–1920)
- ❏ Protective Tariffs
- ❏ Reconstruction Era (1865–1877)
- ❏ Reserved Powers
- ❏ *Roe v. Wade* (1973)
- ❏ Segregation
- ❏ Seneca Falls Convention (1848)
- ❏ Separation of Powers
- ❏ September 11, 2001
- ❏ Social Security Act (1935)
- ❏ Spanish-American War (1898)
- ❏ Truman Doctrine (1947)
- ❏ United Nations
- ❏ Vietnam War (1962–1973)
- ❏ War of 1812
- ❏ War Powers Act (1973)
- ❏ Watergate Affair (1972–1974)
- ❏ Women's Rights Movement
- ❏ World War I (1914–1918)
- ❏ World War II (1939–1945)

NOTABLE AMERICANS

Following is a checklist of individuals who are frequently the focus of multiple-choice, thematic, and document-based essay questions.

- ❑ Addams, Jane
- ❑ Anthony, Susan B.
- ❑ Bryan, William Jennings
- ❑ Bush, George H.W.
- ❑ Bush, George W.
- ❑ Carnegie, Andrew
- ❑ Carson, Rachel
- ❑ Carter, Jimmy
- ❑ Carver, George Washington
- ❑ Clinton, Bill
- ❑ Coolidge, Calvin
- ❑ Douglass, Frederick
- ❑ DuBois, W.E.B.
- ❑ Edison, Thomas
- ❑ Eisenhower, Dwight D.
- ❑ Ford, Gerald
- ❑ Ford, Henry
- ❑ Friedan, Betty
- ❑ Garvey, Marcus
- ❑ Gompers, Samuel
- ❑ Grant, Ulysses S.
- ❑ Hamilton, Alexander
- ❑ Harding, Warren
- ❑ Hoover, Herbert
- ❑ Hughes, Langston
- ❑ Jackson, Andrew
- ❑ Jackson, Helen Hunt
- ❑ Jefferson, Thomas
- ❑ Johnson, Andrew
- ❑ Johnson, Lyndon B.
- ❑ Kennedy, John F.
- ❑ King, Martin Luther, Jr.
- ❑ LaFollette, Robert
- ❑ Lincoln, Abraham
- ❑ Lindbergh, Charles
- ❑ MacArthur, Douglas
- ❑ Malcolm X
- ❑ Marshall, George
- ❑ Marshall, John
- ❑ Marshall, Thurgood
- ❑ McCarthy, Joseph
- ❑ McKinley, William
- ❑ Nixon, Richard
- ❑ Obama, Barack
- ❑ Paine, Thomas
- ❑ Parks, Rosa
- ❑ Robinson, Jackie
- ❑ Rockefeller, John D.
- ❑ Roosevelt, Franklin D.
- ❑ Roosevelt, Eleanor
- ❑ Roosevelt, Theodore
- ❑ Rosenberg, Julius and Ethel
- ❑ Scott, Dred
- ❑ Stanton, Elizabeth Cady
- ❑ Steinem, Gloria
- ❑ Stowe, Harriet Beecher
- ❑ Taft, William Howard
- ❑ Tarbell, Ida
- ❑ Truman, Harry S
- ❑ Tubman, Harriet
- ❑ Warren, Earl
- ❑ Washington, Booker T.
- ❑ Washington, George
- ❑ Wilson, Woodrow

PRINCIPLES OF THE U.S. CONSTITUTION

★ **Popular Sovereignty.** The American people hold supreme power in the U.S. government. Through elections, citizens select their own representatives at all levels of government.

★ **Federalism.** Power is shared between the national or federal government and state governments. The federal government deals with matters affecting the whole country, while state governments handle their own matters. Not only is this a more effective way to deal with public needs, but federalism prevents the national government from becoming too strong.

★ **Separation of Powers.** To prevent any one part of the central government from becoming too strong, the authors of the Constitution separated the three main powers of the federal government into three branches:

Legislative (Congress)	**Executive (the President)**	**Judicial (Supreme Court)**

★ **Limited Government.** The Constitution spells out the specific powers of the federal government. All other powers are reserved for the states and the people. However, the federal government has the power to do anything "necessary and proper" to carry out its delegated powers.

★ **Checks and Balances.** To prevent any one branch from becoming too powerful, the Constitution also allows each branch to "check" or limit the others. For example, the President negotiates treaties but the Senate must approve them; Congress passes laws, but the President can veto them.

★ **Flexibility.** The interpretations of the Supreme Court and the process of amendment have allowed the Constitution to adapt to changing conditions.

★ **The Unwritten Constitution.** Our constitutional system of government has allowed the emergence of customary practices not specifically incorporated into the Constitution, such as political parties, the Cabinet, and Congressional Committees.

MILESTONES OF U.S POLITICAL AND SOCIAL HISTORY

Milestone	Description
The American Revolution (1775–1783)	Colonists became alarmed when the British imposed new taxes without their consent. On July 4, 1776, members of the Continental Congress issued the Declaration of Independence, proclaiming that the purpose of government is to protect the rights of the governed.
The Constitutional Convention and Bill of Rights (1787–1791)	After independence, the Articles of Confederation created a central government which could not prohibit states from taxing one another's goods or defend against rebellion or invasion. States sent delegates to Philadelphia to write a new Constitution with a national President, Congress, and Supreme Court. The states ratified the Constitution in 1788. A Bill of Rights was added in 1791.
Westward Expansion (1804–1848)	After the American Revolution, settlers streamed over the Appalachians to settle the Northwest Territory. The Louisiana Purchase (1804) doubled the size of the nation. Americans next annexed California and the Southwest after victory in the Mexican-American War — giving them territory from the Atlantic to the Pacific.
The Civil War (1861–1865)	Sectionalism grew as different ways of life emerged. Southerners relied on slavery, while abolitionism grew stronger in the North. The acquisition of new territories created a crisis as Americans debated whether to extend slavery to these areas. When Lincoln was elected in 1860, Southern states seceded. Determined to preserve the Union, Lincoln led the nation into the Civil War. The North achieved victory but only after four long years of war.
Reconstruction (1865–1877)	During Reconstruction, Americans had to reunify the nation and rebuild the South. Radical Republicans in Congress refused to recognize Southern state governments and imposed military rule. Reconstruction ended in 1877 when Northern troops were withdrawn. White Southerners then deprived African Americans of their voting rights and introduced racial segregation.
Industrialization and the Settlement of the West	After the Civil War, America was transformed by industrialization, urbanization, immigration, the expansion of railroads, and the settlement of the Great Plains and Far West. Native Americans were forced onto reservations.
Grangers and the Populists (1867–1896)	High railroad charges and falling food prices led farmers to organize into Grange associations. Later farmers joined the Populist Party, which sought many reforms, including party primaries and a graduated income tax, which were later adopted by the other political parties.

Milestone	Description
The Progressive Era	Muckrakers and other middle-class reformers exposed the abuses of big business and rapid industrialization. Progressive state governments and Presidents Roosevelt and Wilson helped curb some of the abuses.
The Roaring Twenties (1920s)	The passage of the 19th Amendment and the prosperity of the 1920s saw the rise of new cultural values. Women, African Americans, and youths enjoyed greater freedom than ever before.
Depression, the New Deal, and World War II (1930s–1940s)	The Stock Market Crash of 1929 led to the Great Depression. President Roosevelt's "New Deal" experimented with new programs to find people work and introduced Social Security and many other reforms. World War II restored full employment as the nation fought for victory.
Post-War Prosperity (1950s–1960s)	After W.W. II, America emerged as the world's leading economic super-power. Americans bought millions of autos, refrigerators, and other appliances. War veterans moved to suburbs and started families, creating the baby boom. With the onset of the Cold War, America became concerned with internal security.
Civil Rights Movement (1950s–1960s)	The *Brown* decision (1954) and the Montgomery Bus Boycott (1955) inaugurated the Civil Rights Movement. Under Martin Luther King, Jr. and others, African Americans ended racial segregation and made tremendous strides towards racial equality.
The 1960s: A Decade of Change	The Civil Rights Movement was followed by the Women's Liberation Movement. President Johnson attempted to eliminate poverty with his "Great Society" programs. A new youth culture emerged in which young people experimented with sexual freedom, music, and drugs. The war in Vietnam led to the disillusionment of many with the "establishment."
The Presidency in Crisis (1968–1979)	The New Deal, World War II, the Cold War, and the Vietnam War led to increases in Presidential power. The Vietnam War and Nixon's resignation over the Watergate Scandal led to doubts about our nation's leaders. Presidents Ford and Carter had difficulties coping with rising oil prices, stagflation, and foreign crises.
The New Conservatism (1980–1992)	Presidents Reagan and George H.W. Bush cut federal spending on domestic programs. The Reagan and Bush Presidencies also witnessed the end of the Cold War and the collapse of the Soviet Union.
America Today (1993–Present)	Under President Clinton, Americans benefited from increased foreign trade and improvements in the computer industry. A long period of economic expansion ended with the attack of Sept. 11, 2001. President Bush was given new powers to wage the War on Terror. President Obama was elected to end Iraq's occupation and solve America's financial crisis.

MILESTONES OF AMERICAN ECONOMIC HISTORY

Milestone	Description
Creation of The National Economy	The Commerce Clause of the Constitution and the Supreme Court decision in *Gibbons v. Ogden* (1824) helped create a national economy in which citizens could do business in other states on equal terms — encouraging the free movement of goods, money, and people. This greatly speeded up the growth of the American economy.
Industrial Revolution	Factories and the use of new machines and sources of power greatly increased the scale of production, changed where people lived, and altered what they produced and consumed.
Abolition of Slavery (1865)	After the Civil War, the plantation system of the South was replaced by sharecropping and light industry; the South fell behind the North in economic power and influence.
Building the Transcontinental Railroad (1869)	The construction of railroads opened the interior of the nation for settlement, speeded up the pace of industrialization, and linked production centers to large city markets. In addition, railroads helped settle the prairies, leading to the availability of cheaper food to feed the people living in cities.
Urbanization and Immigration (late 1880s)	A new urban culture developed as America was transformed into a nation of city dwellers. Cities became crowded and faced housing shortages. As the need for labor expanded, immigrants filled jobs in factories and sweatshops. Despite facing many hardships, they contributed greatly to the creation of a prosperous economy.
Business Consolidation in the Gilded Age (late 1880s)	The rise of corporations allowed companies to undertake vast enterprises like the construction of steel mills. The trend toward unfair business practices was limited by federal antitrust laws like the Sherman Antitrust Act of 1890.
Rise of Labor Unions (late 1800s– early 1900s)	Workers gained the right to bargain collectively with their employers over pay and working conditions. Unions obtained better working conditions for U.S. workers. The Wagner Act (1935) gave a decisive push to the growth of unions.
Progressive Reforms (early 1900s)	At the state and federal level, Progressives introduced reforms like the Pure Food and Drug Act (1906) to protect consumers and prevent the worst abuses of big business.

Milestone	Description
Establishment of the Federal Reserve and the Income Tax (1913)	President Wilson introduced a Federal Reserve System to provide stability and flexibility to our national monetary system, and a progressive income tax to raise revenue. The Federal Reserve helped stabilize the economy, while income taxes became the main source of federal revenue, replacing tariffs.
Mass Production of the Automobile	Henry Ford began mass production of the Model T in 1908. The rise of automobiles created a new industry employing millions of Americans. Cars, buses, and trucks increased personal mobility, brought different parts of the country closer together, and transformed the American way of life.
The Great Depression and the New Deal (1929–1939)	The Great Depression of 1929 to 1939 was the greatest economic disaster in American history. People were thrown out of work, families lost their homes, banks failed, and national production was cut in half. The crisis led to increased federal involvement in the economy. President Roosevelt's New Deal introduced Social Security and made the federal government responsible for supervising the performance of the national economy.
World War II and the Post-War Prosperity (1940s–1950s)	The federal government directed national wartime production. War-time research improved our uses of atomic energy, aircraft, and computers. Following the war, America prospered as the world's leading producer of manufactured goods.
The Great Society (1960s)	President Johnson introduced new social programs like Medicare, federal aid to education, and affirmative action. These new programs and the costs of the war in Asia led to increased federal spending and inflation.
Reaganomics (1980s)	President Reagan's deficit spending and easing of government regulations led to economic prosperity for many Americans. However, minority and low income groups suffered from reduced spending on social programs. Deregulation led to stockbroker scandals and increased military spending left a vast national debt.
The Computer Revolution (1990s–2000s)	The spread of computerization led to increased productivity and a period of great prosperity. The introduction and spread of the Internet improved communication and access to information.
Financial Crisis (2008–Present)	The collapse of the housing bubble in the U.S. led to a banking and financial crisis that triggered a worldwide recession in 2008–2009.

MILESTONES OF AMERICAN FOREIGN POLICY

Milestone	Description
Washington's Farewell Address (1796)	President Washington advised Americans to avoid entangling alliances with European nations. This policy helped the United States keep out of war between France and England until 1812.
War of 1812	In 1812, Congress declared war against the British to stop the impressment of American sailors, to halt Native American raids in the Northwest, and to conquer Canada. Americans preserved their independence and the war ended in 1815.
Monroe Doctrine (1823)	President Monroe announced that America would oppose any attempt by European powers to reconquer former colonies in Latin America that had become independent or to establish new colonies. As a result, the newly independent countries of Latin America preserved their independence. Later, the Monroe Doctrine was used by the United States to justify its interference in the Caribbean region.
Manifest Destiny (mid-1800s)	In the mid-19th century, many Americans held the belief that the United States was destined to expand from the Atlantic to the Pacific coast. The desire for territorial expansion led to the Mexican-American War (1846-1848). Mexico was defeated and forced to give up much of its territory to the United States.
Spanish-American War (1898)	After the DeLôme letter and sinking of the *U.S.S. Maine*, Americans went to war with Spain to help Cuban rebels win their independence. After the war, Cuba became independent but fell under U.S. control. Spain lost the Philippines and its possessions in the Western Hemisphere.
American Imperialism (1898–1900)	After the Spanish-American War, the United States became an imperialist power by annexing the Philippines, Puerto Rico, Hawaii, and Samoa. Americans also developed overseas trade with China and Japan.
The Panama Canal and the "Big Stick" Policy (1902–1914)	Theodore Roosevelt helped Panamanian rebels and reached an agreement with a newly independent Panama for construction of the Panama Canal. Roosevelt used his "Big Stick" Policy to assert a greater U.S. presence in the Caribbean. The Caribbean Sea became, in effect, an "American lake" under the control of the United States.

Milestone	Description
World War I (1917–1918)	Events in Europe led to war in 1914. America remained neutral, but entered the war in 1917 after German submarines attacked American ships in the Atlantic. American entry led to Allied victory by 1918. Germany surrendered and a revolution in Germany turned that country into a democracy.
The Fourteen Points and the Treaty of Versailles (1918–1919)	President Wilson announced America's war aims in the Fourteen Points. These sought to create new states in Europe on the basis of nationalism. The Fourteen Points also proposed the creation of a League of Nations — an international peace organization. Many of Wilson's ideas were accepted in the Treaty of Versailles but the U.S. Senate, fearing another foreign war, rejected the treaty and the League of Nations. The United States became isolationist.
World War II (1941–1945)	World War II broke out in Europe when Nazi Germany invaded Poland in 1939. At first, Americans followed a policy of neutrality. Nazi Germany conquered much of Western Europe and attacked Russia in June 1941. In December 1941, Germany's ally, Japan, attacked Pearl Harbor, bringing the United States into the war. World War II was the most destructive war in history. Racial hatred led to the Nazi massacre of European Jews and others in the Holocaust. On the home front, Americans devoted themselves to wartime production, while Japanese Americans were relocated to internment camps in desolate areas. American and other allied forces landed in France on D-Day (June 6, 1944). Germany surrendered in May 1945. The war ended in August 1945, after Americans dropped atomic bombs on two Japanese cities. Nazi leaders were tried at Nuremberg, and Germany and Japan were occupied by allied forces.
The Cold War (1946–1991)	After World War II, America and the Soviet Union emerged as superpowers. When the Soviets established Communist governments in Eastern Europe, the "Cold War" began. The United States countered Soviet Communism by trying to spread its system of democracy. Germany was divided in two, and an Iron Curtain fell over Eastern Europe, cutting it off from the rest of Europe. The Western allies formed NATO, and the Soviet Union and its satellites formed the Warsaw Pact. Although the superpowers never went to war with each other, they stockpiled nuclear weapons and missiles and became involved in regional crises.
Korean War (1950–1953)	In 1950, Communist North Korea invaded South Korea. U.S. troops, acting under a United Nations resolution, sent troops to South Korea to repel the North Korean attack. When U.S. forces repelled the attack and entered North Korea, Communist China entered the war. After three years of war, a truce was signed leaving Korea divided exactly as before the war.

Milestone	Description
Vietnam War (1964–1973)	After achieving independence, Communist North Vietnam began a war against the non-Communist South to reunite the country under Communist rule. Half a million U.S. troops were sent to aid the South Vietnamese government, but they were unable to defeat the Viet Cong and North Vietnamese. America finally withdrew. Thousands of Americans were killed. In Vietnam, a million people were killed, and millions more were left homeless. Fighting spread to neighboring Cambodia, where local Communists massacred millions of innocent civilians. Difficulties in Vietnam also led President Nixon to open relations with Communist China and pursue détente with the Soviet Union.
The Persian Gulf War (1990)	Iraqi dictator Saddam Hussein invaded oil-rich Kuwait. President Bush, with U.N. support, launched an invasion of Kuwait and Iraq, forcing Iraq's withdrawal. The Gulf War was the first example of multi-national cooperation after the end of the Cold War. The allies were able to liberate Kuwait, but ended the war without toppling Hussein in Iraq.
Bosnia and Kosovo (1990–1999)	After the end of the Cold War, several ethnic groups in Yugoslavia declared their independence. Serbs remained in control of "rump" Yugoslavia and attempted to annex parts of Bosnia by murdering or exiling Bosnian Muslims. After years of fighting, U.S. and NATO forces finally intervened with air power and achieved a negotiated settlement. The pattern was repeated in Kosovo where NATO air power was again used to halt Serb attacks on civilians.
The War on Terorism and the Invasion of Afghanistan (2001)	On September 11, 2001, terrorists hijacked four U.S. passenger planes. They crashed two of them into the World Trade Center and one into the Pentagon, causing the deaths of three thousand innocent Americans. President George W. Bush declared a "War on Terrorism" but the Taliban government of Afghanistan refused to turn over members of al-Qaeda responsible for the attack. U.S.-led forces then invaded Afghanistan in October, 2001, overthrew the Taliban, broke up al-Qaeda camps, and introduced democracy to the Afghan people.
The Iraq War (2003–Present)	President Bush became concerned that Iraqi dictator Saddam Hussein might help al-Qaeda or other terrorists or that the Iraqi government might use weapons of mass destruction. U.S.-led forces invaded Iraq in March 2003 and overthrew Hussein's government. Unlike the 1990 Gulf War, the U.S. and its allies acted without the support of the U.N. An occupying force remained in Iraq during its transition to democracy. However, troops faced a rising insurgency from ethnic tensions. President Obama has promised to withdraw American troops as quickly as possible, as soon as their operations are taken over by local Iraqi forces.

CHAPTER 15

A PRACTICE REGENTS EXAMINATION

Now that you have had an opportunity to review the material in this book, you should take a practice examination to measure your progress. To help you in this assessment, this chapter has the actual U.S. History Regents Examination for January 2009. Before you begin, let's look at some common-sense tips for taking such tests:

★ **Answer All Questions.** Don't leave any questions unanswered. Since there is no penalty for guessing, answer all questions — even if only making a guess.

★ **Use the Process of Elimination.** After reading a multiple-choice question, even if you don't know the right answer, it may be clear that certain choices are wrong. Some choices may be irrelevant because they relate to a different time or place. Other choices may have no connection with the question or may be inaccurate statements. After you have eliminated all the wrong choices, choose the *best* response that remains.

★ **Read the Question Carefully.** Underline key words or expressions that are central to the question. If a word in the question is unfamiliar, break the word down into words that are familiar. Look at the prefix (*start of the word*), root, or suffix (*ending*) for clues to the meaning of the word.

Taking the examination that follows will help you to identify any areas that you still need to study. Good luck on this practice test!

U.S. HISTORY AND GOVERNMENT PRACTICE EXAMINATION

This U.S. History and Government Regents Examination contains three parts:

Part I has 50 multiple choice questions

Part II has one thematic essay

Part III has one document-based essay

Part I

Directions (1–50): For each statement or question, circle the *number* of the word or expression that, of those given, best completes the statement or answers the question.

Base your answers to questions 1 and 2 on the map and on your knowledge of social studies.

1 What would be the best title for this map?
   (1) British North America Before 1850
   (2) United States Territorial Expansion
   (3) Colonial North America
   (4) Wartime Land Acquisitions

The shaded ovals next to each question indicate the page(s) in this book where the correct answer can be found.

5–7, 88

2 The Louisiana Purchase was important to the United States because it
   (1) expanded the nation's boundary to the Pacific Ocean
   (2) removed the Spanish from North America
   (3) closed the western territories to slavery
   (4) secured control of the Mississippi River

84

3 Which geographic feature served as the western boundary for British colonial settlements prior to the Revolutionary War?
   (1) Rocky Mountains
   (2) Missouri River
   (3) Appalachian Mountains
   (4) Great Plains   **57**

4 Delegates at the Constitutional Convention of 1787 agreed to the Three-fifths Compromise to solve a dispute directly related to
   (1) the power of the presidency
   (2) representation in Congress
   (3) a decision by the Supreme Court
   (4) the addition of a bill of rights   **63**

5 ". . .That to secure these rights, governments are instituted among men, deriving their just powers from the consent of the governed, . . . "
— Declaration of Independence

Which provision of the original United States Constitution was most influenced by this ideal?
(1) enabling the president to select a cabinet
(2) providing for direct election of the House of Representatives
(3) allowing the Senate to try articles of impeachment
(4) authorizing the Supreme Court to rule on disputes between states   `60, 64, 68`

6 Today, the Federal Reserve System attempts to stabilize the economy of the United States by
(1) requiring federal budgets be prepared and presented to Congress
(2) levying and collecting income taxes
(3) regulating interest rates and the money supply
(4) backing all currency with silver and gold   `187, 307`

7 **"President Wilson Represents the United States at Versailles"**
"President Reagan Meets with Soviet President Gorbachev"
"President Carter Negotiates Camp David Accords"

Each headline illustrates a time when the president of the United States acted as
(1) chief diplomat
(2) chief legislator
(3) commander in chief
(4) head of a political party   `69, 171, 279, 282`

8 Which individual's action was directly protected by the first amendment?
(1) Alexander Graham Bell's invention of the telephone in 1876
(2) Theodore Roosevelt's command of the Rough Riders in 1898
(3) President Franklin D. Roosevelt's election to a third term in 1940
(4) Dr. Martin Luther King Jr.'s leading a march on Washington, D.C., in 1963   `71–72, 171, 245, 249`

Base your answer to question 9 on the quotation below and on your knowledge of social studies.

. . . The nation deserves and I will select a Supreme Court justice that Americans can be proud of. The nation also deserves a dignified process of confirmation in the United States. Senate, characterized by fair treatment, a fair hearing and a fair vote. I will choose a nominee in a timely manner so that the hearing and the vote can be completed before the new Supreme Court term begins. . . .
— President George W. Bush, 2005

9 Which constitutional principle is suggested by this quotation?
(1) federalism
(2) checks and balances
(3) States rights
(4) due process   `66`

10 In his Farewell Address, President George Washington warned against establishing alliances with European countries because he was concerned primarily about
(1) protection of the western frontier
(2) French colonization of the Caribbean
(3) United States involvement in foreign wars
(4) restrictions on trade with Latin America   `84`

11 The Monroe Doctrine (1823) was issued primarily because President James Monroe
  (1) wanted to warn European powers against intervention in Latin America
  (2) opposed the revolutions taking place in South America
  (3) needed to establish a foothold in Panama for a future canal
  (4) believed the United States should pursue overseas colonies **85**

Base your answer to question 12 on the map below and on your knowledge of social studies.

Railroads in 1840 and 1860

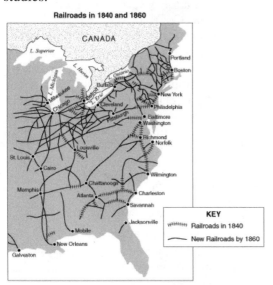

Source: Knownslar and Frizzle, *Discovering American History*, Holt, Rinehart and Winston (adapted)

12 Based on the map, which statement is a valid conclusion?
  (1) Port cities were not connected to railroads.
  (2) Railroads were more expensive to build than canals.
  (3) Most canals were abandoned before the Civil War. **5–7, 92**
  (4) Railroads were expanding more quickly in the North than in the South.

13 President Andrew Jackson's policy toward Native American Indians was created to
  (1) encourage Native American Indians to become part of mainstream American society
  (2) force Native American Indians to move west of the Mississippi River
  (3) improve educational opportunities for Native American Indians
  (4) grant citizenship to Native American Indians **86**

14 The publication of *Uncle Tom's Cabin*, written by Harriet Beecher Stowe, contributed to the start of the Civil War by
  (1) exposing the dangers of cotton manufacturing
  (2) intensifying Northern dislike of slavery
  (3) pressuring the president to support emancipation
  (4) convincing Congress to ban the importation of slaves **89**

15 Following Reconstruction, the passage of Jim Crow laws in the South limited the effectiveness of
  (1) the 14th and 15th amendments
  (2) the Freedmen's Bureau
  (3) Black Codes
  (4) tenant farming and sharecropping **99**

16 During the late 1800s, many United States farmers believed their economic problems would be solved if the federal government would
  (1) raise interest rates
  (2) outlaw strikes by labor unions
  (3) put more money into circulation
  (4) regulate the amount of grain that was produced **149**

17 In the late 19th century, critics of big business claimed that monopolies most harmed the economy by
(1) limiting competition
(2) decreasing the urban growth rate
(3) preventing technological innovation
(4) failing to keep pace with European industries   (120, 151, 156)

18 In the late 19th century, the ideas of Social Darwinism were used primarily to
(1) encourage the passage of compulsory education laws
(2) explain the differences in income between the rich and the poor
(3) urge Congress to end immigration
(4) support the growth of new political parties   (119, 162)

19 The principal reason Congress raised tariff rates in the late 1800s and early 1900s was to
(1) increase personal income taxes
(2) lower prices for American consumers
(3) guarantee high wages to American workers
(4) protect United States businesses from foreign competition   (83, 117, 190)

20 Reformers of the early 20th century frequently attacked political machines because the politicians in these organizations often
(1) denied voting rights to the poor
(2) accepted bribes in return for favors
(3) wasted money on military spending
(4) discriminated against migrant workers   (154)

Base your answer to question 21 on the song lyrics below and on your knowledge of social studies.

The Uprising of the Twenty Thousands
(Dedicated to the Waistmakers
[shirt makers] of 1909)

In the black of the winter of nineteen nine,
When we froze and bled on the picket line,
We showed the world that women could fight
And we rose and won with women's might.

Chorus:
Hail the waistmakers of nineteen nine,
Making their stand on the picket line,
Breaking the power of those who reign,
Pointing the way, smashing the chain.

And we gave new courage to the men
Who carried on in nineteen ten
And shoulder to shoulder we'll win through,
Led by the I.L.G.W.U.

— *Let's Sing!*, Educational Department, International
Ladies' Garment Workers' Union, New York City

21 Which type of labor-related action is best described in this song?   (123, 125)
(1) a strike   (3) a boycott
(2) an open shop   (4) an injunction

22 A major purpose of the Progressive movement (1900–1917) was to
(1) stimulate the economy
(2) support government control of factory production
(3) encourage immigration from southern and eastern Europe
(4) correct the economic and social abuses of industrial society   (151)

23 Which feature of the United States Constitution traditionally gives the states authority over public education?
(1) reserved powers
(2) preamble
(3) fifth amendment
(4) supremacy clause   (64)

Base your answer to question 24 on the graph below and on your knowledge of social studies.

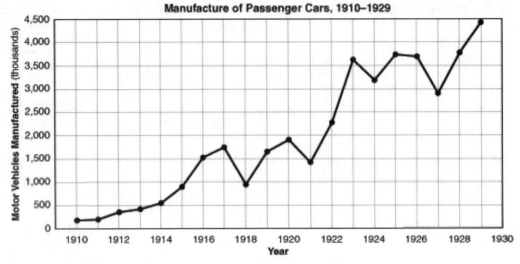

Manufacture of Passenger Cars, 1910–1929

24 The overall trend shown on the graph was primarily the result of
(1) a decline in the economy
(2) the increased use of the assembly line
(3) a shift of the population from urban areas to farms
(4) an increase in the price of automobiles   9–10, 191–192

---

25 What was a major reason the United States entered World War I (1917)?
(1) The Japanese had occupied Manchuria.
(2) Foreign troops had landed on American soil.
(3) The Austro-Hungarian Empire had invaded Belgium.
(4) Germany had resumed unrestricted submarine warfare.   169–170

26 What was one effect of the Bolshevik Revolution (October 1917) on the United States?
(1) Nativism increased, leading to the Red Scare.
(2) Federal courts banned anti-immigrant groups.
(3) Immigration laws were changed to allow refugees from Russia.
(4) The Allied powers needed fewer United States troops.   129, 189

27 What was the effect of the "clear and present danger" ruling established in *Schenck v. United States* (1919)?
(1) placing limits on constitutional freedoms
(2) decreasing the president's powers during wartime
(3) limiting the hours women could work in industry
(4) upholding the right of states to regulate child labor   170–171

28 The Harlem Renaissance promoted African American culture by
(1) increasing factory employment opportunities for minorities
(2) encouraging immigration from Africa
(3) focusing attention on artistic contributions
(4) bringing an end to legalized racial segregation   194

29 During the 1920s, the United States changed its immigration policy by passing new laws that
    (1) provided incentives to attract more immigrants to factory jobs
    (2) encouraged Chinese immigrants to enter the country
    (3) allowed unrestricted immigration of war refugees from Vietnam
    (4) established quotas that reduced the number of immigrants from certain countries   `193`

30 President Franklin D. Roosevelt believed that declaring a bank holiday and creating the Federal Deposit Insurance Corporation (FDIC) would help the nation's banking system by
    (1) restoring public confidence in the banks
    (2) reducing government regulation of banks   `200, 202`
    (3) restricting foreign investments
    (4) granting tax relief to individuals

31 The Social Security Act (1935) is considered an important program because it
    (1) brought about a quick end to the Great Depression
    (2) provided employment for those in need of a job
    (3) established a progressive income tax   `202`
    (4) extended support to elderly citizens

32 The policy of Cash and Carry, the Destroyers for Naval Bases Deal, and the Lend-Lease Act were all designed to
    (1) contribute to the success of the Axis powers
    (2) relieve unemployment caused by the Great Depression
    (3) guarantee a third term to President Franklin D. Roosevelt
    (4) aid the Allies without involving the United States in war   `217–218`

33 Rationing was used in the United States during World War II as a way to
    (1) ensure adequate supplies of scarce natural resources
    (2) increase the number of imports
    (3) raise production of consumer goods
    (4) provide markets for American-made products   `202`

34 The post–World War II trials held by the Allied powers in Nuremberg, Germany, and in Japan set an international precedent by
    (1) placing blame only on civilian leaders
    (2) forcing nations to pay for war damages
    (3) returning conquered territories to their peoples
    (4) holding individuals accountable for their war crimes   `223`

35 The development of the Marshall Plan and the formation of the North Atlantic Treaty Organization (NATO) were part of President Harry Truman's effort to
    (1) promote an isolationist foreign policy
    (2) limit the spread of communism
    (3) provide aid to Asian nations
    (4) end the Korean War   `227–228`

36 **"Jackie Robinson Breaks Color Barrier in Major League Baseball"**
    "President Truman Issues Executive Order Desegregating Armed Forces"
    "NAACP Challenges School Segregation"

    These headlines are most closely associated with
    (1) a decline in African American participation in political activities
    (2) the beginning of the modern civil rights movement
    (3) Southern resistance to the Civil Rights Act of 1964
    (4) the effects of affirmative action programs   `246–247`

Base your answers to questions 37–38 on the graph and on your knowledge of social studies.

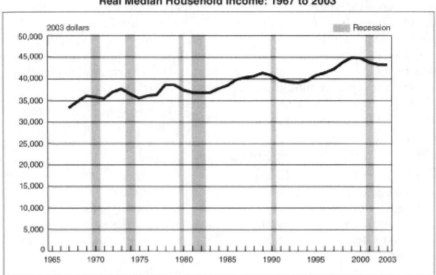

Real Median Household Income: 1967 to 2003

37 Based on the graph, which statement about median household income between 1967 and 2003 is most accurate?
 (1) It doubled.
 (2) It decreased by about $5,000.
 (3) It increased by about $10,000.
 (4) It increased by about $50,000. **9–10**

38 Based on the graph, which development occurred during the year before each recession?
 (1) Median household income decreased.
 (2) Full employment was achieved.
 (3) Median household income stayed the same.
 (4) The United States population decreased. **9–10**

---

39 The passage of the War Powers Act of 1973 was intended to affect the balance of power between the president and Congress by
 (1) allowing troops to be sent overseas without the president's consent
 (2) requiring the president to remove all United States troops from Southeast Asia
 (3) permitting the president to enter treaties without Senate approval
 (4) placing limitations on the president's ability to keep troops in hostile situations **264**

40 Which event led to the investigations that resulted in the resignation of President Richard Nixon?
 (1) a decision to escalate the war in Vietnam
 (2) a presidential decision to freeze wages and prices
 (3) a break-in at the headquarters of the Democratic National Committee
 (4) an oil embargo by the Organization of Petroleum Exporting Countries (OPEC) **276–277**

Base your answer to question 41 on the conversation below and on your knowledge of social studies.

The President:

Helmut! I am sitting in a meeting with members of our Congress and am calling at the end of this historic day to wish you well.

Chancellor Kohl:

Things are going very, very well. I am in Berlin. There were one million people here last night at the very spot where the Wall used to stand—and where President Reagan called on Mr. Gorbachev to open this gate. Words can't describe the feeling. The weather is very nice and warm, fortunately. There were large crowds of young people. Eighty percent were under thirty. It was fantastic. . . .

Source: Telephone conversation between Chancellor Helmut Kohl of Germany and President George H. W. Bush, October 3, 1990

41 This conversation is referring to the
(1) signing of the Nuclear Test Ban Treaty and creation of the Hot Line
(2) expansion of the North Atlantic Treaty Organization (NATO)
(3) end of the Cold War and reunification of Germany
(4) start of the Berlin airlift `284–285`

42 Which heading best completes the partial outline below?

> I. _____
> A. Desire for new markets
> B. Creation of a modern navy
> C. Belief in Anglo-Saxon superiority

(1) Consequences of World War I
(2) Results of the Gentlemen's Agreement
(3) Events Leading to Neutrality
(4) Factors Supporting United States Imperialism `162`

Base your answers to questions 43 and 44 on the cartoon below and on your knowledge of social studies.

Source: Tom Toles, *The Washington Post*, June 26, 2005 (adapted)

43 What is the main idea of this cartoon?
(1) Burning flags is another cause of global warming.
(2) Washington politicians are focusing on the wrong issues.
(3) Respect for the American flag around the world is declining.
(4) Automobiles are mainly responsible for global warming. `13–14, 295`

44 Based on this cartoon, which action by the federal government would the cartoonist most likely support?
(1) restricting first amendment rights
(2) promoting industrial growth
(3) enforcing environmental regulations `295–296`
(4) encouraging globalization

Base your answer to question 45 on the chart below and on your knowledge of social studies.

Political Party	Presidential Nominee	Electoral College Vote	Electoral College Vote Percent	Popular Vote Number	Popular Vote Percent
Republican	George W. Bush	271	50.4	50,456,062	47.9
Democratic	Albert Gore, Jr.	266	49.4	50,996,582	48.4
Green	Ralph Nader	0	0.0	2,858,843	2.7

45 Which generalization about United States presidential elections is most clearly supported by the data in this chart?
(1) A candidate can win the election without a majority of the popular vote.
(2) Third-party candidates have no effect on presidential elections.
(3) Electoral college votes determine the will of the majority of voters.
(4) Voter participation in national elections is declining.   (11–13, 287)

46 "No person in the United States shall, on the basis of sex, be excluded from participation in, be denied the benefits of, or be subjected to discrimination under any education program or activity receiving Federal financial assistance, . . ."
— Title IX, 1972

The passage of this law affected women across the nation by
(1) granting them the right to own property
(2) guaranteeing them the same wages as male workers
(3) increasing their opportunities to participate in school sports
(4) allowing them the right to seek elective offices   (249)

47 The Department of Homeland Security was created as a direct response to the
(1) Persian Gulf War (1991)
(2) Oklahoma City bombing (1995)
(3) terrorist attacks on September 11 (2001)
(4) flooding of New Orleans (2005)   (288)

48 • Establishment of the Peace Corps
• Bay of Pigs invasion
• Cuban missile crisis

These events occurred during the presidency of
(1) John F. Kennedy
(2) Lyndon B. Johnson
(3) Richard Nixon
(4) Jimmy Carter   (252–253)

49 The Anthracite Coal Strike (1902), the Wagner Act (1935), and the founding of the United Farm Workers (1962) were important steps in   (155, 202)
(1) limiting the growth of labor unions
(2) creating greater equality for women
(3) ending discrimination directed at African Americans in the South
(4) promoting fair labor practices and collective bargaining for workers

50 Which book describes how the Dust Bowl of the 1930s affected farmers of the Great Plains?
(1) *How the Other Half Lives*
(2) *The Jungle*
(3) *The Grapes of Wrath*
(4) *Silent Spring*   (197)

Part II
THEMATIC ESSAY QUESTION

Directions Write a well-organized essay that includes an introduction, several paragraphs addressing the task below, and a conclusion.

Theme: Movements of People—Migration

> The movement of people into and within the United States has had a significant impact on the nation. These movements have been both voluntary and involuntary.

Task:

> Select *two* periods of migration that had an impact on the United States and for *each*
> • Describe the historical circumstances that led to the migration
> • Discuss the impact of the migration on the United States

You may use any period of migration from your study of United States history. Some suggestions you might wish to consider include colonial settlement (1600s–1700s), westward expansion (1800s), rural to urban migration (1870s–1920s), European immigration (1880–1910), the Dust Bowl (1930s), suburbanization (1950s–1960s), and illegal immigration (1990 to the present).

You are *not* limited to these suggestions.

Guidelines:

In your essay, be sure to
• Develop all aspects of the task
• Support the theme with relevant facts, examples, and details
• Use a logical and clear plan of organization, including an introduction and a conclusion that are beyond a restatement of the theme

In developing your answer to Part II, be sure to keep these general definitions in mind:

(a) <u>describe</u> means "to illustrate something in words or tell about it"
(b) <u>discuss</u> means "to make observations about something using facts, reasoning, and argument; to present in some detail" Answers to the essay questions are to be written in the separate essay booklet.

In developing your answers to Part III, be sure to keep this general definition in mind:

> discuss **means "to make observations about something using facts, reasoning, and argument; to present in some detail"**

Part III: DOCUMENT-BASED QUESTION

This question is based on the accompanying documents. The question is designed to test your ability to work with historical documents. Some of the documents have been edited for the purposes of the question. As you analyze the documents, take into account the source of each document and any point of view that may be presented in the document.

Historical Context:

Between 1953 and 1969, the Chief Justice of the United States Supreme Court was Earl Warren. Supreme Court decisions made during the "Warren Court" era led to significant changes in various aspects of life in the United States. Several important court cases affected equal protection under the law, separation of church and state, and the rights of individuals accused of crimes.

Task: Using information from the documents and your knowledge of United States history, answer the questions that follow each document in Part A. Your answers to the questions will help you write the Part B essay, in which you will be asked to

> • Discuss how decisions of the Warren Court affected American society

Part A: Short-Answer Questions

Document 1a

> . . . The Warren Court (1953–1969) revolutionized constitutional law and American society. First, the unanimous and watershed [critical] school desegregation ruling, *Brown v. Board of Education*, in 1954 at the end of Warren's first year on the bench. Then, in 1962 *Baker v. Carr* announced the "reapportionment revolution" guaranteeing equal voting rights [to individual voters no matter where they lived]. And throughout the 1960s, the Court handed down a series of rulings on criminal procedure that extended the rights of the accused and sought to ensure equal access to justice for the poor. *Mapp v. Ohio* (1961), extending the exclusionary rule to the states, and *Miranda v. Arizona* (1966), sharply limiting police interrogations of criminal suspects, continue to symbolize the Warren Court's revolution in criminal justice. . . .

Source: David M. O'Brien, "The Supreme Court: From Warren to Burger to Rehnquist," *PS*, Winter 1987

1a   According to David M. O'Brien, what is *one* effect of the Warren Court on American society? [1]

The Warren court extended the rights of the accused and made sure there were equal justice for the poor

Score ☐

Document 1b

> . . .The Warren Court's revolution in public law promoted acrimony [hostility] and bitterness precisely because it empowered those who had previously not had the opportunity to exercise power. Whether we approve of their behavior or not, there is little doubt that these new groups added dramatically and often disturbingly to the contours of American society. Much of what the Warren Court did was to release dissident minorities from long-standing legal and social strictures [limits]. Critics complained that the Court was the root of the problem; it was fostering subversive [disobedient] action by civil rights advocates, Communist agitators, criminals, smut peddlers, and racketeers who hid behind the Fifth Amendment when called to account. . . .

Source: Kermit Hall, "The Warren Court in Historical Perspective," Bernard Schwartz, ed., *The Warren Court: A Retrospective*, Oxford University Press, 1996

1b According to Kermit Hall, what is *one* criticism leveled against the decisions of the Warren Court? [1]

It empowered those who had not been able to exercise power

Score ▢

Document 2

HIGH COURT BANS SEGREGATION IN PUBLIC SCHOOLS

Mrs. Nettie Hunt, sitting on the steps of the U. S. Supreme Court Building in Washington, explains the significance of the Court's May 17, 1954 desegregation ruling to her daughter, Nikie $3\frac{1}{2}$, in this November 19, 1954 photo.

Source: "With an Even Hand," Brown v. Board of Education exhibition, *Library of Congress* (adapted)

2 Based on this photograph and caption, what is the significance of the *Brown v. Board of Education* decision? [1]

It banned segregation in public schools.

Score ▢

Document 3a

> . . . "The promise of Brown was not fulfilled in the way that we envisioned it," says U.S. Secretary of Education Rod Paige, who was a student at Mississippi's all-black Jackson State University when the decision was handed down. Within the first few years after the decision, paratroopers were protecting black students entering Central High School in Little Rock, Ark., schools were shuttered [closed] entirely in Prince Edward County, Va., and white families across the South put their children into private schools. By 1971, the court had endorsed busing to overcome the residential segregation that was keeping black and white children apart. Particularly in the South, the integration drive worked, as the share of black children attending majority white schools rose from 0.1% in 1960 to a high of 44% in 1988. . . .

Source: Rebecca Winters, "No Longer Separate, But Not Yet Equal," *Time*, May 10, 2004

Document 3b

> . . . Even though the effects of *Brown* were slow in coming—real desegregation only occurred with the 1964 Civil Rights Act and aggressive enforcement by the Department of Justice, which denied federal funds to any segregated school—they were revolutionary. Greenberg [Jack Greenberg, a member of the *Brown* legal team] cites encouraging evidence today as the half-full approach: there are black Cabinet members in Democrat and Republican administrations; blacks hold top management positions in major corporations like Citibank, Xerox, Time Warner, and Merrill Lynch. When Greenberg started practicing law in 1949 there were only two black U.S. Congressmen. Today [2004] there are 39.
>
> Brown "broke up the frozen political system in the country at the time," Greenberg notes. Southern congressmen made it a priority to keep African-Americans from obtaining power, but *Brown* allowed for change. Judge Carter [Robert Carter, a member of the *Brown* legal team] believes that the greatest accomplishment of the ruling was to create a black middle class: "The court said everyone was equal, so now you had it by right.". . .

Source: Kristina Dell, "What 'Brown' Means Today," *Time*, May 17, 2004

3 Based on these documents, state *two* effects of the *Brown v. Board of Education* Supreme Court decision on American society. [2]

(1) _It dramatically increased the number of black students attending white schools_

Score ☐

(2) _The ruling created a black middle class which gave everyone equal rights_

Score ☐

Document 4

> ... **QUESTION:** Mr. President, in the furor [uproar] over the Supreme Court's decision [in *Engel v. Vitale*] on prayer in the schools, some members of Congress have been introducing legislation for Constitutional amendments specifically to sanction [permit] prayer or religious exercise in the schools. Can you give us your opinion of the decision itself, and of these moves of the Congress to circumvent [get around] it?
>
> **THE PRESIDENT:** I haven't seen the measures in the Congress and you would have to make a determination of what the language was, and what effect it would have on the First Amendment. The Supreme Court has made its judgment, and a good many people obviously will disagree with it. Others will agree with it. But I think that it is important for us if we are going to maintain our Constitutional principle that we support the Supreme Court decisions even when we may not agree with them.
>
> In addition, we have in this case a very easy remedy, and that is to pray ourselves and I would think that it would be a welcome reminder to every American family that we can pray a good deal more at home, we can attend our churches with a good deal more fidelity, and we can make the true meaning of prayer much more important in the lives of all of our children. That power is very much open to us. ...

Source: President John F. Kennedy, News Conference, June 27, 1962

4a What was **one** effect of the *Engel v. Vitale* decision on public schools in the United States? [1]

Congress is trying to permit prayer and/or religious exercise in schools through constitutional amendments

Score ☐

b What does President John F. Kennedy suggest as a "remedy" to those who disagree with the Supreme Court's decision in *Engel v. Vitale*? [1]

Kennedy suggests that American families should pray more at home and attend their own churches.

Score ☐

Document 5

ATLANTA, Nov. 21 — As President Clinton and the new Republican leadership in Congress consider measures that would return organized prayer to public schools, it is worth remembering one thing.

Prayer is already there.

Despite a Supreme Court ruling [*Engel v. Vitale*] 32 years ago that classroom prayer and Scripture reading are unconstitutional even if they are voluntary, prayer is increasingly a part of school activities from early-morning moments of silence to lunchtime prayer sessions to prefootball-game prayers for both players and fans.

The most common forms are state-mandated moments of silence at the beginning of the day, which are permissible to the extent they are not meant to be a forum for organized prayer. But, particularly in the South, religious clubs, prayer groups and pro-prayer students and community groups are making religion and prayer part of the school day. . . .

Source: Peter Applebome, "Prayer in Public Schools? It's Nothing New for Many,"
New York Times, November 22, 1994

5 According to Peter Applebome, what are *two* ways in which prayer in public schools continued despite the Supreme Court ruling in *Engel v. Vitale*? [2]

(1) _State mandated moments of silence at the beginning of the day_

Score ☐

(2) _Prayed before football games for both fans and players_

Score ☐

Document 6

In the decades following the Engel decision, federal courts have continued to hear cases and make rulings on issues involving separation of church and state.

> FRANKFORT, Ky. — A civic group will send a Ten Commandments monument back to Frankfort only if political leaders give assurances that it will be displayed publicly, as a new law allows. . . .
>
> The Ten Commandments monument was part of an ever-growing list of religious issues that [Governor Ernie] Fletcher and other political leaders have dealt with this year. . . .
>
> The Eagles [a fraternal organization] donated the Ten Commandments monument to the state in 1971. It was removed from the Capitol grounds and placed in storage in the mid-1980s during a construction project. When political leaders tried to display it again in 2000, the American Civil Liberties Union went to court, claiming the monument was an unconstitutional endorsement of religion. The ACLU won the case. . . .
>
> Lawmakers passed a bill calling for the return of the monument. The same bill granted permission to local governments to post displays of the commandments in courthouses and other public buildings.
>
> Kentucky has been at the center of legal fights in recent years on the posting of the commandments. In one case, *McCreary County v. ACLU* [2005], the U.S. Supreme Court ruled displays inside courthouses in McCreary and Pulaski counties were unconstitutional. In another [lower court case], *Mercer County v. ACLU*, the 6th U.S. Circuit Court of Appeals said a similar display in the Mercer County Courthouse is constitutional because it included other historic documents. . . .

Source: "Ten Commandments, other issues generating debate in Ky.," *Associated Press*, April 13, 2006

6 Based on this article, what is **one** issue in the continuing debate on separation of church and state? [1]

Whether or not lawmakers could post The ten commandments in court houses and other public buildings

Score ☐

Document 7

... along with other Warren Court decisions, Miranda has increased public awareness of constitutional rights. The *Miranda* warnings may be the most famous words ever written by the United States Supreme Court. With the widespread dissemination [distribution] of *Miranda* warnings in innumerable [numerous] television shows as well as in the movies and contemporary fiction, the reading of the *Miranda* rights has become a familiar sight and sound to most Americans; *Miranda* has become a household word. As Samuel Walker writes, "[e]very junior high school student knows that suspects are entitled to their '*Miranda* rights.' They often have the details wrong, but the principle that there are limits on police officer behavior, and penalties for breaking those rules, is firmly established." As we have seen, a national poll in 1984 revealed that 93% of those surveyed knew that they had a right to an attorney if arrested, and a national poll in 1991 found that 80% of those surveyed knew that they had a right to remain silent if arrested. Perhaps it should not be surprising that, as many of my research subjects told me, some suspects assert their rights prior to the *Miranda* admonition [warning] or in situations where police warnings are not legally required. Indeed, in the last thirty years, the *Miranda* rights have been so entrenched [well-established] in American popular folklore as to become an indelible part of our collective heritage and consciousness. ...

Source: Richard A. Leo, "The Impact of 'Miranda' Revisited,"
The Journal of Criminal Law and Criminology, Spring 1996 (adapted)

7 According to Richard A. Leo, what is *one* effect of the *Miranda* decision on American society? [1]

Have the right to an attorney if arrested and a right to remain silent under the Miranda law

Score ☐

Document 8a

Source: Charles Brooks, *Birmingham News* (adapted)

Document 8b

... The familiar fact is that the vastly troubled criminal-justice system often exacts no price at all for crime. An adult burglar has only one chance in 412 of going to jail for any single job, according to Gregory Krohm of the Virginia Polytechnic Institute's Center for the Study of Public Choice. For juveniles under 17, the figure is one in 659 burglaries, with a likelihood of only a nine-month term if the 659-to-1 shot comes in. Many critics are convinced that such odds were created in large part by those constitutional-law rulings of the Warren Court that expanded the rights of criminal defendants. Mapp, Escobedo, Miranda and Wade* are still names that enrage law-and-order advocates. But despite all the years of talk and four Nixon appointments, the court has so far been willing only to trim some of the rules, not reverse them. The new rulings obviously add to the work of the courts, and some experts believe that they have hampered the criminal-justice system's capacity to convict guilty offenders, though as yet there have been no studies demonstrating any such significant damage. . . .

Source: "The Crime Wave," *Time*, June 30, 1975

*In *United States v. Wade* (1967), the Court ruled that defendants have a right to counsel during police lineups. This does **not** refer to *Roe v. Wade*.

8 Based on the cartoon and the *Time* article, what is *one* impact of the rulings of the Warren Court on crime? [1]

criminals were given too much leeway in the courts and often were not even put in jail. The rights of criminal defendants was expanded.

Score ☐

Document 9

> WASHINGTON — Refusing to overturn more than three decades of established law enforcement practice, the Supreme Court yesterday strongly reaffirmed its landmark Miranda [Miranda v. Arizona] decision, which requires police to inform criminal suspects of their rights to remain silent and to be represented by an attorney during interrogation.
>
> In a 7-2 opinion written by Chief Justice William H. Rehnquist, the high court ruled that the requirement that criminal suspects be read their "Miranda rights" is rooted in the Constitution and cannot be overturned by an act of Congress. Federal lawmakers passed legislation seeking to undo the Miranda decision in 1968, two years after the ruling.
>
> The seven justices in the majority left open the question of whether they would have reached the same conclusion as the original five-justice Miranda majority about the constitutional rights of criminal suspects. But citing the court's long tradition of respect for precedent, the justices said there were compelling reasons not to overrule it now.
>
> "Miranda has become embedded in routine police practice to the point where the warnings have become part of our national culture," wrote Rehnquist, a frequent and vocal critic of the Miranda decision during his earlier years on the bench. . . .

Source: "Miranda warnings upheld, Supreme Court says right now deeply rooted,"
Florida Times Union, June 27, 2000

9 Based on this article, why did the Supreme Court decide not to overturn the decision in *Miranda v. Arizona*? [1]

The decision to overturn the Miranda rights is rooted in the constitution and congress cannot overturn it

Score ☐

Part B: Essay

Directions: Write a well-organized essay that includes an introduction, several paragraphs, and a conclusion. Use evidence from *at least five* documents in your essay. Support your response with relevant facts, examples, and details. Include additional outside information.

Historical Context:

Between 1953 and 1969, the Chief Justice of the United States Supreme Court was Earl Warren. Supreme Court decisions made during the "Warren Court" era led to significant changes in various aspects of life in the United States. Several important court cases affected equal protection under the law, separation of church and state, and the rights of individuals accused of crimes.

Task: Using information from the documents and your knowledge of United States history, write an essay in which you

> • Discuss how decisions of the Warren Court affected American society

Guidelines:

In your essay, be sure to
- Develop all aspects of the task
- Incorporate information from *at least five* documents
- Incorporate relevant outside information
- Support the theme with relevant facts, examples, and details
- Use a logical and clear plan of organization, including an introduction and a conclusion that are beyond a restatement of the theme

INDEX

A

A Century of Dishonor, 134, 144
Acid Rain, 296
Addams, Jane, 153
Affirmative Action, 250
Agricultural Adjustment Act, 201
Alliance for Progress, 252
Alliance System, 168
American Federation of Labor, 123
American Indian Movement, 259
American Revolution, 59–61, 308
Americans with Disabilities Act, 283
Anthony, Susan, B., 159
Anti-War Movement, 251
Articles of Confederation, 61
Atlantic Charter, 218
Atomic bomb, 223

B

Baker v. *Carr*, 260
Bay of Pigs Invasion, 252
Berlin Airlift, 227
Big Stick Policy, 167
Bill of Rights, 63, 65, 71–72, 308
Bills of Attainder, 65
Bin Laden, Osama, 286–287
Black Codes, 94
Black Power Movement, 258–259
Boston Tea Party, 59, 78
Boxer Rebellion, 164
Brown v. *Board of Education*, 245, 246–247, 260, 309
Bryan, William Jennings, 150
Bull Moose Party, 157
Bush, George, 283–284
Bush, George Walker, 286–289
Business cycle, 195

C

Cabinet, 67
Camp David Accords, 279
Captains of Industry, 119
Carnegie, Andrew, 119–120
Carpetbaggers, 95
Carson, Rachel, 144
Carter, Jimmy, 278–279
Carver, George Washington, 100
Census, 68
Checks and balances, 66, 307
Chinese Exclusion Act, 130
Civil Disobedience, 247

Civil Rights Act of 1964, 154, 249
Civil Rights Movement, 242, 246–48, 256, 309
Civil War, 80, 88–93, 308
Civilian Conservation Corps, 200
Clayton Antitrust Act, 125, 157
Clinton, Bill, 284–286
Coal Miners' Strike of 1902, 155
Cold War, 224–228, 284, 313
Collective Security, 216, 228
Command Economy, 113
Compromise of 1850, 88
Computer Revolution, 294, 311
Concurrent powers, 64
Constitutional Convention, 62, 308
Containment, 226
Coolidge, Calvin, 191
Court packing scheme, 203
Critical Period, 54, 61
"Cross of Gold" Speech, 150
Cuban Missile Crisis, 214, 252

D & E

Dawes Act, 134
Declaration of Independence, 2, 54, 56, 60, 179
Delegated powers, 64, 65
DeLôme Letter, 161
Democracy, 3, 303
Denied powers, 65
Détente, 276
Domino Theory, 261
Double Jeopardy, 72
Douglass, Frederick, 89
Dred Scott v. Sandford, 90, 323
DuBois, W.E.B., 103
Due Process of Law, 72, 304
Dust Bowl, 197
Eakins, Thomas, 145
Economic system, 113
Edison, Thomas, A., 119
Eighteenth Amendment, 193
Einstein, Albert, 223
Eisenhower, Dwight, D., 230, 250–251
Elastic clause, 65
Electoral College, 69
Emancipation Proclamation, 92
Environment, 296–297
Equal Protection Clause, 304
Ethnocentrism, 273
Ex Post Facto laws, 65

Executive branch, 55, 68–69
Executive Privilege, 277

F

Federal Deposit Insurance Corporation, 202
Federal Emergency Relief Act, 200
Federal Reserve Act, 157, 187, 188, 311
Federal Trade Commission Act, 157
Federalism, 64, 307
Feminist Movement, 255
Fifteenth Amendment, 105
Financial Crisis of 2008, 291–292, 311
Fireside Chat, 199
Fitzgerald, F. Scott, 194
Ford, Gerald, 277–278
Ford, Henry, 192
Foreign Policy, 85, 211–214, 312–314
Four Freedoms, 218
Fourteen Points, 171, 313
Fourteenth Amendment, 94, 105
Freedman's Bureau, 93, 95
Freedom of Expression, 304
Freedom of the Seas, 169–179, 181
French and Indian War, 59
Friedan, Betty, 144, 256
Fugitive Slave Law, 90

G

Gadsden Purchase, 87
Garrison, William Lloyd, 89
Garvey, Marcus, 194
Genetic engineering, 294
Geneva Conference of 1954, 261
Gentlemen's Agreement, 130
Geography, 48–52, 81–82, 84, 121, 132, 147, 163, 197, 222, 251, 281
Gibbons v. *Ogden*, 71
Gideon v. *Wainwright*, 245, 260
Gilded Age, 119, 310
Glenn, John, 253
Global warming, 296
Globalization, 295
Gompers, Samuel, 123
Good Neighbor Policy, 215
Grandfather clause, 97
Grange Movement, 148
Great Compromise, 62
Great Depression, 195–199, 311

Great Society, 253–254, 311
Greenhouse effect, 296
Gross Domestic Product, 185
Guadalupe-Hidalgo, Treaty of, 87
Gulf of Tonkin Resolution, 262

H
Hamilton, Alexander, 63, 144
Harding, Warren, 190
Harlem Renaissance, 194
Haymarket Affair, 125
Hearst, William Randolph, 161
Historical periods, 47
Hitler, Adolf, 216
Ho Chi Minh, 261
Holocaust, 223
Homeland Security, 287
Homer, Winslow, 145
Homestead Act of 1862, 132
Hoover, Herbert, 191, 198, 240
House of Burgesses, 58
House of Representatives, 68
House Un-American Activities
    Committee, 231
Hughes, Langston, 195
Hurricane Katrina, 289
Hussein, Saddam, 284, 288

I & J
"I Have A Dream" Speech, 249
Immigration, 127–130, 193, 281, 306
Imperial Presidency, 275
Imperialism, 162, 304
Implied powers, 65
Indian Wars, 133
Industrial Revolution, 310
Interstate Commerce Act, 120, 149
Iran-Contra Affair, 282
Iron Curtain, 226, 228
Isolationism, 189, 215, 304
Jackson, Helen Hunt, 134
Jefferson, Thomas, 60
Jim Crow Laws, 97, 106
Job Corps, 254
Johnson, Andrew, 85–86, 93
Johnson, Lyndon B., 253–254, 262
Judicial Branch, 55, 70–71
Judicial Review, 67, 70, 71

K
Kansas-Nebraska Act, 90
Kellogg-Briand Peace Pact, 215
Kennedy, John F., 252–253, 261

Kerner Commission, 258
Keynes, John Maynard, 186
King, Martin Luther, Jr., 247, 249
Knights of Labor, 123
Korean War, 229–230, 313
Korematsu v. *United States*,
    220–221, 236
Ku Klux Klan, 95–96, 190

L
LaFollette, Robert, 154
Laissez-faire, 116, 304
Lange, Dorothea, 146, 197
League of Nations, 171, 216
Legislative branch, 55, 67–68
Lend-Lease Act, 218
Letter from a Birmingham Jail, 248
Lewis, Sinclair, 194
Limited government, 65, 307
Lincoln, Abraham, 91, 93, 179
Lindbergh, Charles, 195
Literacy Tests, 98
Locke, John, 60
Louisiana Purchase, 84
Loyalty Review Boards, 231
Lusitania, sinking of, 170, 181

M
MacArthur, Douglas, 224, 230
Magna Carta, 58
Mahan, Alfred Thayer, 163
Malcolm X, 259
Manifest Destiny, 84, 312
Mao Zedong, 228
Mapp v. *Ohio*, 245, 260
Maps, 5–7
Marbury v. *Madison*, 71, 245
March on Washington, 249
Market Economy, 113
Marshall Plan, 227
Marshall, John, 70
Mayflower Compact, 58
Mazzoli-Simpson Act of 1986, 281
McCarthyism, 231
McCulloch v. *Maryland*, 71, 245
McKinley, William, 150, 155,
    161–162
Meat Inspection Act, 156
Medicare Act of 1965, 254
Mercantilism, 58
Merit System, 155
Mexican-American War, 85
Miranda v. *Arizona*, 245, 261
Missouri Compromise, 90

Monarchy, 55
Monetary Policy, 187
Monroe Doctrine, 85, 312
Montgomery Bus Boycott, 248
Mott, Lucretia, 158
Muckrakers, 153
Multi-national corporations, 291
Munich Conference, 216
Munn v. *Illinois*, 148

N
N.A.A.C.P., 98, 153, 247
N.A.F.T.A., 285
National Convention, 68
National Debt, 185
National Industrial Recovery Act, 202
National Organization for Women,
    256
National Recovery Administration,
    201
Native Americans, 132–133
Nativism, 129–130, 190
NATO, 228
Neutrality, 84, 217, 304
New Deal, 184, 198–203
New Federalism, 280
New Immigrants, 127–128
New York Stock Market Crash, 197
Nineteenth Amendment, 160
Nixon, Richard, 263–265, 275–277
Non-violence, 247
Noriega, Manuel, 283
Norris, Frank, 153
Norris-LaGuardia Act, 202
Northwest Ordinance, 61
Nuremberg Trials, 223
Nye Commission, 217

O & P
Obama, Barack, 291–293
O.P.E.C., 277
Open Door Policy, 164
Opinion, 22
Oregon Territory, 87
Paine, Thomas, 59, 144
Palmer Raids, 189
Panama Canal Treaty, 279
Panama Canal, 166–167, 279
Paris Peace Accords of 1973, 276
Parks, Rosa, 248
Patriot Act, 287, 290
Peace Corps, 253
Pearl Harbor, 219
Per Capita Income, 185

Perry, Matthew, Commodore, 165
Persian Gulf War, 284, 288, 314
Platt Amendment, 166
Plessy v. *Ferguson*, 97, 107, 245–246
Poll Taxes, 96
Popular Sovereignty, 64, 90, 307
Populists, 142, 149, 151, 308
Potsdam Conference, 225
Powderly, Terrence, 123
Preamble, 64, 65
Primaries, 68
Profit motive, 113
Progressive Movement, 142, 151–155, 172, 304, 309, 310
Prohibition, 193
Protective Tariffs, 117
Public Works Administration, 200
Pulitzer, Joseph, 161, 180
Pure Food and Drug Act, 156

Q & R
Quarantine Speech, 218
Radical Republicans, 94
Rationing, 220
Reagan, Ronald, 280–282
Reaganomics, 281, 311
Reconstruction Finance Corporation, 198
Reconstruction, 80, 92–95, 308
Red Power, 259
Red Scare, 189
Remington, Frederick, 145
Representative democracy, 55
Reserved powers, 64
Riis, Jacob, 153
Roaring Twenties, 189, 309
Robber Barons, 119
Robinson, Jackie, 246
Rockefeller, John D., 120, 140
Roe v. *Wade*, 245, 257–258
Roosevelt, Eleanor, 199
Roosevelt, Franklin D., 4, 68, 199–203, 218–220
Roosevelt, Theodore, 154–156, 165, 238
Rosenberg, Julius and Ethel, 231

S
Sacco, Nicola, 189
Sadat, Anwar, 279
SALT I Accord, 276
SALT II Treaty, 279
Schechter Poultry v. *United States*, 203, 245
Schenck v. *United States*, 170–171, 245
Scopes "Monkey Trial," 193
Secondary sources, 47
Sectionalism, 88–89
Securities and Exchange Commission, 202
Selma Marches, 249
Seneca Falls Convention, 158–159
Separation of powers, 65, 307
Sharecropping, 95
Shays Rebellion, 62
Sherman Antitrust Act, 120
Sinclair, Upton, 144, 153
Sixteenth Amendment, 157
Social Darwinism, 119, 162
Social Gospel Movement, 152
Social Security Act, 202
Solid South, 96
Space Race, 231, 253
Spanish-American War, 160–161, 163, 168, 180, 312
Square Deal, 156
Stagflation, 277, 278
Stanton, Elizabeth Cady, 158
States' Rights, 91
Steffens, Lincoln, 153
Steinbeck, John, 197
Steinem, Gloria, 256
Stowe, Harriet Beecher, 87, 144
Submarine warfare, 170
Supply-side economics, 281
Sussex Pledge, 170

T
Taft, William, 156, 238
Taft-Haftley Act, 203
Taliban, 287
Tarbell, Ida, 153
Teapot Dome Scandal, 190
Technology, 294
Tennessee Valley Authority, 202
Tenure of Office Act, 95
Terrorism, 286–287, 290, 297, 309
Tet Offensive, 262
The Crisis, 100
The Federalist Papers, 63, 144
The Feminine Mystique, 144, 256
The Grapes of Wrath, 197
The Jungle, 144, 153
Thirteenth Amendment, 93, 105
Three Mile Island, 278, 294
Three-fifths Compromise, 63

Traditional economy, 113
Treaty of Portsmouth, 165
Treaty of Versailles, 171, 313
Truman Doctrine, 226, 230
Truman, Harry, 223, 226
Tubman, Harriet, 89
Turner, Frederick Jackson, 144
Twenty-fifth Amendment, 276
Twenty-first Amendment, 193
Twenty-fourth Amendment, 249
Twenty-second Amendment, 68

U, V, & W
U.S. Constitution, 54, 56
U.S. Senate, 67
U.S.S. Maine, 161
Uncle Tom's Cabin, 87, 144
Unemployment rate, 185
Unions, 122–124, 304, 310
United States v. *Nixon*, 277
University of California v. *Bakke*, 250
Unwritten Constitution, 67, 307
Urbanization, 125, 304, 310
Vanzetti, Bartolomeo, 189
Versailles Treaty, 171–172
Vietnam War, 242, 261–264, 276–277, 314
Voting Rights Act of 1965, 249
Wabash v. *Illinois*, 148
Wagner Act, 202
War of 1812, 84, 312
Warren, Earl, 247, 260
Washington Naval Conference, 215
Washington, Booker T., 98, 103
Washington, George, 61, 85, 312
Watergate Scandal, 276–277
Wilson, Woodrow, 156–157, 171–172, 239
Women's Liberation Movement, 255–256
Women's Rights Movement, 142, 158–160
World War I, 168–171, 313
World War II, 216–224, 309, 311, 313
Wright, Orville and Wilbur, 119
Writ of Habeas Corpus, 65

X, Y, & Z
Yalta Conference, 225
Zimmerman Telegram, 169, 182